AUTO-BIOGR[

This page enables you to compile a list of useful data on your car, so that whether you're ordering spares or just checking the tyre pressures, all the key information - the information that is 'personal' to your car - is easily within reach.

Registration number: ....

Model: ....

Engine type/size: ....

Fuel type/grade: ....

Body colour: ....

Paint code number: ....

Date of first registration: ....

Date of manufacture (if different): ....

VIN (or 'chassis') number: ....

Engine number: ....

Ignition key/key tag number: ....

Door lock key/s number/s: ....

Fuel locking cap key number (if fitted): ....

Alarm remote code (if fitted): ....

Radio/cassette security code (if fitted): ....

Tyre size

Front: ....Rear: ....

Tyre pressures (normally laden)

Front: ....Rear: ....

Tyre pressures (fully laden)

Front: ....Rear: ....

Insurance

    Name and address of insurer: ....

....

    Policy number: ....

Modifications

    Information that might be useful when you need to purchase parts: ....

....

Suppliers

    Address and telephone number of your local dealership: ....

....

....

First published in 1997 by: **Porter Publishing Ltd.**

The Storehouse
Little Hereford Street
Bromyard
Hereford HR7 4DE
England

Tel: 01885 488800
Fax: 01885 483012

British Library Cataloguing in Publication Data.

A catalogue record for this book is available from the British Library.

ISBN 1-899238-23-9

Series Editor: Lindsay Porter
Front cover design: Crazy Horse 1842 Ltd and Porter Publishing Ltd.
Back cover design: Porter Publishing Ltd.
Layout and Typesetting: Mark Leonard at Porter Publishing Ltd.
Printed in England by The Trinity Press, Worcester.

PORTER MANUALS AND VIDEO ON THE INTERNET!

http://www.porter-publish.com

GREAT CARS ON VIDEO

PP Video has a truly great range of video tapes, mostly original 'archive' footage, and covering the finest cars ever built. We present the official Jaguar Cars Archive, Dunlop Archive, Audi AG Archive films, among others. There are profiles on the greatest classic cars, motor racing from the '30s, the '50s, the '60s and '70s, and much more besides. For a FREE VIDEO CATALOGUE, please write to: PP Video Ltd, at the address shown at the top of this page.

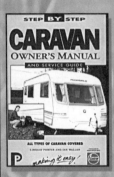

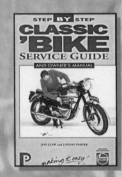

FIAT Uno

Repair Manual and Service Guide

by
Lindsay Porter
and Ivor Carroll

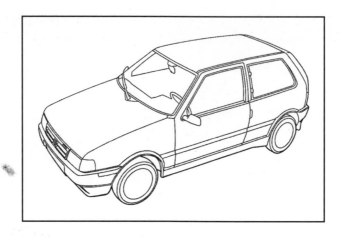

Detailed Contents are shown at the start of each chapter.

CONTENTS

FACT FILE: 'LEFT AND 'RIGHT' SIDES OF THE CAR

● Throughout this manual, we refer to the 'left' and 'right' sides of the car. They refer to the sides of the car that you would see if you were sitting in the driver's seat, looking forwards.

CHAPTER 1
SAFETY FIRST!

You must always ensure that safety is the first consideration in any job you carry out. A slight lack of concentration, or a rush to finish the job quickly can easily result in an accident, as can failure to follow the precautions outlined in this manual.

Be sure to consult the suppliers of any materials and equipment you may use, and to obtain and read carefully any operating and health and safety instructions that may be available on packaging or from manufacturers and suppliers.

GENERAL

Raising the Car Safely

ALWAYS ensure that the vehicle is properly supported when raised off the ground. Don't work on, around, or underneath a raised vehicle unless axle stands are positioned under secure, load bearing underbody areas, or the vehicle is driven onto ramps, with the wheels remaining on the ground securely chocked to prevent movement.

NEVER work on a vehicle supported on a jack. Jacks are made for lifting the vehicle only, not for holding it off the ground while it is being worked on.

ALWAYS ensure that the safe working load rating of any jacks, hoists or lifting gear used is sufficient for the job, and that lifting gear is used only as recommended by the manufacturer.

NEVER attempt to loosen or tighten nuts that require a lot of force to turn (e.g. a tight oil drain plug) with the vehicle raised, unless it is safely supported. Take care not to pull the vehicle off its supports when applying force to a spanner. Wherever possible, initially slacken tight fastenings before raising the car off the ground.

ALWAYS wear eye protection when working under the vehicle and when using power tools.

Working On The Vehicle

ALWAYS seek specialist advice unless you are justifiably confident about carrying out each job. The safety of your vehicle affects you, your passengers and other road users.

DON'T lean over, or work on, a running engine unless it is strictly necessary, and keep long hair and loose clothing well out of the way of moving mechanical parts. Note that it is theoretically possible for fluorescent striplighting to make an engine fan appear to be stationary - double check whether it is spinning or not! This is the sort of error that happens when you're really tired and not thinking straight. So...

...DON'T work on your car when you're over tired.

ALWAYS work in a well ventilated area and don't inhale dust - it may contain asbestos or other harmful substances.

NEVER run the engine indoors, in a confined space or over a pit.

REMOVE your wrist watch, rings and all other jewellery before doing any work on the vehicle - and especially when working on the electrical system.

DON'T remove the radiator or expansion tank filler cap when the cooling system is hot, or you may get scalded by escaping coolant or steam. Let the system cool down first and even then, if the engine is not completely cold, cover the cap with a cloth and gradually release the pressure.

NEVER drain oil, coolant or automatic transmission fluid when the engine is hot. Allow time for it to cool sufficiently to avoid scalding you.

ALWAYS keep antifreeze, brake and clutch fluid away from vehicle paintwork. Wash off any spills immediately.

TAKE CARE to avoid touching any engine or exhaust system component unless it is cool enough not to burn you.

Running The Vehicle

NEVER start the engine unless the gearbox is in neutral (or 'Park' in the case of automatic transmission) and the hand brake is fully applied.

NEVER run catalytic converter equipped vehicles without the exhaust system heat shields in place.

TAKE CARE when parking vehicles fitted with catalytic converters. The 'cat' reaches extremely high temperatures and any combustible materials under the car, such as long dry grass, could be ignited.

Personal Safety

NEVER siphon fuel, antifreeze, brake fluid or other such toxic liquids by mouth, or allow contact with your skin. Use a suitable hand pump and wear gloves.

BEFORE undertaking dirty jobs, use a barrier cream on your hands as a protection against infection. Preferably, wear suitable gloves, available from DIY outlets.

WEAR IMPERVIOUS GLOVES for sure when there is a risk of used engine oil coming into contact with your skin. It can cause cancer.

WIPE UP any spilt oil, grease or water off the floor immediately.

MAKE SURE that spanners and all other tools are the right size for the job and are not likely to slip. Never try to 'double-up' spanners to gain more leverage.

SEEK HELP if you need to lift something heavy which may be beyond your capability. Don't forget that when lifting a heavy weight, you should keep your back straight and bend your knees to avoid injuring your back.

NEVER take risky short-cuts or rush to finish a job. Plan ahead and allow plenty of time.

BE METICULOUS and keep the work area tidy - you'll avoid frustration, work better and lose less.

KEEP children and animals right-away from the work area and from unattended vehicles.

ALWAYS tell someone what you're doing and have them regularly check that all is well, especially when working alone on, or under, the vehicle.

HAZARDS

Fire!

Petrol (gasoline) is a dangerous and highly flammable liquid requiring special precautions. When working on the fuel system, disconnect the vehicle battery earth (ground) terminal whenever possible and always work outside, or in a very well ventilated area. Any form of spark, such as that caused by an electrical fault, by two metal surfaces striking against each other, by a central heating boiler in the garage 'firing up', or

even by static electricity built up in your clothing can, in a confined space, ignite petrol vapour causing an explosion. Take great care not to spill petrol on to the engine or exhaust system, never allow any naked flame anywhere near the work area and, above all, don't smoke.

Invest in a workshop-sized fire extinguisher. Choose the carbon dioxide type or preferably, dry powder but NEVER a water type extinguisher for workshop use.

DON'T disconnect any fuel pipes on a fuel injected engine without following the advice in this manual. The fuel in the line is under very high pressure - sufficient to cause serious injury. Remember that many injection systems have residual pressure in the pipes for days after switching off. If necessary seek specialist advice.

Fumes

Petrol (gasoline) vapour and that given off by many solvents, thinners, and adhesives are highly toxic and under certain conditions can lead to unconsciousness or even death, if inhaled. The risks are increased if such fluids are used in a confined space so always ensure adequate ventilation. Always read the maker's instructions and follow them with care.

Never drain petrol (gasoline) or use solvents, thinners adhesives or other toxic substances in an inspection pit. It is also dangerous to park a vehicle for any length of time over an inspection pit. The fumes from even a slight fuel leak can cause an explosion when the engine is started.

Mains Electricity

Avoid the use of mains electricity when working on the vehicle, whenever possible. Use rechargeable tools and a DC inspection lamp, powered from a remote 12V battery - both are much safer. However, if you do use mains-powered equipment, ensure that the appliance is wired correctly to its plug, that where necessary it is properly earthed (grounded), and that the fuse is of the correct rating for the appliance. Do not use any mains powered equipment in damp conditions or in the vicinity of fuel, fuel vapour or the vehicle battery.
Always use an RCD (Residual Current Device) circuit breaker with mains electricity. Then, if there is a short, the RCD circuit breaker minimises the risk of electrocution by instantly cutting the power supply.

Ignition System

Never work on the ignition system with the ignition switched on, or with the engine being turned over on the starter, or running and you are recommended never to do so.

Touching certain parts of the ignition system, such as the HT leads, distributor cap, ignition coil etc., can result in a severe electric shock or physical injury as a hand is pulled sharply away. Voltages produced by electronic ignition systems are much higher than those produced by conventional systems and could prove fatal, particularly to people with cardiac pacemaker implants. Consult your handbook or main dealer if in any doubt.

Cooling Fan

On many vehicles, the electric cooling fan can switch itself on even with the ignition turned off. This is especially likely after driving the car and parking it before turning off, after which heat rises to the top of the engine and turns the fan on, suddenly and without warning. If you intend working in the engine bay, it's best to do so when the engine is cold, to disconnect the battery, or keep away from the fan, if neither of these are possible.

Battery

Never cause a spark, smoke, or allow a naked light near the vehicle's battery, even in a well ventilated area. Highly explosive hydrogen gas is given off as part of the charging process.

Battery terminals on the car should be shielded, since a spark can be caused by any metal object which touches the battery's terminals or connecting straps.

IMPORTANT NOTE: Before disconnecting the battery earth (ground) terminal read the relevant FACT FILE in Chapter 5 regarding saving computer and radio settings.)

When using a battery charger, switch off the power supply before the battery charger leads are connected or disconnected. If the battery is not of the 'sealed-for-life' type, loosen the filler plugs or remove the cover before charging. For best results the battery should be given a low rate trickle charge overnight. Do not charge at an excessive rate or the battery may burst.

Always wear gloves and goggles when carrying or when topping up the battery. Acid electrolyte is extremely corrosive and must not be allowed to contact the eyes, skin or clothes.

Brakes and Asbestos

Obviously, a car's brakes are among its most important safety related items. ONLY work on your vehicle's braking system if you are trained and competent to do so. If you have not been trained in this work, but wish to carry out the jobs described in this book, we strongly recommend that you have a garage or qualified mechanic check your work before using the car.

Whenever you work on the braking system components, or remove front or rear brake pads or shoes: i) wear an efficient particle mask; ii) wipe off all brake dust from the brakes after spraying on a proprietary brand of brake cleaner (never blow dust off with compressed air); iii) dispose of brake dust and discarded shoes or pads in a sealed plastic bag; iv) wash your hands thoroughly after you have finished working on the brakes and certainly before you eat or smoke; v) replace shoes and pads only with asbestos-free shoes or pads. Note that asbestos brake dust can cause cancer if inhaled; vi) always replace brake pads and/or shoes in complete 'axle' sets of four - never replace the pads/shoes on one wheel only.

Brake Fluid

Brake fluid absorbs moisture rapidly from the air and can become dangerous resulting in brake failure. You should change the fluid in accordance with your vehicle manufacturer's recommendations or as advised in this book. Never store (or use) an opened container of brake fluid. Dispose of the remainder at your Local Authority Waste Disposal Site, in the designated disposal unit, not with general waste or with waste oil.

Engine Oils

Always wear disposable plastic or rubber gloves when draining the oil from your engine. i) Note that the drain plug and the oil are often hotter than you expect. Wear gloves if the plug is too hot to touch and keep your hand to one side so that you are not scalded by the spurt of oil as the plug comes away; ii) There are very real health hazards associated with used engine oil. In the words of one manufacturer's handbook "Prolonged and repeated contact may cause serious skin disorders, including dermatitis and cancer." Use a barrier cream on your hands and try not to get oil on them. Always wear gloves and wash your hands with hand cleaner soon after carrying out the work. Keep oil out of the reach of children; iii) NEVER, EVER dispose of old engine oil into the ground or down a drain. In the UK, and in most EC countries, every local authority must provide a safe means of oil disposal. In the UK, try your local Environmental Health Department for advice on waste disposal facilities.

Plastic Materials

Many of the materials used (polymers, resins, adhesives and materials acting as catalysts and accelerators) contain dangers in the form of poisonous fumes, skin irritants, and the risk of fire and explosions. Do not allow resin or 2-pack adhesive hardener, or that supplied with filler or 2-pack stopper, to come into contact with skin or eyes. Read carefully the safety notes supplied on the can, tube or packaging and always wear impervious gloves and goggles when working with them.

Fluoroelastomers

Fluoroelastomers are commonly used for oil seals, wiring and cabling, bearing surfaces, gaskets, diaphragms, hoses and 'O' rings. If they are subjected to temperatures greater than 315 degrees C, they will decompose and can be potentially hazardous. Some decomposition may occur at temperatures above 200 degrees C, and it is obvious that when a car has been in a fire or has been dismantled with the assistance of a cutting torch or blow torch, the fluoroelastomers can decompose in the manner indicated above.

According to the Health and Safety Executive, "Skin contact with this liquid or decomposition residues can cause painful and penetrating burns. Permanent irreversible skin and tissue damage can occur". Damage can also be caused to eyes or by the inhalation of fumes created as fluoroelastomers are burned or heated.

After a vehicle has been exposed to fire or high temperatures:

1. Do not touch blackened or charred seals or equipment.

2. Preferably, don't handle parts containing decomposed fluoroelastomers, but if you must, wear goggles and PVC (polyvinyl chloride) or neoprene protective gloves whilst doing so. Never handle such parts unless they are completely cool.

3. Contaminated parts, residues, materials and clothing, including protective clothing and gloves, should be disposed of by an approved contractor to landfill or by incineration according to national or local regulations. Oil seals, gaskets and 'O' rings, along with contaminated material, must not be burned.

WORKSHOP

1. Always have a fire extinguisher of the correct type at arm's length when working on the fuel system. If you do have a fire, DON'T PANIC. Use the extinguisher effectively by directing it at the base of the fire.

2. NEVER use a naked flame anywhere in the workplace.

3. KEEP your inspection lamp well away from any source of petrol (gasoline) such as when disconnecting a carburettor float bowl or fuel line.

4. NEVER use petrol (gasoline) to clean parts. Use paraffin (kerosene), white spirits, or, a proprietary degreaser.

5. NO SMOKING. There's a risk of fire or of transferring dangerous substances to your mouth and, in any case, ash falling into mechanical components is to be avoided.

FACT FILE: FOUR WHEEL DRIVE CARS

● Whenever you have to raise a wheel off the ground and turn it by hand, always ensure that the opposite-side's wheel to the one being lifted is also off the ground and free to turn and that both wheels remaining on the ground are held by the parking brake (if possible) and securely chocked in both directions.

● ALWAYS have the gearbox in neutral (or 'N' in the case of automatics). In the case of some 4 wheel drive automatics and those with permanent 4WD, it is necessary to disengage the 4WD system by special means.

● Consult your handbook or seek advice from your main dealer.

6. BE METHODICAL in everything you do, use common sense, and think of safety at all times.

ENVIRONMENT FIRST!

The used oil from the sump of just one car can cover an area of water the size of two football pitches, cutting off the oxygen supply and harming swans, ducks, fish and other river lift.

When you drain your engine oil - don't oil the drain!

Pouring oil down the drain will cause pollution. It is also an offense. Don't mix used oil with other materials, such as paint and solvents, because this makes recycling difficult. Take used oil to an oil recycling bank. Telephone FREE on 0800 663366 to find the location of your nearest oil bank, or contact you local authority recycling officer.

OIL POLLUTES WATER
USE YOUR BRAIN-
NOT THE DRAIN!

CHAPTER 2 USING YOUR CAR

This Chapter is taken from FIAT's own official Handbooks on the Uno. It contains important and helpful information for the operation of your FIAT Uno.

We recommend that you read this chapter carefully, so that you will become familiar with your vehicle's controls and instruments.

KEYS AND LOCKS

❏ 1. DOORS AND BONNET

DOOR LOCKS
Most FIAT Unos have manual locking. You turn the key in the lock in the normal way to lock and unlock the door.

CHILDPROOF LOCKS
1A. 5-door models are fitted with childproof locks. Find them in the ends of the rear doors, when open.

● **A** - Lock not engaged.

● **B** - Lock engaged.

IMPORTANT NOTE: On models fitted with power locks the childproof locks remain engaged even if the doors are opened with the remote control.

REMOTE LOCKING/UNLOCKING
Remote Operation:
1B. A directional signal is emitted when you press button **D** on your remote unit.

IMPORTANT NOTE: The presence of dirt, snow or ice on the side windows may prevent operation.

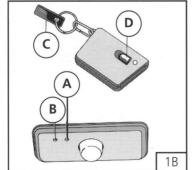

Receiving Unit In Car: The receiving unit can store up to 6 codes. Tag **C**, supplied with every receiver, has a code number stamped on it. **Keep this tag in a safe place - replacements are very expensive.**

To Store the Code of Your Transmitter:
● Press and hold down button **A** with a ball-point pen. The red LED **B** illuminates, indicating that the receiving unit is ready to store the code.

● Hold down button **D** on your remote unit.

● The LED at **B** turns off, indicating that the receiver has stored the code.

● Release Button **A**. Red LED **B** flashes for about 8 seconds to confirm that the code has been stored.

If you press button **A** again within 8 seconds, the red LED **B** illuminates indicating that the receiving unit is ready to store another code. Repeat the procedure.

If you lose a remote unit there are two ways to store a new code:

Using a Remote Unit With Code Already Stored:
● Press and hold down button **A**. After about 2 seconds red LED **B** flashes once.

● Press button **D** on the remote unit whose code has been stored. Red LED **B** illuminates.

● Release button **A**. Red LED **B** flashes for 8 seconds indicating new code has been stored.

Manual Operation: ● Have tag **C** ready. The four numbers stamped on the tag will be used in this procedure:

● Press Button **A** twice . Red LED **B** flashes 3 times and then turns off for about 2 seconds.

● Release button **A** (see illustration *1B*). Red LED **B** flashes for 8 seconds indicating the new remote units code has been stored.

IMPORTANT NOTE: If the LED does not illuminate when remote unit button (illustration *1B*, button *D)* is pressed, change the remote units battery.

1C. Locking and Unlocking the Hatchback Door:

Most hatchback models have manual locking. You turn the key in the lock in the normal way to lock and unlock the the door. Some models have a hatchback door release lever **A** near the driver's seat which, when pulled upwards, can be used to open the hatchback door.

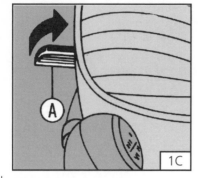

1C

☐ 2. IGNITION SWITCH AND STEERING COLUMN LOCK

IGNITION SWITCH

2. The ignition/steering column lock key, once inserted in the ignition lock, can be placed in any of the following four positions:

● **PARK** - With the key in this position the side and tail lights can be turned on, the steering column locked and the keys can be removed. Press button **A** to turn the key to PARK.

2

● **STOP** - When the key is turned to the STOP position the steering column will be locked, and the keys can be removed.

● **MAR** - This is the driving position. When the key is in this position all the electrical devices are energised.

● **AVV** - Turning the key to this position starts the engine.

STEERING COLUMN LOCK

● **LOCKING** - To apply the steering wheel lock turn the steering wheel slightly to the left or right when the key is at STOP or PARK.

SAFETY FIRST!

● *Never remove the key when the car is moving. If you do, the steering wheel will lock the first time you turn it.*

● *If the ignition lock has been tampered with or shows any sign of damage (e.g. attempted theft), have the lock checked at your nearest FIAT Service Centre.*

● **UNLOCKING** - Rock the steering wheel gently back and forth while turning the ignition key to MAR unlocks the steering wheel.

DASHBOARD

☐ 3. PANEL INDICATORS

Instrument Display Panel

3A. These are the instrument panel warning LED indicators for all FIAT Uno models. Your vehicle will only have Panel Indicators relevant to your particular car.

⎢↗⎢	Choke	🛢	Oil pressure warning
⇦⇨	Direction indicators	(⚠)	Handbrake engaged
⯬◑	Side lights	🔲	Rear window defroster
☰D	High beam lights		Injection system warning light
(⫢	Rear fog lights	🔋	Battery warning
⚠	Hazard warning lights		Seat belts not buckled
(⏹)	ABS brake warning		Automatic transmission fluid warning
⭕	Brake pad wear warning		Doors improperly closed
	Turbo pressure warning		Trailer direction indicators
⫢D	Front fog lights		

3A

IMPORTANT NOTE: The check panel will not indicate if the side and tail light fuses blow at the same time, or if there is a circuit failure within the panel display.

Turbocharger Pressure Gauge (Petrol Models)

3B. Under normal conditions the pressure gauge should indicate:
- Between 0 and 0.75 bar.

IMPORTANT NOTE: If the turbo pressure exceeds the maximum figures shown, have your car checked at a FIAT service centre.

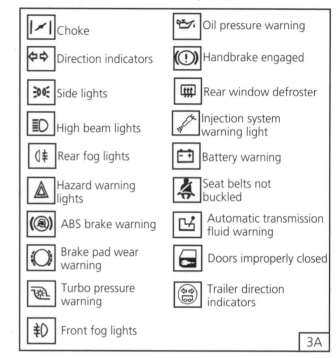

3B

☐ 4. ELECTRONIC CHECK PANEL

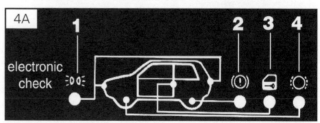

EXTERIOR LIGHT FAILURE

4A. When the ignition key is at MAR, the check panel LED (**1**) light up when one or more of the following circuits is open:

● side and tail lights ● rear fog guard lights ● number plate lights

IMPORTANT NOTE: The check panel does not indicate if the side and tail light fuses blow at the same time.

BRAKE FLUID WARNING LIGHT
When the ignition is at MAR, the brake fluid warning light (**2**) lights up if the brake fluid is low.

DOOR OPEN WARNING LIGHT
With the ignition key at MAR, LED (**3**) lights up if one or more of the doors is not properly closed.

BRAKE PAD WEAR WARNING LIGHT
With the ignition key at MAR, the brake pad wear warning LED (**4**), will light up intermittently. As the brake pads wear increases the warning light remains on constantly.

❏ 5. HEATING AND VENTILATION CONTROLS

The heating and ventilation control panel on all Unos is situated in the centre of the dashboard underneath the central air vents.

EARLY MODELS

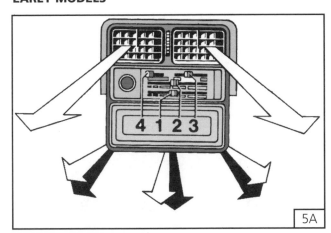

5A

5A. The controls for the early models are:
- **1** - Heater temperature (hottest to right).
- **2** - Air flow (strongest flow to right).
- **3** - Air distribution (screen to left; footwell to right).
- **4** - Fan control.

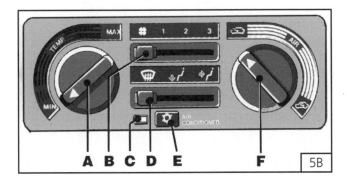

A B C D E F 5B

5B. The controls for later Uno models are:
- **A** - Air temperature adjustment knob.
- **B** - Three speed fan lever.
- **C** - Automatic temperature control ON/OFF indicator or air conditioner ON/OFF indicator (if fitted).

- **D** - Air distributor lever.
- **E** - Air conditioner ON/OFF switch (if fitted).
- **F** - Air volume knob or if fitted air conditioner recirculation knob.

HEATING
Heat Distribution - With the air temperature knob **A** turned to the red zone and the air volume knob **F** turned to the MAX position, select a desired fan speed and place the air distribution lever **B** at:

- Central setting - For defrosting or cold outside temperatures.
- Right-hand setting - For normal heating.

Automatic Heating - Turn the air temperature regulation knob **A** to the desired position, place the air volume control knob **F** in any position except OFF (MAX is recommended), and move the fan lever **B** to AUTO. The red LED **C** will light up indicating that the system is operating automatically.

The fan speed can be controlled manually by moving lever **B** to the right. The automatic system LED turns off, but the passenger compartment temperature will still be regulated automatically.

Demist the Windows - By turning the air temperature knob **A** to the red zone.

- Turn the air volume **F** knob to the MAX setting.
- Move the fan lever (**B**) to maximum speed.
- Place the air distribution lever (**D**) in the far left-hand position.

Turn on the rear window demister if the rear window fogs up.

VENTILATION
- Turn the air temperature knob **A** to MIN in the blue zone.
- Turn the air volume **F** knob to MAX.
- Place the fan lever **B** at the desired speed.

AIR CONDITIONING
Air conditioning is an optional extra fitted to some models of Uno.

- **Air Conditioning Switch** - When you press the air conditioning switch **E**, the air conditioning will initially operate at the first fan speed even if the fan is at the OFF position.

- **Air Recirculation Knob** - The following two selections can be made using the recirculation knob **F** - see illustration *5B*

- **Recirculation** - When knob **F** is turned fully to the right no outside air enters the passenger compartment. Use this feature for fast cooling or heating. Select this position in conditions where the air is heavily polluted.

- **Outside Air** - Turn the recirculation selector fully left so that outside air enters the passenger compartment.

Air Conditioner Cooling: (see illustration **5B**).
- Turn the air temperature knob **A** to the blue zone.
- Turn the knob **F** fully left to the outside air position.
- Select the desired fan setting with lever **B**.
- Slide the air distribution lever **D** to the far right.
- Press button **E** to turn on the air conditioner.
- When the blue LED **C** lights up the air conditioning system is operating.

Air Conditioner Heating: (see illustration **5B**).
- Turn the air temperature control **A** to the red zone.
- Turn the knob **F** to the outside air position.
- Place the air distribution lever **D** in the centre position - DO NOT SWITCH ON THE AIR CONDITIONER!

Defrosting the Windsceen and Windows:
- Turn the air temperature knob **A** to the red zone.
- Turn the knob **F** fully to the outside air position.
- Place fan speed **B** lever at the maximum setting.
- Place the air distribution lever **D** in the far left setting.
- Use the air conditioner when the air is very damp.

CONTROLS - pre-1990

❑ 6. SWITCH BANKS

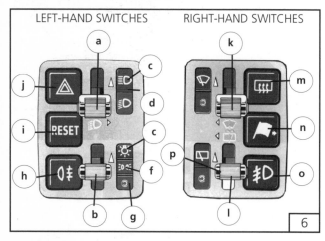

LEFT-HAND SWITCHES   RIGHT-HAND SWITCHES

6

HEADLIGHT MAIN BEAMS
Bring the upper switch (**a**) to (**c**) and lower switch to (**e**).

HEADLIGHT DIPPED BEAMS
Bring the upper switch to (**d**) and lower switch to (**e**).

HEADLIGHT FLASHER
Press the upper switch (**a**) towards the steering wheel.

SIDE LIGHTS
With lower switch at (**e**) side lights will operate with headlights.

With the lower switch at (**f**), side lights only will operate. Also, see PARK position, *page 10*.

Positions (**g**, **p** and **r**) are OFF.

HAZARD WARNING LIGHTS
Depress button (**j**) and all direction indicators will flash.

TRIP MASTER CONTROL (if fitted). Press button (**i**).

REAR FOG-GUARD LIGHTS
Depress button (**h**) and move upper switch to (**d**) and lower switch (**c**).

The two vertical switches on the right-hand side of the binnacle are for the operation of front and rear screen wipers, washers and heated rear window.

WINDSCREEN WIPER (k)
Top = continuous fast. Centre = continuous slow (some cars). Intermediate down = intermittent operation. Down = Off.

WINDSCREEN WASHER (l)
Move the upper switch (**k**) towards the steering wheel (some versions are fitted with a manual pump located near the steering column).

REAR WINDOW WIPER
To operate move the switch (**l**) to position (**p**).

REAR WINDOW WASHER
To operate, move the switch (**e**) towards the steering wheel, then release.

HEATED REAR WINDOW
Push button (**m**). The engine should be running to protect the battery.

CONTROL FOR TRIP MASTER (if fitted) - press button (**n**).

FRONT FOG LAMPS (if fitted)

Press button (**o**) when side lights are on and engine is running.

CONTROLS - 1990-on

❑ 7. LIGHTS AND INDICATORS

7A. The lights only operate when the ignition key is at MAR, **except** when the key is in the PARK position - see page 10.

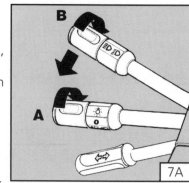

7A

- Move the stalk towards the steering wheel to flash the high beam headlights.

SIDE AND TAIL LIGHTS
- Rotate the end of the left-hand stalk (**A**) in the direction of the arrow. The panel side light LED will light up.

IMPORTANT NOTE: The lever cannot be moved down while in this position.

LOW BEAM HEADLIGHTS
- Rotate the stalk from position **A** to **B**.

HIGH BEAM HEADLIGHTS
- Rotate the stalk to the low beam position **B**.
- Push the stalk down to switch on the high beam.

DIRECTION INDICATORS

7B. Move the left-hand stalk:

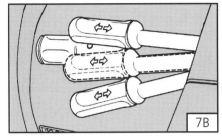

- Up - right turn.
- Down - left turn.

The panel direction indicator light flashes when the direction indicators are operating. The stalk returns to the centre position after completing the turn.

❏ 8. WINDSCREEN WASHER/WIPER

FRONT WASHER/WIPERS

8. The washers and wipers (right-hand stalk) only operate when the ignition key is at MAR.

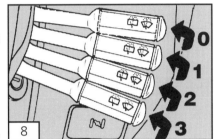

- **0** - Wipers OFF.
- **1** - Intermittent operation.
- **2** - Slow with continuous operation (except base version).
- **3** - Fast and continuous operation.
- Pull the right-hand stalk towards the steering wheel to turn on the windscreen washer (and headlight washer, if installed).

REAR WASHER/WIPER
- Press the lever forward towards the dashboard to turn on the rear window washer/wiper (if installed). The washer/wiper turns off when you release the stalk.

❏ 9. SWITCH BANK

9A. Some models are fitted with a switch bank, which is located in the centre of the dashboard above the air vents. The switch bank replaces

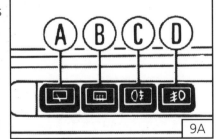

some of the controls which would normally be on the direction indicator and wiper control stalks.

- **A** - **Rear Window Wiper** (if installed). - Press this button when the ignition key is at position MAR.
- **B** - **Rear Window Defroster**. - Press this button when the ignition key is at MAR to demist the rear window. The rear demister panel LED will light up when this button is pressed.

- **C** - **Rear Fog Lights** - These lights can be turned on when the low beam headlights are on. The rear fog light panel LED will light up when this button is pressed.
- **D** - **Front Fog Lights** (if installed) - The front fog lights can be switched on when the low beam headlights are on. The front fog light panel LED will light up when the button is pressed.

9B. HAZARD WARNING LIGHTS
Press the hazard light switch (arrowed) to turn the hazard warning lights. All the directional indicator lamps and the panel indicator will flash. The hazard warning lights work whether the key is inserted or not.

INDIVIDUAL SETTINGS

❏ 10. FRONT SEAT ADJUSTMENT

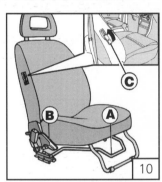

10. LEG ROOM ADJUSTMENT
- Lift lever **A** and exert body pressure in the direction desired to set the seats fore and aft position.
- Release the lever, ensuring that the seat is locked in the desired position.

FRONT SEAT ANGLE ADJUSTMENT
- To adjust the angle of the front seats backrest cushion lift lever **B** to recline the or raise the backrest.

Some models are fitted with an optional lumbar support. To adjust the lumbar support to the desired position turn the knob located on the side of the seats back rest.

ACCESS TO REAR SEATS (3-DOOR MODELS)
The front seats can be released and tilted forward by pulling up the levers **C** on the sides of both the front seats back rests.

IMPORTANT NOTE: The front seats are fitted with headrests which cannot be removed.

❏ 11. DOOR MIRROR ADJUSTMENT

11A. MANUAL ADJUSTMENT
When the door mirror **A** is in position **1** you can adjust the door mirrors angle using lever **B** from inside the passenger compartment.

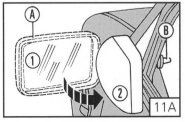

- The mirror can be folded flush against the car (position **2**) when driving through a car wash.
- Adjustable door mirrors are available as an option.

11B. POWER ADJUSTMENT

The two electric powered window switches are located in the driver's side armrest, to operate the power windows when the key is at MAR:

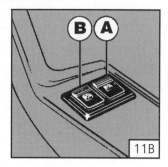

- **A** - Opens and closes the driver's door window.
- **B** - Opens and closes the passenger door window.

There is also a single switch in the passenger's side door armrest which will only open and close the front passenger window.

BONNET AND LUGGAGE COMPARTMENT

❑ 12. BONNET

OPENING THE BONNET

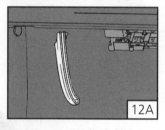

- **12A.** First pull the bonnet release lever, located to the right of the steering column (or on passenger's side, early cars)

- **12B.** Positioned underneath the front of the bonnet is the bonnet release catch (arrowed). Lift the catch up to release.
- Lift the bonnet and pull the support rod out of its holder.
- When the bonnet is fully raised, place the tip of the rod in the recess located in the bonnet.

❑ 13. LUGGAGE COMPARTMENT

13A. INCREASING THE CARGO AREA
Folding the Back Seats - Use the following procedure to fold the rear seat forwards:

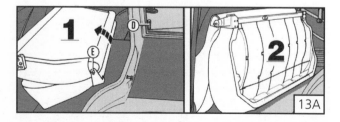

- Press lever **D** down to release the seat backrest.
- Push the entire seat forwards **1**, then upwards **2** (as shown).

Repositioning the Back Seats - When repositioning the rear seat ensure that:

- The pegs **E** are properly engaged in the slots.
- Make sure that the outer seat belts are put in front of the backrests.
- Pull the centre seat belt webbing and buckle through gap where both the rear seat cushion and backrest meet.

- **13B.** The rear seat backrest cushion can be placed in two different positions depending on which slots the backrest side pins are inserted into. Models with split rear seats have only one slot position.

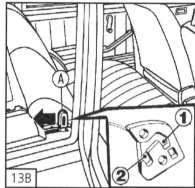

- Pull levers **A** towards the rear of the car.
- **1** - Normal backrest position.
- **2** - In this position there is increased storage space in the luggage compartment.

ACCESSORIES

❑ 14. INTERIOR LIGHTS

COURTESY LIGHT
On most models the courtesy light is positioned in the centre of the roof. However, on models fitted with a sunroof the courtesy lights are located on the centre pillars. The light turns on when either of the front doors is opened.

- When the doors are closed pressing the sides of the courtesy light lens will switch the light ON/OFF.

14. MAP LIGHT (if fitted)
- Press button **A** to switch on the map light.
- Turn the map light housing **B** to adjust the direction of the beam.

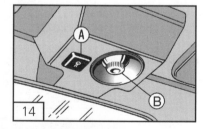

❑ 15. SUNROOF OPERATION

15A. SUNROOF CONTROLS
As an optional extra some models are fitted with a sunroof. To operate the sunroof.

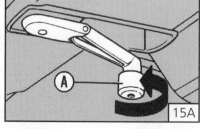

- Pull handle **A** down and turn anti-clockwise. The sunroof lifts up and then slides back.

• A sliding louvre provides shade and decreases the air flow inside the passenger compartment.

15B. Some models are fitted with a sliding-open sunroof.

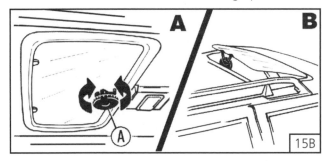

15B

• OPEN - Turn knob **A** anti-clockwise to raise the sunroof fully from the back **B**.
• CLOSE - Turn knob **A** clockwise to close sunroof.
• Ensure that the sunroof is fully sealed, by turning the handle/knob slightly past the closed position, then back.

WHEEL CHANGING

❏ 16. CHANGING THE WHEEL IN AN EMERGENCY

CHANGING THE WHEEL
Whenever possible park the car on firm level ground. Put the car into first or reverse gear and pull on the handbrake. It's a good idea to keep a chock or piece of wood in the boot of your car, which can be wedged under the wheels to prevent the car from rolling. If you haven't got a piece of wood handy you can always use a large rock or stone.

The spare wheel, jack and tools are located in the luggage compartment under the mat.

• **16A. Early Models:**
Pull tab (**A**) to release the jack from the support.

16A

• **16B.** To release the support and toolkit squeeze the retaining tabs (**B**), lift and remove the support and spare wheel.

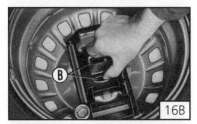

16B

• **16C. Later Models:**
Release the jack from the tool kit housing by unhooking the elastic strap (**a**) and then by lifting the base of the stand (**b**), which contains the

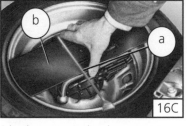

16C

jack and tools, from inside the spare wheel.

• **16D.**
Release the jack from the stand by lifting tab **A**.

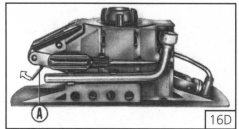

16D

❏ 17. RAISING THE VEHICLE

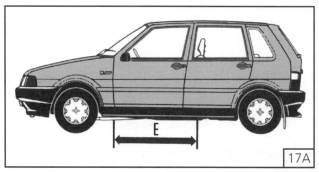

17A

17A. To raise the vehicle, position the jack (in zone **E** only) under the side member.

17B. Turn the jack handle until the jack's grooved head **C** engages the flange at the base of the sill **D**.

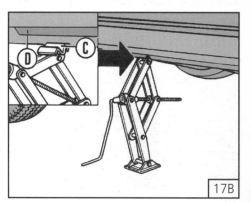

17B

REMOVING THE WHEEL
17C. Using the wrench provided, loosen all the wheel bolts about one turn, in the order shown in the inset illustration.

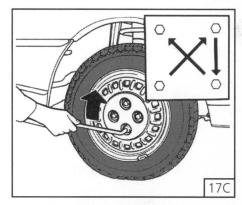

17C

SAFETY FIRST!

• *Before jacking the car, always make sure that the vehicle is on firm even ground.*

• *Always place the spare wheel, or the wheel you've just removed, under the car: partly for safety to guard against being crushed; partly so that if the car topples off the jack you won't damage the underneath of the car and you'll be able to reposition the jack.*

• Lift the car until the wheel is about 25 mm (1 in.) off the ground.

• The hub cap is only secured by three of the four wheel bolts.

• Remove the hub cap by unscrewing the three bolts, then unscrew the fourth wheel bolt, and remove the wheel.

• Put the spare wheel on, making sure that the aligning peg on the hub fits into one of the holes in the rim.

• Attach the wheel with a single bolt and then put the wheel cover back on so that the largest hole fits over the bolt holding on the wheel. Screw in the other three bolts, which also hold on the wheel cover.

• Lower the car and remove the jack. Tighten the wheel bolts evenly in a criss-cross fashion, as shown in illustration **17D** (inset).

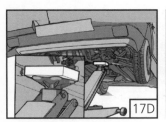 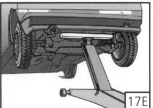

RAISING THE VEHICLE WITH A TROLLEY JACK

• **17D. From The Front** - Place a hardwood board between the jack and the car, see inset. The jack must ONLY be positioned under the gearbox case support on the side of the differential gears.

• **17E. From The Rear** - Put a hardwood board between the jack and the car ONLY at the back of the spare wheel housing.

EMERGENCY STARTING

❑ 18. ENGINE STARTING

See **FACT FILE: DISCONNECTING THE BATTERY** on **page 36**.

JUMP STARTING YOUR CAR

Choose a fully charged battery with the same or higher capacity than the flat battery in your car, then proceed as follows:

• Make sure that the car with the flat batteries electrical equipment is turned off and that the ignition keys are removed.

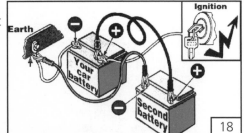

18. Connect one of the jump lead clamps to the positive battery post of your flat battery.

Then clamp the other end of the same lead on to the positive post of the second (charged) battery.

• Connect one end of the second jump lead to the negative pole of the charged battery, and attach the other end to the metal terminal (as shown) of the earth cable from your car's flat battery.

• Run the engine of the car with the charged battery at a medium to slow speed.

• Start the engine of the car with the flat battery, and run the engines of both cars for about three minutes.

• To reduce voltage peaks when disconnecting the jump leads, turn on the air fan and the heated rear screen of the car that had the flat battery.

• Remove the jumpleads, starting with the negative clamp connected to the car with the flat battery's earth.

IMPORTANT NOTE: When disconnecting the jump leads DO NOT switch on the headlights in place of the heated rear screen, as the peak voltage may blow the headlight bulbs.

BUMP STARTING

The best method of starting the engine in an emergency is using an auxiliary battery and jump leads, as described above. But in the case of extreme emergency, as long as your car does not have automatic transmission and is not fitted with a catalytic converter, the alternative method would be to bump start your car.

IMPORTANT NOTES: 1) Never bump start a car fitted with a catalytic converter, as the sudden rush of unburnt fuel into the catalytic converter during the initial moments of engine operation could damage the converter beyond repair.

2) On models fitted with automatic transmission bump starting is made impossible by the features of the automatic transmission (i.e. no manual clutch).

To bump start a car not fitted with automatic transmission or a catalytic converter:

• Place the key in the ignition and turn to MAR.

• Engage a high gear (3rd or 4th), NOT REVERSE.

• Hold the clutch pedal down and get someone to push the car.

• When the pushed car has reached a fair speed, with the car still in gear, gradually release the clutch pedal.

• As soon as the gear kicks in, the engine should turn over and start running. Keep the engine running!

Get the battery charged and the car checked immediately.

IMPORTANT NOTE: Ensure that the key is in the ignition and is turned to MAR while the car is being pushed. If it is not, the steering wheel will lock the first time you turn it.

CHAPTER 3
FACTS AND FIGURES

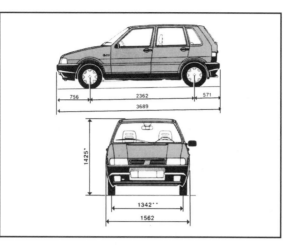

This chapter provides you with all the information you will need about your car, especially in connection with servicing and repairing it. First, you'll need to identify the engine type. If you don't know it already, see *Chapter 6, Repairs and Replacements*.

Before buying parts, be sure to take your vehicle's chassis (VIN) and spares numbers with you - see *Auto-Biography* on *page 1* and *PART G: IDENTIFICATION NUMBERS* in this chapter.

Chapter Contents

IMPORTANT NOTE: Many detail changes have taken place over the years, and there have been many different Special Editions and Options available. The following information will be true of most cases but can only be taken as a general guide. Consult your local FIAT dealer for confirmation.

PART A: MAJOR MILESTONES

Overview When introduced, the Uno was available with ● a 903cc Overhead Valve (OHV) engine (*45* and *Super ES 45*), ●1116cc Overhead Camshaft (OHC) engine (*Comfort 55* and *Super 55*), ● or 1301cc OHC engine (*Super 70*). ● All models with front disc, rear drum brakes. ● All (except commercial vehicles) are hatchbacks. ● Some models with 3 doors; some with 5. ● Some with 4-speed gearboxes; some with 5-speed (and some models available with either).

Later, the smaller versions of the OHC engine were dropped in favour of the Fully Integrated Robotised Engine (FIRE) unit. 1372cc versions of the non-FIRE OHC engine continued to be used, in Turbo and injection forms. Latest cars had sophisticated engine management and catalytic converter fitted. A non-Turbo diesel engine was available and an automatic on some petrol engine types.

Uno 'One' (so to speak!) was replaced by Uno 'Two' in January 1990, with body revisions.

The Uno Van is essentially a Uno car, but with panels in place of the rear side-windows and suitably adapted 'furniture' at the rear.

FACT FILE: NON-FIRE, OHC PETROL ENGINE TYPES

● 1. The top-end appearance of different versions of the non-FIRE OHC engine can lead you to believe that they are 'different' engines when, essentially, they are not! Some have block-mounted distributors; others have horizontal, head-mounted distributors. Air filter housings and oil filler caps can both be either round or rectangular, and both camshaft and cam belt covers can vary in appearance - but it's all the same 'family' of non-FIRE OHC engines!

● 2. Some engines, other than those shown here (such as a 1.5 petrol and 1.4 Turbo Diesel) were only available outside the UK.

● 3. The 1301cc 'regular' engine and the 1301cc Turbo i.e. engines have different bores and strokes from each other.

Limited Editions Too many were produced to list here. Only those which throw up anomalies are shown.

May 1983 Uno first introduced in 903cc OHV, 1116cc OHC and 1301cc OHC forms, as described above.

July 1985 903cc *Uno 45* and *Super 45 S* now fitted with 999cc FIRE engine. *Uno 55* gains twin choke carburettor and electronic ignition and becomes *Uno 60,* still with 1116cc non-FIRE OHC engine. Early 1984 *Uno 70 SL* introduced, with 1299cc (virtually identical to 1301cc) non-FIRE OHC engine. Same capacity engines fitted to new *Uno Turbo i.e.*, producing 105 BHP (compared with the *Uno 70's* 65 BHP).

July 1986 Reintroduction of basic *Uno Formula* version with 903cc OHV engine.

July 1987 Selecta constantly variable automatic transmission (CVT) introduced, on *Uno 60* only.

September 1987 *Uno 60 DS* with 1697cc Diesel engine introduced, in 5 door version only.

January 1990 'New' *Uno* range introduced with restyled front end, more rounded tailgate, larger bumpers and rear light clusters. New fascia and instruments. Available as 903cc OHV (*Uno 45 Formula*); 999cc FIRE OHC (*45 FIRE* and *1.0 i.e.*); 1108cc FIRE OHC (*60 1.1 i.e.*); 1116cc non-FIRE OHC (*60 Selecta*); 1372cc non-FIRE OHC (*70 range* and *Turbo i.e.*) 1697cc non-turbo Diesel in 3-door and 5-door versions (*60 D* and *60 DS*). All (except rear-disc brake Turbo) still with rear drum brakes.

January 1991 *Selecta 70 i.e. auto.* introduced with 1372cc non-FIRE OHC engine. *Uno Van* introduced with 903cc OHV petrol or 1697cc diesel engine, with payloads of 460 kg and 450 kg respectively.

June 1992 *Selecta 60* discontinued. Other petrol versions now with catalyst/injection and rebadged with i.e. suffix.

August 1992 903cc OHV engined *Uno 45 Formula* discontinued.

January 1993 *Selecta 70 i.e.* discontinued.

December 1993 *Uno Petrol Van* discontinued.

March 1994 1108 cc FIRE-engined *60 1.1*, and *Uno Turbo i.e.* discontinued.

End 1995 All remaining Uno versions discontinued.

PART B: VITAL STATISTICS

Wheels and tyres

The following information has been extracted from FIAT's published data. In case of doubt, please ask your local FIAT main dealer.

WHEELS

Base Models: 4.50 B 13 H steel, or 4.50 J 13 H2 alloy (option)

Turbo i.e.: 5 1/2 J x 13 AH2 alloy

TYRE SIZES: All Base models: 135 SR-13
All other Super versions: 155/70 SR-13
SX models: 165/65 R 13 S
Turbo i.e.: 175/60 R 13 H

TYRE PRESSURES (cold)

Pressures relate to your tyre size EXCEPT in the case of specific models shown below.

	Normal Load		Fully Loaded	
	Front	**Rear**	**Front**	**Rear**
135 SR 13	1.9 bar/28 psi	1.9 bar/28 psi	2.2 bar/32 psi	2.2 bar/32 psi
155/70 SR 13	1.9 bar/28 psi	1.9 bar/28 psi	2 bar/29 psi	2.2 bar/32 psi
165/65 SR13	1.9 bar/28 psi	1.9 bar/28 psi	2 bar/29 psi	2.2 bar/32 psi
175/60R 13H	2.2 bar/32 psi	2.2 bar/32 psi	2.3 bar/33 psi	2.5 bar/36 psi
Uno Diesel	2.0 bar/29 psi	1.9 bar/2.8 psi	2.2 bar/32 psi	2.2 bar/3.2 psi
Selecta models	1.9 bar/28 psi	1.9 bar/28 psi	2 0 bar/29 psi	2.2 bar/32 psi

Weights

All weights are given in kilograms (kg). The following are typical Uno model vehicle weights - they may differ according to age of vehicle and specification. NB Maximum load capacity = (Maximum Laden Weight) minus (Unladen Weight). Trailer weights are maximum loaded weight. See your vehicle's VIN plate for definitive information.

MODEL	Unladen Weight	Maximum Laden Weight	Unbraked trailer	Braked trailer	Towball, max. load
1 and 1.1 litre cars	700 to 810	1220	400	800	56
1 litre vans	740	1220	400	800	56
Diesel vans	870	1320	400	900	70
1.4 litre cars	810 to 870	1270	400	900	63
Selecta i.e.	880 to 895	1280	400	900	63
Turbo i.e.	940	1280	400	1000	70
Uno D cars	885 to 900	1320	400	900	70

Max. roof load - 50 kg, all models.

Dimensions (vehicle unladen)

NB There may be very small variations across certain models.

'Mk I' Uno - Overall length: 3644 mm; Overall width: 1555 mm; Wheelbase: 2362 mm; Front track: 1330/1340 mm; Rear track: 1300 mm; Height: 1425/1432 mm.

'Mk II' Uno - Overall length: 3689 mm; Overall width: 1558 mm; Wheelbase: 2362 mm; Front track: 1343 mm; Rear track: 1300 mm; Height: 1415 mm.

PART C: CAPACITIES

All fluid figures are given in litres.

FUEL TANK: Early models - 42. Later models - 38. 1372 Turbo i.e. - 46. Diesels all years - 42

COOLANT CAPACITY INC. HEATER: 903cc OHV - 4.6. 1 litre and 1.1 FIRE OHC - 4.6. 1.1 and 1.3 NON-FIRE OHC - 6.2. 1372cc Turbo i.e. - 7.7. Diesel - 8.

ENGINE OIL CAPACITIES - OIL CHANGE CAPACITY GIVEN, FOLLOWED BY TOTAL CAPACITY IN BRACKETS: 903cc OHV, and 1.0 and 1.1 FIRE OHC - 3.75 (3.9). All NON-FIRE OHC - 4.05 (4.4). Diesel - 4.05 (4.4). Selenia engine oil of appropriate type.

GEARBOX/TRANSAXLE: All manual transmission models - 2.4. **Tutela ZC 90** or **Tutela ZC80/S**, see *page 153*. Selecta - 4.8 (max.), 3.5 (change). **Tutela CVT**. Figures vary - check dipstick reading as confirmation.

STEERING GEAR: All models - 0.14. **Tutela K 854**.

CV JOINT CAVITIES AND BOOTS: All models - 0.08 kg. **Tutela MRM 2** grease.

BRAKE FLUID: All models 0.33 to 0.37 (anti-lock brakes - 0.45) (depending on model). **Tutela Plus 3 - 270 degrees C**.

PART D: SERVICE DATA

Petrol Engine

FIRING ORDER: All models 1-3-4-2
DISTRIBUTOR POINTS GAP (NON-ELECTRONIC IGNITION ONLY): M.Marelli - 0.42 to 0.48. Ducellier - 0.39 to 0.43.
DWELL ANGLE (NON-ELECTRONIC IGNITION ONLY): 52 to 55 degrees.
IGNITION TIMING in degrees Before Top Dead Centre - BTDC:

1. NON-ELECTRONIC IGNITION: OHV: 5 degrees. 1.1
2. NON-ELECTRONIC, NON-DIGIPLEX IGNITION: 999cc and 1108cc FIRE with Ducellier distributor: 2 degrees. 1108cc FIRE with M.Marelli: 3 degrees. 1.1 and 1.3 litre NON-FIRE: 10 degrees. 1.4 litre: 4 degrees. 1.5/Selecta: 3 to 7 degrees. Turbo i.e.: 8 to 12 degrees.
3. DIGIPLEX ELECTRONIC IGNITION: Sensor set with special equipment: 0-1,000 rpm - 2 to 6 degrees. 4,500 - 6,200 rpm @ 0.6 bar - 44 to 48 degrees.

SPARK PLUG TYPES AND GAPS

Model	FIAT	Champion	Gap (mm)
NON ELECTRONIC IGNITION			
All types	V4LSR	RN9Y	0.7
ELECTRONIC IGNITION			
1.0 and 1.1	9GYSSR	RC9YCC	0.85 to 0.95
1.4	9FYSSR	RN9YCC	0.85 to 0.95
Turbo i.e.		Bosch FR 6 DTC	0.7 to 0.8

IDLE SPEED: All petrol models: 750 to 800 up to 1991 except Turbo i.e.: 800 to 900. 1991-on: 800 to 900 except Turbo i.e.: 850 to 950.
CO CONTENT AT IDLE (MAX): Early models: 2 to 3%. Later carburettor models: 1.0 to 2%. Fuel injected models (not adjustable): All models: 0.35.
UNBURNED HYDROCARBONS: <70 p.p.m at idle (1992-on)

VALVE CLEARANCES(mm)	Inlet	Exhaust
OHV ENGINES		
	0.15	0.2

	Inlet	Exhaust
NON-FIRE OHC Engines		
All types	0.4	0.5
FIRE OHC Engines	0.3	0.4
DIESEL 1697cc	0.3	0.35

Diesel Engines

INJECTOR SETTING PRESSURE: Bosch - 125-133 bar.
CAV Nozzle Type BDN - 124-131 bar.
CAV Nozzle Type RDN - 116-123 bar.

INJECTOR PUMP WITH No. 1 PISTON AT TDC, COMPRESSION STROKE: Bosch - -1 to 1 degree, Piston travel 1 mm. CAV - -1 to 1 at TDC.
IDLE SPEED: Bosch 740 to 780 rpm. CAV - 790 to 830 rpm.
MAX. FREE RUNNING ENGINE SPEED: 5100 to 5200 rpm - all types.
VALVE CLEARANCES (mm): Inlet - 0.3. Exhaust - 0.4

Other Settings

CLUTCH ADJUSTMENT: Pedal free play: nil
BRAKE DISC PAD MINIMUM THICKNESS: 1.5 mm
BRAKE SHOE FRICTION LINING MINIMUM THICKNESS: 1.5 mm
TYRE PRESSURES: See **PART A: VITAL STATISTICS.**

PART E: REPAIR DATA

Engine 'bottom end'

	903cc OHV	999cc and 1108cc-FIRE	1116cc OHC NON-FIRE	1301cc OHC NON-FIRE	1301cc Turbo i.e.	1372cc OHC NON-FIRE	1697cc Diesel
BORE:	65-65.05	70-70.05	80 to 80.05	86.4 to 86.45	80.5	80.5 to 80.55	82.6 to 82.65
MAX. BORE TAPER OR OVALITY:	0.015	0.015	0.01	0.01	0.01	0.01	0.015
ENGINE CAMSHAFT BEARING DIAMETERS - FRONT (TIMING GEAR) END (OHV engines only):							
Grade B	50.5 - 50.51	N/A	N/A	N/A	N/A	N/A	N/A
Grade C	50.51 - 50.52	N/A	N/A	N/A	N/A	N/A	N/A
Grade D	50.7 - 50.71	N/A	N/A	N/A	N/A	N/A	N/A
Grade E	50.71 - 50.72	N/A	N/A	N/A	N/A	N/A	N/A

NOTE: Oversize bearings are not available for centre and rear camshaft bearings.

	903cc OHV	999cc and 1108cc-FIRE	1116cc OHC NON-FIRE	1301cc OHC NON-FIRE	1301cc Turbo i.e.	1372cc OHC NON-FIRE	1697cc Diesel
STROKE:	68.0	64.9 (1108: 72)	55.5	55.5 (1299cc: 55.4)	63.9	67.4	79.2
PISTON SIZES:							
Size A	64.94-64.95	69.96-69.97	79.94-79.95	86.36-86.37	80.45-80.46	80.46-80.47 (Turbo: 80.45-80.46)	82.53-82.54
Size C	64.96-64.97	69.98-69.99	79.96-79.97	86.38-86.39	80.47-80.48	80.48-80.49 (Turbo: 80.47-80.48)	82.55-82.56
Size E	64.98-64.99	70-70.01	79.98-79.99	86.4-86.41	80.49-80.5	80.5-80.51 (Turbo: 80.49-80.5)	82.57-82.58

OVERSIZES: 0.2, 0.4, 0.6 (all models)

	903cc OHV	999cc and 1108cc-FIRE	1116cc OHC NON-FIRE	1301cc OHC NON-FIRE	1301cc Turbo i.e.	1372cc OHC NON-FIRE	1697cc Diesel
PISTON CLEARANCES IN BORE:	0.05-0.07	0.03-0.05	0.05-0.07	0.03-0.05	0.04-0.06	0.03-0.05 (Turbo: 0.3-0.06)	0.06-0.08
PISTON PROJECTION ABOVE BLOCK AT TOP DEAD CENTRE:							0.667-1.132
PISTON RING THICKNESS:							
TOP	1.728-1.74	1.478-1.49	1.478-1.49	1.478-1.49	1.478-1.49	1.478-1.49	2.075-2.095
SECOND	1.978-1.99	1.478-1.49	1.978-1.99	1.978-1.99	1.978-1.99	1.728-1.74 (Turbo: 1.978-1.99)	1.978-1.99
BOTTOM	3.925-3.937	2.975-2.99	3.925-3.937	3.925-3.937	3.922-3.937	2.975-2.99	2.975-2.99
PISTON RING CLEARANCES - RING-TO-GROOVE:							
TOP	0.045-0.077	0.04-0.072	0.045-0.047	0.045-0.077	0.045-0.077	0.045-0.077	0.08-0.13
SECOND	0.025-0.057	0.025-0.057	0.025-0.057	0.04-0.072	0.02-0.072	0.040-0.072 (Turbo: 0.02-0.052)	0.02-0.055
BOTTOM	0.020-0.052	0.020-0.055	0.020-0.052	0.03-0.062	0.03-0.085	0.03-0.065	0.03-0.065
PISTON RING END GAP:	All 3: 0.2-0.45	All 3: 0.2-0.45	1: 0.3-0.45 2 &3: 0.2-0.35	1 & 2: 0.3-0.45 3: 0.25-0.4	1 & 2: 0.3-0.5 3: 0.25-0.5	1 & 2: 0.3-0.5 3: 0.25-0.5	1 & 2: 0.3-0.5 3: 0.25-0.5

PISTON RING OVERSIZES: 0.2, 0.4, 0.6 (All models)

	903cc OHV	999cc and 1108cc-FIRE	1116cc OHC NON-FIRE	1301cc OHC NON-FIRE	1301cc Turbo i.e.	1372cc OHC NON-FIRE	1697cc Diesel
CRANK MAIN JOURNAL DIAMETER:	Size 1: 50.785-50.805	Size 1: 43.99-44.0	50.785-50.805	50.79-50.81	Size 1: 50.785-50.795	Size 1: 50.79-50.8	Size 1: 52.995-53.004
	Size 2: 50.785-50.795	Size 2: 43.98-43.99			Size 2: 50.775-50.785	Size 2: 50.78-50.79	Size 2: 52.986-52.995
CRANK, BIG-END DIAMETER:	39.985-40.005	37.988-38.008	45.498-45.518	45.503-45.525	Size 1: 45.508-45.518	Size 1: 45.513-45.523	Size 1: 50.796-50.805
					Size 2: 45.498-45.508	Size 2: 45.503-45.513	Size 2: 50.787-50.796

	903cc OHV	999cc and 1108cc-FIRE	1116cc OHC NON-FIRE	1301cc OHC NON-FIRE	1301cc Turbo i.e.	1372cc OHC NON-FIRE	1697cc Diesel
MAIN BEARING SHELL THICKNESS:							
Size 1	1.832-1.838	1.834-1.84	1.825-1.831	1.825-1.831	1.833-1.842	1.84-1.844	1.839-1.843
Size 2	1.837-1.843	1.839-1.845	N/A	N/A	1.838-1.847	1.845-1.849	1.843-1.847
MAIN BEARING CLEARANCE:							
	0.028-0.073	0.025-0.06	0.026-0.071	0.35-0.08	0.028-0.069	0.019-0.05	0.027-0.062
MAIN BEARING UNDERSIZES: All models: 0.254-0.508							
BIG-END BEARING SHELL THICKNESS (STANDARD):							
	1.807-1.813	1.542-1.548	1.531-1.538	1.531-1.538	Size A: 1.534-1.543	Size A: 1.535-1.541	Size A: 1.528-1.533
					Size B: 1.539-1.548	Size B: 1.54-1.546	Size B: 1.533-1.537
BIG-END BEARING CLEARANCE:							
	0.026-0.071	0.024-0.068	0.036-0.086	0.031-0.081	0.026-0.07	0.025-0.063	0.026-0.06
BIG-END BEARING UNDERSIZES: All models: 0.25, 0.5, 0.76, 1.0							
THRUST WASHER THICKNESS:							
	2.31-2.36	2.31-2.36	2.31-2.36	2.31-2.36	2.31-2.36	2.31-2.36	2.31-2.36
THRUST WASHER OVERSIZE:							
	0.127	0.127	0.127	0.127	0.127	0.127	0.127
CRANKSHAFT END FLOAT:							
	0.055-0.265	0.055-0.265	0.055-0.265	0.055-0.265	0.055-0.265	0.055-0.265	0.06-0.3

Engine 'top end' and valve gear

	903cc OHV	999cc and 1108cc-FIRE	1116cc OHC NON-FIRE	1301cc OHC NON-FIRE	1301cc Turbo i.e.	1372cc OHC NON-FIRE	1697cc Diesel
ENGINE CAMSHAFT BEARING OUTER DIAMETERS (OHC Engines only):							
FRONT	N/A	24.045-24.070	N/A	N/A	N/A	N/A	N/A
CENTRE	N/A	23.545-23.57	N/A	N/A	N/A	N/A	N/A
REAR	N/A	24.045-24.070	N/A	N/A	N/A	N/A	N/A
CAM FOLLOWER DIAMETER:							
	13.982-14	34.975-34.995	36.975-36.995	36.975-36.995	36.975-36.995	36.975-36.995	36.975-36.995
OVERSIZES AVAILABLE:							
	0.05-0.1	N/A	N/A	N/A	N/A	N/A	N/A
INLET VALVE HEAD SIZE:							
	28.8-29.1	30.2-30.5	35.85-36.15	35.85-36.15	43.3-43.7	37.35-37.65 Turbo: 35.85-36.15	37.3-37.6
EXHAUST VALVE HEAD SIZE:							
	28.8-29.1	27.2-27.5	30.85-31.15	30.85-31.15	32.85-33.45	30.85-31.15 Turbo: 32.85-33.45	33.3-33.6

VALVE SEAT RE-CUTTING ANGLE: 45 degrees, +/-5' (all types)

VALVE FACE RE-CUTTING ANGLE: 45 degrees 30', +/-5' (all types)

OHC VALVE SHIM THICKNESSES: Between 3.2 and 4.7 mm in shim increments of 0.05 mm

Cooling system

All figures in degrees Celsius unless stated otherwise.

	903cc OHV	999cc and 1108cc-FIRE	1116cc OHC NON-FIRE	1301cc OHC NON-FIRE	1301cc Turbo i.e.	1372cc OHC NON-FIRE	1697cc Diesel
THERMOSTAT:							
Starts to open	85-89	85-89	80-84	80-84	78-82	80-84	78-82
Fully open	100	100	96	96	95	96	90
PRESSURE CAP RATING: All models: 0.98 bar (14 lbf/sq.in.) - except Diesel models: 0.78 bar (11 lbf/sq.in.)							
COOLING FAN - Switches on:							
	90-94	90-94	90-94	90-94	Low: 86-90 High: 90-94	90-94	Low: 86-90 High: 90-94
COOLING FAN - Switches off:							
	85-89	85-89	85-89	85-89	Low: 81-85 High: 85-89	85-89	Low: 81-85 High: 85-89

WATER TIGHTNESS PRESSURE CHECK: All models: 0.98 bar (14 lbf/sq.in.) - except Diesel models: 0.78 bar (11 lbf/sq.in.)

Brakes

Brakes	903cc OHV	999cc and 1108cc-FIRE	1116cc OHC NON-FIRE	1301cc OHC NON-FIRE	1301cc Turbo i.e.	1372cc OHC NON-FIRE	1697cc Diesel

GAP - SERVO PISTON PUSHROD FROM SUPPORT PLATE (d):
N/A   All other models: 0.825-1.025 mm

Servo

MINIMUM ALLOWED FRONT DISC THICKNESS (mm):
9   9   9   9
18.2   9   10.8
Turbo: 18.2

MINIMUM ALLOWED REAR DISC THICKNESS (mm):
N/A   N/A   N/A   N/A   9   N/A   N/A
                              Turbo: 9

MINIMUM ALLOWED BRAKE DRUM INTERNAL DIAMETER (mm): All models except Turbo i.e.: 186.33

Running gear/suspension - front

CAMBER - **All models:** Front - 25' +/-30' (not adjustable). Rear - N/A (not adjustable)
FRONT CASTER - **All models:** 2 degrees 15' +/-30' (not adjustable)
TOE-IN - **All models:** Front - 0 to 2 mm. Rear N/A
FRONT SPRING HEIGHT RELEASED (mm):
c. 329   c. 329   337   337   334   431.5   344
                                          Turbo: 334

FRONT SPRING HEIGHT-LOAD REQUIRED TO COMPRESS TO 205 mm:
2100 Nm   2100 Nm   2650 Nm   2650 Nm   2850 Nm   2650 Nm   3050 Nm
                                                        Turbo: 2850 Nm

REPLACEMENT FRONT SPRING COLOURS: If new springs fail to give the above heights, YELLOW springs give LOWER heights; GREEN springs give HIGHER. ALWAYS use them in pairs of the same colour.

Rear suspension

REAR COIL SPRING HEIGHT, RELEASED (mm):
c. 242   c. 242   c. 242   c. 242   231   c. 269.5   c. 242
                                                Turbo: 231

REAR COIL SPRING HEIGHT, LOAD REQUIRED TO COMPRESS TO 155 mm. (1372 i.e. = 162 mm):
3200 Nm   3200 Nm   3200 Nm   3200 Nm   3030 Nm   3110 Nm   3200 Nm
                                                        Turbo: 3030 Nm

REPLACEMENT REAR SPRING COLOURS: If new springs fail to give the above heights, YELLOW springs give LOWER heights; GREEN springs give HIGHER. ALWAYS use them in pairs of the same colour.

PART F: TORQUE WRENCH SETTINGS

IMPORTANT NOTE: All torque settings shown in Newton-meters (Nm). Bolt, nut or screw sizes in brackets.

Key for engine types and sizes: A - OHV 903cc; B - FIRE 999cc and 1108cc; C - 1.1cc and 1.3cc; D - 1372 ie; E - 1372 ie; F - 1697cc diesel.

Engine

	A	B	C	D	E	F	Torque (Nm)
Crankshaft support caps to crankcase fixing, bolt (M10 x 1.25)	•						70
Main bearing cap, bolt (M10 x 1.25)		•					40 + 90 degrees
Main bearing cap, bolt (M10 x 1.25)			•	•	•		80
Engine breather body to crankcase fixing, bolt (M8 x 1)						•	20
Engine breather to crankcase fixing, bolt (M8 x 1.25)			•	•	•		23
Intermediate and centre caps to crankcase fixing, bolt (M12 x 1.25)						•	113
Front and rear caps to crankcase fixing, bolt (M12 x 1.25)						•	113
Lower belt shield fixing, bolt (M8 x 1.25)				•			25
Power unit mounting support to crankcase fixing, bolt (M10 x 1.25)			•				59
Crankcase front cover fixing, bolt							
(M10 x 1.25)				•			49
(M8 x 1.25)				•			25
Cylinder head, bolt (M9)	•						55
Cylinder head, bolt (M9 x 1.25)		•					30 + 90 degrees + 90 degrees
Cylinder head, bolt (M10 x 1.25)			•	•	•		40 + 90 degrees + 90 degrees

	A	B	C	D	E	F	Torque (Nm)
Cylinder head, bolt (M8 x 1.25)			●	●	●	●	30
Camshaft housing to lower cylinder head fixing, bolt (M8 x 1.25)			●	●	●		20
Cylinder head to crankcase fixing, bolt (M12 x 1.25)						●	100 + 90 degrees + 90 degrees
Crankcase cover, flywheel side fixing, bolt (M6 x 1)				●			10
Ante-chamber to head fixing, ring nut (M32 x 1.5)						●	118
Complete support for engine mounting fixing, bolt (M8 x 1.25)	●						25
Exhaust manifold to cylinder head fixing, nut (M8 x 1.25)	●						20
Inlet and exhaust manifold fixing, nut (M8 x 1.25)						●	25
Bracket connecting exhaust manifold to crankcase fixing, nut (M8 x 1.25)					●		29
Inlet and exhaust manifold to cylinder head fixing, nut (M8 x 1.25)		●					27
Inlet and exhaust manifold to cylinder head fixing, nut (M8 x 1.25)			●	●			28
Connecting rod bolt (M8 x 1)	●	●					41
Nut for connecting rod bolt (M9 x 1)			●	●			51
Nut for connecting rod bolt (M8 x 1)				●			51
Flywheel to crankshaft fixing, bolt (M8 x 1.25)	●	●					44
Con rod, bolt (M10 x 1)						●	25 + 50 degrees
Flywheel to crankshaft fixing, bolt (M10 x 1.25)			●	●	●		83
Flywheel to crankshaft fixing, bolt (M12 x 1.25)						●	142
Crankshaft front and rear covers to crankcase fixing, bolt (M6 x 1)		●					10
Camshaft caps fixing, bolt (M8 x 1.25)		●					20
Camshaft caps fixing, bolt (M6 x 1)		●					10
Water pump inlet pipe fixing, bolt (M6 x 1)		●					10
Belt tensioner fixing, nut (M8 x 1.25)		●					28
Fixed belt tensioner bearing fixing, bolt (M10 x 1.25)						●	44
Bearing to belt tensioner mounting fixing, nut (M10 x 1.25)			●				44
Bearing to bolt tensioner mounting fixing, nut (M8 x 1.25)				●			22
Injection pump driven gear fixing, nut (M12 x 1.75)						●	49
Camshaft driven gear fixing, bolt (M10 x 1.25)			●	●	●		83
Camshaft cap fixing, nut for stud (M8 x 1.25)						●	20
Front and rear support for camshaft and vacuum pump fixing, nut (M8 x 1.25)						●	20
Camshaft driven gear fixing, bolt (M12 x 1.25)						●	118
Steel tappets cover fixing, nut (M6 x 1)		●					8.5
Timing drive gear fixing, bolt (M10 x 1.25)		●					70
Tappet cover fixing, bolt (M6 x 1)		●		●			8
Auxiliary shaft drive gear fixing, bolt (M10 x 1.25)			●	●	●		83
Oil pump to crankcase fixing, bolt (M8 x 1.25)				●			25
Water pump to crankcase fixing, bolt (M6 x 1)		●					8
Water pump to crankcase fixing, bolt (M8)				●			25
Water pump cover fixing, bolt (M8 x 1.25)				●			15
Gear to crankshaft fixing, bolt (M10 x 1.25)		●					80
Crankshaft pulley fixing, bolt (M8 x 1.25)		●					25
Plate to oil pump casing fixing, bolt (M6 x 1)		●					7
Petrol pump to head fixing, nut (M6 x 1)		●					8
Driven gear and petrol pump cam to camshaft fixing, bolt (M10 x 1.25)	●						49
Oil sump to crankcase fixing, bolt (M6 x 1)		●		●			10
Oil sump fixing, nut (M6 x 1)				●			10
Sump to covers fixing, nut (M6 x 1)		●					8
Alternator to crankcase fixing and adjustment, bolt (M10 x 1.25)		●					60
Engine mounting fixing, nut (M10 x 1.25)		●					60
Engine mounting fixing, nut (M8 x 1.25)		●					25
Flexible mounting to water pump casing fixing, nut (M12 x 1.25)						●	80
Timing shield fixing, bolt (M6 x 1)						●	8
Flexible engine mounting to water pump fixing (M10 x 1.25)						●	50
Rocker arm support to cylinder head fixing, nut for stud (M10 x 1.25)	●						40
Drive pulley fixing, nut (M18 x 1.5)	●						100
Alternator to crankcase fixing, nut for stud (M10 x 1.25)	●						50
Thermostatic switch (M16 x 1.5)	●						50
Water temperature thermostatic switch (smear a layer of hermetical sealant on the thread) (M16 x 1.5 tapered)				●			30
Water temperature sender unit and thermostatic switch (M14 x 1.25)		●					25
Oil pressure switch (M14 x 1.5)		●	●	●	●	●	32
Water temperature gauge switch unit (M16 x 1.5 tapered)			●				49
Thermal valves on inlet manifold (tapered thread) (M10 x 1.25)				●			20
(M8 x 1.25)				●			9.5
Water temperature gauge sender unit (smear a layer of hermetic sealant on the thread) (M16 x 1.5 tapered)				●			30
Water temperature sender unit (M16 x 1.5 conico)						●	34
Oil pressure sender unit (M14 x 1.5)						●	30
Oil temperature sender unit (M16 x 1.5 conico)					●		50
Oil pressure sender unit (M14 x 1.5)					●		37

	A	B	C	D	E	F	Torque (Nm)
Spark plugs (M14 x 1.25)	●						32
Spark plugs (M14) all models - **petrol**		●		●	●		37
Complete injector (M24 x 2)						●	55
Heater plugs (M12 x 1.25)						●	15
Fuel supply pipes to injection pump and injector fixing, nut (M12 x 1.5)						●	24
Flywheel cover to flywheel side fixing, bolt (M6)	●						10
Carburettor to inlet manifold fixing, bolt (M6 x 1)		●					10
Inlet manifold to cylinder head fixing, bolt (M8 x 1.25)		●					27
Water pump to crankcase fixing, nut (M6 x 1)		●					8
Turbine to exhaust manifold and head fixing, nut (M8 x 1.25)					●		29
Oil pump shaft driven gear fixing, bolt (M10 x 1.25)				●			83
Crankshaft pulley fixing, nut (M20 x 1.5)			●	●	●		137
Mounting support to fixing, nut (M10 x 1.25)		●					59
Engine mounting fixing, bolt (M10 x 1.25)		●					59
Accelerator bracket to inlet manifold fixing, bolt (M8 x 1.25)		●					25
Union on inlet manifold for brake servo vacuum pick up (M14 x 1.5 tapered)		●					35
Oil temperature switch (M8 x 1.25)		●					20
Alternator to upper bracket fixing, bolt (M8 x 1.25)				●			23
Alternator to upper bracket fixing, nyloc nut for bolt (M10 x 1.25)			●	●			49
Alternator to lower mounting fixing, nut (M10 x 1.25)			●	●	●		49
Engine flexible mounting fixing, bolt (M10 x 1.25)					●		59
Inlet manifolds to head fixing, nut (M8 x 1.25)					●		25
Bracket connecting camshaft housing to inlet manifold fixing, bolt (M8 x 1.25)					●		25
Lower alternator mounting to crankcase fixing, bolt (M10 x 1.25)			●	●	●		49
Exhaust manifold to cylinder head fixing, nut (with flexible washer) (M8 x 1.25)					●		25
Water temperature sender unit (M14 x 1.5 tapered)					●		27
Bearing to belt tensioner mounting fixing, nut (M8 x 1.25)					●		29
Alternator to bracket fixing, bolt (M10 x 1.25)					●		49
Oil seal cover on crankcase fixing, bolt (M6 x 1)			●	●	●		8
Water pump mounting and engine mounting to crankcase fixing, bolt (M8 x 1)						●	25
Water pump pulley fixing, bolt (M8 x 1.25)						●	23
Fuel supply union on injection pump (M12 x 1.5)						●	30
Union on injection pump (M12 x 1.5)						●	32
Injection pump drive gear fixing, nut (M12 x 1.75)						●	50
Injection pump fixing, nut for stud (M8 x 1.25)						●	25
Injection pump fixing, bolt (M8 x 1.25)						●	25
Rear bracket to injection pump mounting fixing, bolt (M8 x 1.25)						●	30
Lower oil filter mounting and injection pump fixing, bolt (M10 x 1.25)						●	71
Upper oil filter mounting and injection pump fixing, nut (M12 x 1.25)						●	98
Drive gear to crankshaft fixing, bolt (without lubrication) (M14 x 1.5 left hand)						●	19
Flywheel damper to drive gear fixing, bolt (M8 x 1.25)						●	28
Cover and bracket to water pump casing fixing, bolt (M8 x 1.25)						●	23
Oil filter mounting union (M20 x 1.5)						●	50

Exhaust

	A	B	C	D	E	F	Torque (Nm)
METEX joint fixing, nut (M8 x 1.25)				●	●	●	15
Flange to exhaust manifold fixing, nut (M8 x 1.25)		●	●	●	●	●	18
Flange to exhaust manifold fixing, nut (M8 x 1.25)				●	●	●	24

Clutch

	A	B	C	D	E	F	Torque (Nm)
Clutch plate mounting to flywheel fixing, bolt (M6 x 1)	●	●	●	●	●	●	16
Clutch release fork fixing, bolt (M8 x 1.25)	●	●	●	●	●	●	26

Gearbox and Differential

	A	B	C	D	E	F	Torque (Nm)
Speedometer mounting fixing, bolt (M6 x 1)	●	●	●	●	●	●	12
Gearbox tapered, oil drain filler plugs (M22 x 1.5) all models	●	●	●	●	●	●	46
Right drive-shaft cap fixing, bolt (M6 x 1)				●	●	●	10
Reversing light switch (M14 x 1.5)				●	●	●	40

External Gearbox Controls

	A	B	C	D	E	F	Torque (Nm)
Gear lever to selector rod fixing, nut (M6 x 1)	●	●					11
Engagement lever bracket with cover to gearbox fixing, nut (M8 x 1.25)	●	●					15
Selector rod bracket to gearbox fixing, bolt (M8 x 1.25)	●	●					24
Gear lever to mounting fixing, nut (M10 x 1.25)				●	●	●	49
Gear lever with selector and engagement rod fixing, nut (M6 x 1)				●	●	●	11
Lever support to gearbox control fixing, nut (M6 x 1)				●	●	●	4.4
Gear lever support plate fixing, nut (M6 x 1)				●	●	●	4.4
Gear lever support plate fixing, bolt (M6 x 1)				●	●	●	4.4
Gear selector and engagement rods fixing, nut (M8 x 1.25)				●	●	●	15
Gear selector and engagement pipe to idler lever fixing, nut (M8 x 1.25)				●	●	●	15
Idler lever to lever fixing, nut (M8 x 1.25)				●	●	●	15

	A	B	C	D	E	F	Torque (Nm)
Selector lever on gearbox to idler cover fixing, nut (M8 x 1.25)				●	●	●	15
Allen keys fixing bracket to gearbox (M8 x 1.25)				●	●	●	15
Gearbox support plate to bodyshell fixing, nut (M6 x 1)						●	4.4
Complete selector and engagement idler lever mounting to gearbox fixing, bolt (M8 x 1.25)						●	15
Selector lever on gearbox to idler lever cover fixing, nut (M8 x 1.25)						●	15
Mounting to bodyshell fixing, nut (M6 x 1)			●	●			4.4
Mounting to bracket fixing, nut (M6 x 1)			●	●			4.4
Bracket to gearbox fixing, nut (M8 x 1.25)			●	●			15

Various Fixings in Power Unit

	A	B	C	D	E	F	Torque (Nm)
Bell housing to engine fixing, nut (M12 x 1.25)	●	●	●	●	●	●	78
Bell housing to engine fixing, bolt (M12 x 1.5)	●						78
Bell housing to engine fixing, bolt (M12 x 1.25)			●	●	●	●	78
Starter motor to upper engine mounting fixing, bolt (M8 x 1.25)					●		25
Starter motor to lower engine mounting fixing, bolt (M8 x 1.25)					●		25
Starter motor to engine mounting fixing, bolt (M8 x 1.25)	●	●	●	●			25
Bell housing to engine fixing, nut (M12 x 1.25)		●					65
Gearbox casing fixing, bolt (M12 x 1.25)		●					65

Front Suspension

	A	B	C	D	E	F	Torque (Nm)
Front wheel bearing retaining, ring nut (M62 x 1.5)	●	●	●			●	50
Track rod end to steering knuckle fixing, nut with polyammide ring for bolt (M10 x 1.25)	●	●	●	●	●	●	49
Track rod end to steering knuckle fixing, nut with metal insert for bolt (M10 x 1.25)	●	●	●	●	●	●	49
Front track control arm to crossmember fixing, nut with polyammide ring (M12 x 1.25)	●	●	●	●	●	●	88
Shock absorber upper flexible mounting to bodywork fixing, nut (M8 x 1.25)	●	●	●	●	●	●	24
Upper shock absorber to flexible mounting fixing, nut with polyammide ring (M12 x 1.25)	●	●	●	●	●	●	59
Upper shock absorber to steering knuckle fixing, nut with polyammide ring (M10 x 1.25)	●	●	●	●	●	●	49
Rear suspension arm and crossmember to bodywork fixing, bolt (M10 x 1.25)	●	●	●	●	●	●	60
Front crossmember to bodywork fixing, bolt (M10 x 1.25)	●	●	●	●	●	●	60
Wheel bolts/nuts (M12 x 1.25)	●	●	●	●	●	●	86
Front wheel hub fixing, nut with collar for staking (M20 x 1.5)	●	●	●	●	●	●	294
Front wheel brake caliper bleed screw (M8 x 1.25)	●	●	●	●	●	●	6.4
Complete caliper to steering knuckle fixing, bolt (M10 x 1.25)	●	●	●	●	●	●	53
Front suspension anti-roll bar centre mounting fixing, bolt (M8 x 1.25)				●	●		24
Anti-roll bar to front suspension track control arm fixing, nut (M8 x 1.25)				●	●		15

Rear Suspension

	A	B	C	D	E	F	Torque (Nm)
Brake back plate to rear axle lower fixing, bolt (M8 x 1.25)	●	●	●	●		●	24
Brake back plate upper fixing, bolt (M8 x 1.25)					●		24
Rear stub axle fixing, nut with collar for staking (M20 x 1.5)	●	●	●	●	●	●	216
Bracket fixing axle to bodywork fixing, bolt (M8 x 1.25)	●	●	●	●	●	●	24
Rear axle to bodywork bracket fixing, nut with polyammide ring for bolt (M10 x 1.25)	●	●	●	●	●	●	55
Lower shock absorber to rear axle fixing, nut with polyammide ring (M10 x 1.25)	●	●	●	●	●	●	31
Upper shock absorber to flexible mounting fixing, nut with polyammide ring (M10 x 1.25)	●	●	●	●	●	●	31
Upper shock absorber flexible mounting to bodywork fixing, nut (M8 x 1.5)	●	●	●	●	●	●	15
Rear wheel brake cylinder bleed screw (M8 x 1.25)	●	●	●	●	●	●	6.4
Brake caliper carrier plate fixing, bolt (M8 x 1.25)					●		24
Brake caliper bleed screw (M8 x 1.25)					●		6.4
Rear brake caliper mounting fixing, bolt (M10 x 1.25)					●		53

Steering

	A	B	C	D	E	F	Torque (Nm)
Steering wheel to steering control shaft fixing, nut (M16 x 1.25)	●	●	●	●	●	●	49
Universal joint fork to steering control shaft fixing, nut with polyammide ring (M8 x 1.25)	●	●	●	●	●	●	20
Ball joint on side steering rod fixing, nut (M12 x 1.25)	●	●	●	●	●	●	34
Ball joint to lever on steering knuckle fixing, nut with polyammide ring (M10 x 1.25)	●	●	●	●	●	●	34
Steering box to crossmember fixing, bolt with unlosable flexible washer (M8 x 1.25)	●	●	●	●	●	●	24
Upper steering control shaft complete mounting fixing, nut (M6 x 1)	●	●	●	●	●	●	64

Braking System

	A	B	C	D	E	F	Torque (Nm)
Lever to bodywork fixing, bolt with flexible washer (M8 x 1.25)	●	●	●	●	●	●	15
Cylinder to brake back plate fixing, bolt (M6 x 1)	●	●	●	●	●	●	10
Load proportioning valve adjustment, screw (M8 x 1.25)	●	●	●	●	●	●	24
Brake master cyl. to pedals mounting fixing, nut (M8 x 1.25)	●						25
Brake master cyl to brake servo fixing, nut (M8 x 1.25)		●	●	●	●	●	20
Brake servo to pedals mounting fixing, nut with wide type B edge (M8 x 1.25)		●	●	●	●	●	25

Pedals

	A	B	C	D	E	F	Torque (Nm)
Brake and clutch pedal mounting to bodywork fixing, special nut (M8 x 1.25)	●						147
Brake servo for right hand drive versions fixing, bolt (M8 x 1.25)					●	●	15

PART G: IDENTIFICATION NUMBERS

Finding the Numbers

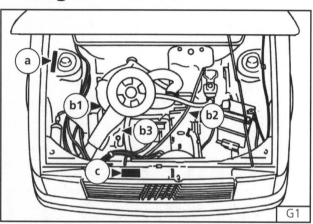

G1

G1: There are four sets of identification numbers in all. First, there is the Vehicle Identification (V.I.N.) Number, or chassis number (**a**). Second, is the engine number. Position (**b1**) is the engine number on OHV engines; (**b2**) the position non-FIRE OHC and 1697cc Diesel engines; (**b3**) the position on FIRE OHC engines. Also, see **G4, G5, G6** and **G7**.

Third, there is the Model and Data Plate (**c**). See **G3**.

G2: Fourth, you will need the Paint Identification Plate if you need to need to buy paint. You'll find it on the inside of the

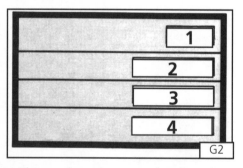

G2

hatchback door. The numbers shown on the plate give the following information: **1** - Paint manufacturer; **2** - Colour name; **3** - Colour code; **4** - Respray and touch-up code.

Vehicle Identification Numbers

See illustration **G1**, part **a**. There are two groups of codes which are unique to your car. You should never buy a car without checking first that the V.I.N. shown on the car matches that on the vehicle registration document. The vehicle code is also shown at position **C** on the Model and Data Plate and the chassis serial number is also shown at position **D**.

Model and Data Plate

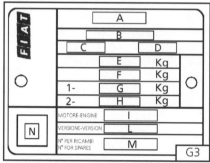

G3

G3: The numbers stamped on the plate stand for the following: **A** - Manufacturer; **B** - Homologation number; **C** - Vehicle identity code; **D** - Chassis serial number; **E** - Maximum authorised weight of vehicle, fully laden; **F** - Maximum authorised weight of vehicle, fully laden plus trailer; **G** - Maximum authorised weight on front axle; **H** - Maximum authorised weight on rear axle; **I** - Engine type; **L** - Body code (see below); **M** - Number for buying spares; **N** - Smoke opacity index (diesel engines only).

Engine Numbers

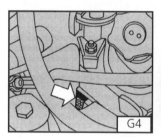

G4

G5

G4: This is the position of the engine numbers on OHV engines. Note the position relative to the oil filler cap.

G5: On all non-FIRE OHC engines, the number is on the top of the crankcase at the gearbox end.

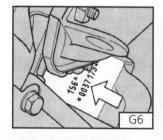

G6

G7

G6: It's on the crankcase, above the water pump housing on all FIRE OHC engines.

G7: On diesel engines, look on the crankcase, above the water pump housing.

CHAPTER 4
GETTING THROUGH THE MOT

This chapter is for owners in Britain whose vehicles need to pass the 'MoT' test. Obviously, you won't be able to examine your car to the same degree of thoroughness as the MoT testing station. But you can reduce the risk of being one of the 4 out of 10 who fail the test first time by following this check-list.

The checks shown below are correct at the time of writing but do note that they are becoming stricter all the time. Your local MoT testing station will have the latest information, should you need it.

Chapter Contents

PART A: INSIDE THE CAR

Steering Wheel and Column

◯ **1.** Try to move the steering wheel towards and away from you and then from side to side. There should be no appreciable movement or play. Check that the steering wheel is not loose on the column.

◯ **2.** Lightly grip the steering wheel between thumb and finger and turn from side to side. **Cars with a steering rack:** free play should not exceed approximately 13 mm (0.5 in.), assuming a 380 mm (15 in.) diameter steering wheel. **Cars fitted with a steering box:** free play should not exceed approximately 75 mm (3.0 in.), assuming a 380 mm (15 in.) diameter steering wheel.

◯ **3.** If there is a universal joint at the bottom of the steering column inside the car, check for movement. Place your hand over the joint while turning the steering wheel to-and-fro a little way with your other hand. If ANY free play can be felt, the joint must be replaced.

◯ **4.** Ensure that there are no breaks or loose components on the steering wheel itself.

Electrical Equipment

◯ **5.** With the ignition turned on, ensure that the horn works okay.

◯ **6.** Check that the front wipers work.

◯ **7.** Check that the windscreen washers work.

◯ **8.** Check that the internal warnings for the indicator and hazard warning lights work okay.

Checks With An Assistant

◯ **9.** Check that the front and rear side lights and number plate lights work and that the lenses and reflectors are secure, clean and undamaged.

◯ **10.** Check the operation of the headlights (you won't be able to check the alignment yourself) and check that the lenses are undamaged. The reflectors inside the headlights must not be tarnished, nor must there be condensation inside the headlight.

◯ **11.** Turn on the ignition and check the direction indicators, front and rear and on the side markers.

◯ **12.** Check that the hazard warning lights operate on the outside of the vehicle, front and rear.

◯ **13.** Check that the rear fog light/s, including the warning light inside the car, all work correctly.

◯ **14.** Check that the rear brake lights work correctly. These checks are carried out all around the vehicle with all four wheels on the ground.

◯ **15.** Operate the brake lights, side lights and each indicator in turn, all at the same time. None should affect the operation of the others.

SAFETY FIRST!

• *Follow the Safety information in **CHAPTER 1, SAFETY FIRST!** but bear in mind that the vehicle needs to be even more stable than usual when raised off the ground.*

• *There must be no risk of it toppling off its stands or ramps while suspension and steering components are being pushed and pulled in order to test them.*

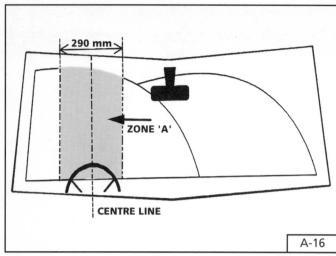

290 mm

ZONE 'A'

CENTRE LINE

A-16

Windscreen and Mirrors

○ **16.** In zone '**A**' of your windscreen, no items of damage larger than 10 mm in diameter will be allowed. In the rest of the area swept by the windscreen wipers, no damage greater than 40 mm in diameter will be allowed, nor should windscreen stickers or other obstructions encroach on this area.

○ **17.** Check that the exterior mirror on the driver's side is in good condition.

○ **18.** There must be one other mirror in good condition, either inside the car or an external mirror on the passenger's side.

Brakes

○ **19.** You cannot check the brakes properly without a rolling road brake tester but you can carry out the following checks:

○ **20.** Pull on the handbrake. It should be fully ON before the handbrake reaches the end of its travel.

○ **21.** Knock the handbrake from side to side and check that it does not then release itself.

○ **22.** Check the security of the handbrake mountings and check the floor around it for rust or splits.

○ **23.** Check that the brake pedal is in good condition and that, when you take hold of it and move it from side to side, there is not too much play.

○ **24.** Push the footbrake down hard, with your foot. If it creeps slowly down to the floor, there is probably a problem with the master cylinder. Release the pedal, and after a few seconds, press down again. If the pedal feels spongy or it travels nearly to the floor, there is air in the system or another MoT-failing fault with the brakes.

○ **25.** Check the servo unit (when fitted) as follows: Pump the pedal several times then hold it down hard. Start the engine. As the engine starts, the pedal should move down slightly. If it doesn't the servo or the vacuum hose leading to it may be faulty.

Seat Belts and Seats

○ **26.** Examine all of the webbing (pull out the belts from the inertia reel if necessary) for cuts, fraying or deterioration.

○ **27.** Check that each inertia reel belt retracts correctly.

○ **28.** Fasten and unfasten each belt to ensure that the buckles work correctly.

○ **29.** Tug hard on each belt and inspect the mountings, as far as possible, to ensure that all are okay.

IMPORTANT NOTE: Checks apply to rear seat belts as much as front ones.

○ **30.** Make sure that the seat runners and mountings are secure and that the back rest locks in the upright position.

Doors and Door Locks

○ **31.** Check that both front doors latch securely when closed and that both can be opened and closed from both outside and inside the car.

PART B: VEHICLE ON THE GROUND

Electrical Equipment

See *Part A: INSIDE THE CAR* for checks on the operation of the electrical equipment.

○ **1.** Examine the wiper blades and replace those that show any damage.

Vehicle Identification Numbers (VIN)

○ **2.** The VIN (or chassis number on older vehicles) must be clearly displayed and legible.

○ **3.** Number plates must be secure, legible and in good condition with correct spacing between letters and numbers. Any non-standard spacing will not be accepted.

Braking System

○ **4.** Inside the engine bay inspect the master cylinder, servo unit (if fitted), brake pipes and mountings. Look for corrosion, loose fitting or leaks.

Steering and Suspension

○ **5.** While still in the engine bay, have your assistant turn the steering wheel lightly from side to side and look for play in steering universal joints or steering rack mountings and any other steering connections.

○ **6.** If your vehicle is fitted with power steering, check the security and condition of the steering pump, hoses and drivebelt, in the engine bay.

○ **7.** Look and reach under the car while your assistant turns the steering wheel more vigorously from side to side. Place your hand over each track rod end in turn and inspect all of the steering linkages, joints and attachments for wear.

○ **8.** Go around the vehicle and 'bounce' each corner of the vehicle in turn. Release at the lowest point and the vehicle should rise and settle in its normal position without continuing to 'bounce' of its own accord.

PART C: VEHICLE RAISED OFF THE GROUND

Bodywork Structure

◯ **1.** Any sharp edges on the external bodywork, caused by damage or corrosion will cause the vehicle to fail.

◯ **2.** Check all load bearing areas for corrosion. Open the doors and check the sills inside and out, above and below. Any corrosion in structural metalwork within 30 cm (12 in.) of seat belt mounting, steering and suspension attachment points will cause the vehicle to fail.

Wheels and Tyres

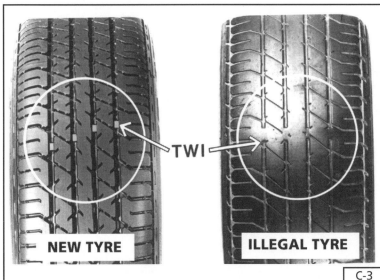

NEW TYRE   ILLEGAL TYRE   TWI   C-3

◯ **3.** To pass the test, the tread must be at least 1.6 mm deep throughout a continuous band comprising the central three-quarters of the width of the tread. The Tread Wear Indicators (TWI) will tell you when the limit has been reached, on most tyres.

IMPORTANT NOTE: Tyres are past their best, especially in wet conditions, well before this point is reached!

◯ **4.** Check that the front tyres match and that the rear tyres match each other - in terms of size and type but not necessarily make. They must be the correct size for the vehicle and the pressures must be correct.

◯ **5.** With each wheel off the ground in turn, check the inside and the outside of the tyre wall for cuts, lumps and bulges and check the wheel for damage. Note that tyres deteriorate progressively over a period of time and if they have degraded to this extent, replace them.

Under the Front of the Car

You will need to support the front of the car on axle stands with the rear wheels firmly chocked in both directions.

◯ **6.** Have your helper turn the steering from lock to lock and check that the steering turns smoothly and that the brake hoses or pipes do not contact the wheel, tyre or any part of the steering or suspension.

◯ **7.** Have your assistant hold down the brake pedal firmly. Check each brake flexible hose for bulges or leaks.

◯ **8.** Inspect all the rigid brake pipes underneath the front of the vehicle for corrosion or leaks and also look for signs of fluid leaks at the brake calipers. Rigid fuel pipes need to be checked in the same way.

◯ **9.** At each full lock position, check the steering rack rubber gaiters for splits, leaks or loose retaining clips.

◯ **10.** Check the track rod end dust covers to make sure they are in place.

◯ **11.** Inspect each constant velocity joint gaiter - both inners and outers - for splits or damage. You will have to rotate each wheel to see the gaiters all the way round.

◯ **12.** Check all of the suspension rubber mountings, including the anti-rollbar mountings (when fitted). Take a firm grip on each shock absorber in turn with both hands and try to twist the damper to check for deterioration in the top and bottom mounting bushes.

◯ **13.** Underneath the front wheel arches, check that the shock absorbers are not corroded, that the springs have not cracked and that there are no fluid leaks down the body of the shock absorber.

◯ **14.** While under the front end of the car, check the front of the exhaust system for security of fixing at the manifold, for corrosion and secure fixing to the mounting points.

◯ **15.** Preferably working with a helper, grasp each front road wheel at the 12 o'clock and 6 o'clock positions and try rocking the wheel. Look for movement or wear at the suspension ball joints, suspension mountings, steering mountings and at the wheel bearing - look for movement between the wheel and hub. Repeat the test by grasping the road wheel at 3 o'clock and 9 o'clock and rocking once more.

◯ **16.** Spin each wheel and check for noise or roughness in the wheel bearing and binding in either the wheel bearing or the brake.

IMPORTANT NOTE: Don't forget that on front wheel drive cars, the gearbox must be in neutral. There will be a certain amount of noise and drag from the drivetrain components.

◯ **17.** If you suspect wear at any of the suspension points, try levering with a screwdriver to see whether or not you can confirm any movement in that area.

◯ **18.** Vehicles fitted with other suspension types such as hydraulic suspension, torsion bar suspension etc. need to be checked in a similar way with the additional point that there must be no fluid leaks or damaged pipes on vehicles with hydraulic suspension.

Underneath the Rear of the Car

◯ **19.** Inspect the rear springs for security at their mounting points and for cracks, severe corrosion or damage.

◯ **20.** Check the rear shock absorbers in the same way as the checks carried out for the fronts.

◯ **21.** Check all rear suspension mounting points, including the rubbers to any locating rods or anti-rollbar that may be fitted.

◯ **22.** Check all of the flexible and rigid brake pipes and the fuel pipes just as for the front of the vehicle.

23. Have your assistant press down firmly on the brake pedal while you check the rear brake flexible hoses for bulges, splits or other deterioration.

24. Check the fuel tank for leaks or corrosion. Remember also to check the fuel filler cap - a correctly sealing filler cap is a part of the MoT test.

25. Examine the handbrake mechanism. Frayed or broken cables or worn mounting points, either to the bodywork or in the linkage will all be failure points.

26. Check each of the rear wheel bearings as for the fronts.

27. Spin each rear wheel and check that neither the wheel bearings nor the brakes are binding. Pull on and let off the handbrake and check once again to make sure that the handbrake mechanism is releasing.

SAFETY FIRST!

- *Only run the car out of doors.*
- *Beware of burning yourself on a hot exhaust system.*

28. While you are out from under the car, but with the rear end still raised off the ground, run the engine. Hold a rag over the end of the exhaust

pipe and listen for blows or leaks in the system. You can now get back under the car and investigate further if necessary.

29. Check the exhaust system mountings and check for rust, corrosion or holes in the rear part of the system.

30. Check the rear brake back plate or calipers (as appropriate) for any signs of fluid leakage.

31. Check the insides and the outsides of the tyres as well as the tyre treads for damage, as for the front tyres.

PART D: EXHAUST EMISSIONS

This is an area that is impossible to check accurately at home. However, the following rule-of-thumb tests will give you a good idea whether your car is likely to fail or not.

i INSIDE INFORMATION: If you feel that your car is likely to fail because of the emission test, have your MoT testing station carry out the emission part of the test first so

that if it fails, you don't waste money on having the rest of the test carried out. *i*

1. PETROL ENGINES BEFORE 1 AUGUST 1973 AND DIESEL ENGINES BEFORE 1 AUGUST 1979 only have to pass visible smoke check. Rev the engine to about 2,500 rpm (about half maximum speed) for 20 seconds and then allow it to return to idle. If too much smoke is emitted (in the opinion

of the tester) the car will fail.

2. DIESEL ENGINES FROM 1 AUGUST 1979 The engine will have to be taken up to maximum revs several times by the tester, so make certain that your timing belt is in good condition, otherwise severe damage could be caused to your engine. If the latter happens, it will be your responsibility!

FACT FILE: VEHICLE EMISSIONS

PETROL ENGINED VEHICLES WITHOUT CATALYSER

Vehicles first used before 1 August 1973
- visual smoke check only.

Vehicles first used between 1 August 1973 and 31 July 1986
- 4.5% carbon monoxide and 1,200 parts per million, unburned hydrocarbons.

Vehicles first used between 1 August 1986 and 31 July 1992
- 3.5% carbon monoxide and 1,200 parts per million, unburned hydrocarbons.

PETROL ENGINED VEHICLES FITTED WITH CATALYTIC CONVERTERS

Vehicles first used from 1 August 1992 (K-registration on)

- All have to be tested at an MoT Testing Station specially equipped to handle cars fitted with catalytic converters whether or not the vehicle is fitted with a 'cat'. If the test, or the garage's data, shows that the vehicle was not fitted with a 'cat' by the manufacturer, the owner is permitted to take the vehicle to a Testing Station not equipped for catalysed cars, if he/she prefers to do so (up to 1998-only). Required maxima are - 3.5% carbon monoxide and 1,200 parts per million, unburned hydrocarbons. The simple emissions test (as above) will be supplemented by a further check to make sure that the catalyst is maintained in good and efficient working order.

- The tester also has to check that the engine oil is up to a specified temperature before carrying out the test. (This is because 'cats' don't work properly at lower temperatures - ensure *your* engine is fully warm!)

DIESEL ENGINES' EMISSIONS STANDARDS

- The Tester will have to rev your engine hard, several times. If it is not in good condition, he is entitled to refuse to test it. This is the full range of tests, even though all may not apply to your car.

Vehicles first used before 1 August, 1979
- Engine run at normal running temperature; engine speed taken to around 2,500 rpm (or half governed max. speed, if lower) and held for 20 seconds. FAILURE, if engine emits dense blue or black smoke for next 5 seconds, at tick-over. (NOTE: Testers are allowed to be more lenient with pre-1960 vehicles.)

Vehicles first used on or after 1 August, 1979
- After checking engine condition, and with the engine at normal running temperature, the engine will be run up to full revs between three and six times to see whether your engine passes the prescribed smoke density test. (For what it's worth - 2.5k for non-turbo cars; 3.0k for turbo diesels. An opacity meter probe will be placed in your car's exhaust pipe and this is not something you can replicate at home.) Irrespective of the meter readings, the car will fail if smoke or vapour obscures the view of other road users.

- IMPORTANT NOTE: The diesel engine test puts a lot of stress on the engine. It is IMPERATIVE that your car's engine is properly serviced, and the cam belt changed on schedule, before you take it in for the MoT test. The tester is entitled to refuse to test the car if he feels that the engine is not in serviceable condition and there are a number of pre-Test checks he may carry out.

Please read the whole of the Introduction to this Chapter before carrying out any work on your car.

CHAPTER 5   SERVICING YOUR CAR

CHAPTER 5
SERVICING YOUR CAR

Everyone wants to own a car that starts first time, runs reliably and lasts longer than the average. And it's all a question of thorough maintenance!

If you follow the FIAT-approved Service Jobs listed here you can almost guarantee that your car will still be going strong when others have fallen by the wayside - or the hard shoulder.

How To Use This Chapter

This chapter contains all of the servicing Jobs recommended by FIAT for all models of Uno imported into the UK. To use the schedule, note that:

- Each letter code tells you the Service Interval at which you should carry out each Service Job.
- Look the code up in the Service Intervals Key.
- Each Service Job has a Job number. Look up the number in the relevant part of this chapter and you will see a complete explanation of how to carry out the work.

SAFETY FIRST!

- *SAFETY FIRST information must always be read with care and always taken seriously.*
- *In addition, please read the whole of **Chapter 1, Safety First!** before carrying out any work on your car.*
- *There are many hazards associated with working on a car but all of them can be avoided by adhering strictly to the safety rules.*
- *Don't skimp on safety!*

SERVICE INTERVALS - INTRODUCTION

making it easy! • We think it is very important to keep things as straight forward as possible. And where you see this heading, you'll know there's an extra tip to help 'make it easy' for you!

Over the years, FIAT, in common with all other manufacturers, have lengthened their recommended service intervals. For instance, oil changes on later FIATs don't have to take place as often as earlier ones. In the main, these changes have not come about because of specific modifications to the cars themselves. They have come about because of a number of factors: Lubricants, spark plugs, seals and other components have improved and mechanical parts are better made due to improved materials and production techniques.

As a result, you are recommended to follow the maker's recommendations on how often to service your car. If your car lies right on a change-over point, the choice of which schedule to follow will be yours, unless the specific advice given here recommends otherwise - as we said earlier, most change points came about for a number of reasons, so it generally isn't necessary to identify with pinpoint accuracy which bracket your car belongs to, if it isn't obvious.

Some of the suggested inspection/replacement intervals may not correspond to those shown in the original handbook. The suggested schedule takes into account the age of the vehicle and the annual MoT test in the UK.

IMPORTANT NOTE: Each service should be carried out at EITHER the recommended mileage OR the recommended time interval, whichever comes first.

SERVICE INTERVALS: KEY

A - Every week, or before every long journey.
B - Every year or 9,000 miles.
C - Every 2 years or 18,000 miles.
D - Every 3 years or 27,000 miles.

E - Every 4 years or 36,000 miles.
F - Every 5 years or 45,000 miles.
G - Every 6 years or 54,000 miles.
H - Every 7 years or 63,000 miles.
I - Every 8 years or 72,000 miles..

SERVICE INTERVAL CHART

PART A: REGULAR CHECKS

	SERVICE INTERVALS
Job 1. Engine oil - check level	A
Job 2. Cooling system - check level	A
Job 3. Hydraulic fluid - check level/s	A
Job 4. Battery - check electrolyte level	A
Job 5. Screen washer fluid - check level	A
Job 6. Tyres - check pressures and condition (road wheels)	A
Job 7. Check lights/change bulbs	A

PART B: THE ENGINE AND COOLING SYSTEM

Job 8 - Petrol. Change engine oil and filter	C
Job 8 - Diesel. Change engine oil and filter	B
Job 9 - Petrol. Check/adjust valve clearances	C
Job 9 - Diesel. Check/adjust valve clearances	C
Job 10. Check crankcase ventilation	H
Job 11. Check camshaft timing belt (OHC AND DIESEL ENGINES ONLY)	F
Job 12. Change camshaft timing belt (OHC AND DIESEL ENGINES ONLY)	I
Job 13. Check cooling system	C
Job 14. Change engine coolant	E

PART C: TRANSMISSION

Job 15. Check manual gearbox oil level	C
Job 16. Change manual gearbox oil	J
Job 17. Check auto. transmission fluid level	C
Job 18. Change auto. transmission fluid and filter	F
Job 19. Check driveshaft gaiters	C
Job 20. Check/adjust clutch pedal/cable	C
Job 21. Check auto. transmission selector cable	E

PART D: IGNITION AND ELECTRICS

	SERVICE INTERVALS
Job 22. Check/clean/gap spark plugs	B
Job 23. Change spark plugs	D
Job 24. Check/clean HT leads and distributor cap	C
Job 25. Check/adjust contact breaker points (DISTRIBUTORS WITH CONTACT BREAKERS ONLY)	B
Job 26. Replace contact breaker points (DISTRIBUTORS WITH CONTACT BREAKERS ONLY)	C
Job 27. Check ignition timing	C
Job 28. Check/adjust alternator drive belt	D
Job 29. Check electric fan operation	C

PART E: FUEL AND EXHAUST

	SERVICE INTERVALS
Job 30. Check fuel pipes for leaks	C
Job 31. Change air filter (*petrol*)	D
(*diesel*)	C
Job 32. Change petrol fuel filter	F
Job 33. Drain diesel fuel filter	B
Job 34. Change diesel fuel filter	C
Job 35. Check/adjust petrol engine idle and emissions	C
Job 36. Check emission control systems	F
Job 37. Check Lambda sensor	F
Job 38. Check/adjust diesel idle speed	C
Job 39. Check/adjust diesel injection timing	E
Job 40. Check inlet and exhaust manifold fixings	D
Job 41. Check exhaust system	C

PART F: STEERING AND SUSPENSION

	SERVICE INTERVALS
Job 42. Check front wheel bearings	C
Job 43. Check front suspension	C
Job 44. Check track rod ends	C
Job 45. Check steering column and rack	C
Job 46. Check rear wheel bearings	C
Job 47. Check rear suspension	C
Job 48. Check wheel bolts for tightness	C

PART G: BRAKING SYSTEM

	SERVICE INTERVALS
Job 49. Check front brakes, change pads	C
Job 50. Check rear brakes	C
Job 51. Check/adjust handbrake	C

Job 52. Check brake pipes	C
Job 53. Change brake hydraulic fluid	E

PART H: BODYWORK & INTERIOR

	SERVICE INTERVALS
Job 54. Lubricate hinges and locks	C
Job 55. Check windscreen	C
Job 56. Check seat and seat belt mountings	C
Job 57. Check headlight alignment	C
Job 58. Check underbody	C
Job 59. Check spare tyre	B
Job 60. Change pollen filter	C

PART I: ROAD TEST

Job 61. Road test and specialist check *AFTER EVERY SERVICE*

ENGINE BAY LAYOUTS

These are the engine bay layouts common to almost all Unos. Note that there is no carburettor fitted to fuel-injected vehicles.
N.B. On right-hand drive cars the brake fluid reservoir may be on the driver's side of the car.

1 - 1.1 NON-FIRE OHC (EARLY)

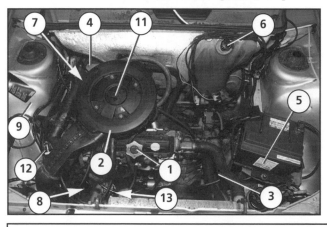

2 - OHV 903cc (EARLY)

1 - oil filler cap	7 - alternator location	13 - oil filter location
2 - engine oil dipstick	8 - distributor (ignition)	14 - fuel pump (mechanical)
3 - coolant filler cap	9 - coil (ignition)	15 - diesel injection pump
4 - brake fluid reservoir	10 - electronic control unit (ECU)	16 - air flow meter
5 - battery	11 - air filter housing	
6 - screenwash reservoir cap	12 - fuel filter	

3 - FIRE OHC

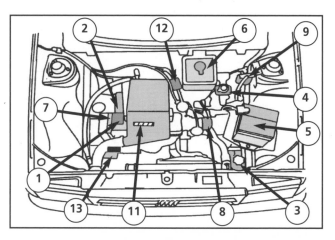

4 - DIESEL

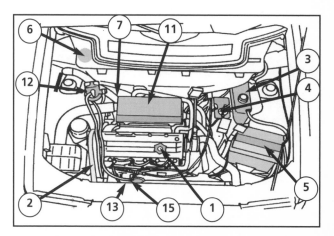

1 - oil filler cap	7 - alternator location	13 - oil filter location
2 - engine oil dipstick	8 - distributor (ignition)	14 - fuel pump (mechanical)
3 - coolant filler cap	9 - coil (ignition)	15 - diesel injection pump
4 - brake fluid reservoir	10 - electronic control unit (ECU)	16 - air flow meter
5 - battery	11 - air filter housing	
6 - screenwash reservoir cap	12 - fuel filter	

NON-FIRE OHC 1372cc i.e. (SINGLE POINT)

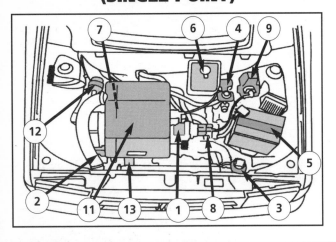

TURBO i.e.

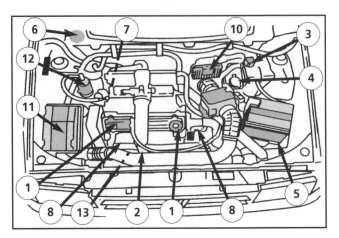

FACT FILE: UNO ENGINE TYPES

● There have been several basic Uno engine types. The OHV engine is a 903cc unit of older design. It was progressively replaced by a modern 999cc and 1108cc FIRE (Fully Integrated Robotised Engine) in the late Eighties/early Nineties.

● In addition, an OHC engine has powered certain models in several different capacities - 1116cc, 1299cc, 1301cc and 1372cc. The 1299cc and 1301cc units are effectively the same engine deliberately 'tweaked' by FIAT so that they fit into certain countries' tax bands.

Turbo i.e. models are powered either by the 1301cc engine, or latterly by a 1372cc version. The 1372cc engine was introduced in 1991 as both a Turbo (multi-point injection) and non-turbo (single-point injection) unit.

● Finally, the Uno Diesel is powered by an indirect-injection diesel engine of 1697cc and of similar design to the OHC petrol engine. A 1367cc Turbo diesel engine was also available outside the UK.

PART A: REGULAR CHECKS

We recommend that these Jobs are carried out on a weekly basis, as well as before every long journey. They consist of checks essential for your safety and for your car's reliability.

☐ Job 1. Engine oil - check level.

Check the engine oil level with the car on level ground. If the engine has been running, leave it turned off for several minutes to let the oil drain into the sump.

IMPORTANT NOTE: Some Turbo i.e. models have an oil level check light on the dashboard and a sensor on the dipstick. Disconnect the sensor before removing the dipstick.

1A. The dipstick is located at the rear of the engine on the OHV unit, near the distributor.

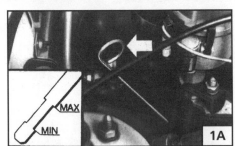

1B. The FIRE engine's dipstick is also at the back, between alternator and engine.

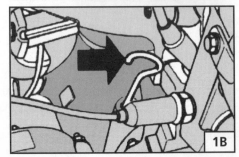

1C. OHC non-FIRE engines have the dipstick at the front of the block, towards the timing belt end...

1D. ...while the diesel's dipstick is located at the front edge of the timing cover, behind the right-hand headlight.

Lift the dipstick out, wipe it dry and re-insert it. The oil level is correct when between the MAX and MIN marks.

i INSIDE INFORMATION: The difference between MIN and MAX marks is approximately one litre of oil. *i*

TOPPING-UP

1E. On OHV engines the oil filler cap is at the end of the rocker cover adjacent to the distributor. On OHC (non-FIRE) engines, including diesel, the cap can be at either end of the cam cover. The cap is removed by turning a quarter-turn to the left and lifting.

1F. On FIRE engines the oil filler cap is a square plastic moulding on the cam cover. Remove it by pulling upwards.

1G. Pour in the fresh oil carefully, ideally using a funnel. Pour particularly slowly into FIRE engines.

IMPORTANT NOTE: Regularly check the ground over which the car has been parked for traces of

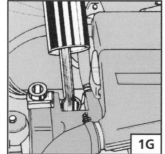

oil or other fluid leaks. If a leak is found, don't drive the car without first finding out where the leak is from, and ideally, repairing it.

☐ Job 2. Cooling system - check level.

Never allow the coolant level to fall below the MIN mark on the expansion tank. It is vitally important that all engines have the correct proportion of anti-freeze in the coolant all year round to prevent corrosion. A 50% mix of distilled water with **FL Paraflu** coolant gives the best protection.

DIESEL AND TURBO i.e. WITH SEPARATE HEADER TANK.

2A. The coolant should be just below the header tank filler neck - about 25 mm (1 in.) above the MIN mark on the tank. This is the header tank (screw-on cap,

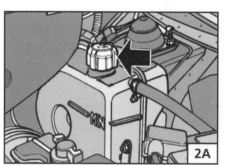

arrowed), in the passenger-side bulkhead corner of the engine bay.

ALL OTHER MODELS WITH HEADER TANK INTEGRAL WITH RADIATOR

2B. The coolant should be 5-7 cm above the MIN mark on the header tank (engine cold).

2C. Unscrew the coolant filler cap anti-clockwise and remove it. Top-up using a 50:50 mixture of **Paraflu** distilled water and anti-freeze.

☐ Job 3. Hydraulic fluid - check level/s.

On all models the brake fluid reservoir is positioned above the master cylinder either in the rear right-hand or rear left-hand corner of the engine bay, according to model. The reservoir is semi-transparent so the level can be checked without disturbing the cap.

- *If brake fluid should come into contact with skin or eyes, rinse immediately with plenty of water.*

- *It is acceptable for the brake fluid level to fall slightly during normal use, but if it falls significantly below the MIN mark on the reservoir there is probably a leak or internal seal failure. Stop using the car until the problem has been put right.*

- *If you let dirt get into the hydraulic system it can cause brake failure. Wipe the filler cap clean before removing it.*

- *You should only ever use new brake fluid from a sealed container - FIAT recommend **FL Tutela DOT 3** brake fluid. Old fluid absorbs moisture and this could cause the brakes to fail when carrying out an emergency stop or during another heavy use of the brakes - just when you need them most and are least able to do anything about it, in fact!*

IMPORTANT NOTE: On very latest models, the clutch is also hydraulically operated. The position of the remote filler can be seen in *Chapter 6, PART B: TRANSMISSION AND CLUTCH, Job 13.*

3A. If brake fluid topping-up is required, turn the cap without allowing the centre section to turn. This section, with two wires attached, swivels in the cap. Place the cap and float to one side - take care not to drip fluid from the float - and top up with **FL Tutela DOT 3**.

IMPORTANT NOTE: Ensure the fluid level is high enough to allow fluid to flow internally between front and rear sections of the reservoir.

3B. Check that the brake fluid-level warning-light is operating. Turn the ignition key to the MAR (ignition-ON) position and press down the button between the two terminals on the reservoir cap - when fitted. The warning light on the dash should light up. When no button is fitted, unscrew and raise the cap (ignition key ON) to check the warning

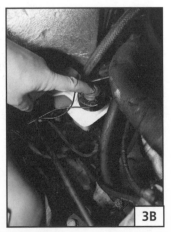

light. Check the bulb, check the fuse, or have your FIAT dealer repair the warning system, if faulty.

❑ Job 4. Battery - check electrolyte level.

FACT FILE: DISCONNECTING THE BATTERY

- Many vehicles depend on a constant power supply from the battery; with these you find yourself in trouble if you simply disconnect the battery. You might find the car alarm goes off, or that the engine management system forgets all it ever 'learned', making the car feel odd to drive until it has re-programmed itself. You might also find that the radio refuses to operate until its correct security code is keyed into it.

- On cars with engine management systems and/or coded radios, you must ensure the car has a constant electrical supply, even with the battery removed. You will need a separate 12 volt battery; put a self-tapping screw into the positive lead near the battery terminal before disconnecting it, and put a positive connection to your other battery via this screw.

- Be EXTREMELY CAREFUL to wrap insulation tape around the connection so that no short is caused. The negative terminal on the other battery must be connected to the car's bodywork.

- *The gas given off by a battery is highly explosive. Never smoke, use a naked flame or allow a spark in the battery compartment.*

- *Never disconnect the battery (it can cause sparking) with the battery caps removed.*

- *All vehicle batteries contain sulphuric acid. If the acid comes into contact with the skin or eyes, wash immediately with copious amounts of cold water and seek medical advice.*

- *Do not check the battery levels within half an hour of the battery being charged with a separate battery charger because the addition of fresh water could cause electrolyte to flood out.*

4. Check the electrolyte level in the battery. MAX and MIN lines (arrowed) are moulded into the translucent battery casing. In the case of non-FIAT-

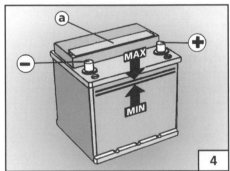

supplied batteries, the cell caps or strip (**a**) may need to be removed to see the level.

Original FIAT batteries are of the 'maintenance-free' type and usually do not need topping-up. However, if necessary, top up after prising off the cell sealing strip with a screwdriver. Top-up each cell ONLY with distilled or de-ionised water.

Job 5. Screen washer fluid - check level.

Top up with a mixture of water and screen-wash additive, mixed according to the instructions on the container. FIAT recommend **Arexons DP1**. The reservoir takes different forms depending on the model of Uno. A few models may have a separate rear screenwash reservoir mounted on one side of the boot/hatch area.

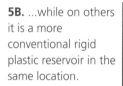

5A. On many it is one or more plastic 'bags' mounted on the bulkhead...

5B. ...while on others it is a more conventional rigid plastic reservoir in the same location.

The **Diesel Uno** has a washer reservoir directly under the windscreen. The **Uno Turbo i.e**. has a screenwash filler cap which protrudes through a plastic cover in the bulkhead scuttle. The reservoir itself is not visible.

Job 6. Tyres - check pressures and condition (road wheels).

6A. Check the tyre pressures using a reliable and accurate gauge. Note that the recommended pressures (see **Chapter 3, Facts and Figures**) are given for COLD tyres. Tyres warm up as the car is used - and warm tyres give a false (high) reading. You should also check for wear or damage at the same time.

SAFETY FIRST!

- *If a tyre is worn more on one side than another, consult your FIAT dealer or a tyre specialist. It probably means the tracking needs re-setting, though it could indicate suspension damage, so have it checked.*
- *If a tyre is worn more in the centre or on the edges, this indicates incorrect tyre pressures.*
- *Incorrectly inflated tyres wear rapidly, can give dangerous handling, and can worsen fuel consumption.*

6B. Every few weeks, examine the tyre treads for wear using a tread-depth gauge. This will help you keep safe and on the right side of the law! Check treads visually every time you check the pressures.

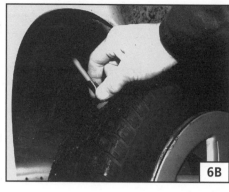

Every three months, raise each wheel off the ground and turn it slowly between your hands, looking and feeling for any bulges, tears or splits in the tyre walls, especially the inner sidewalls. (See **Job 59** for spare tyre checks.)

i INSIDE INFORMATION: In time, rubber deteriorates, increasing the risk of a blow-out. Keep your eye on the sidewalls of older tyres. If you see any cracking, splits or other damage scrap the tyre. If you're not sure, consult your FIAT dealer or tyre specialist. **i**

Job 7. Check lights/change bulbs.

making it easy!
- *Whenever a light fails to work, check its fuse before replacing the bulb.*
- *A blown bulb often causes a fuse to 'go' in sympathy.*

See **Job 7L, FACT FILE: FUSES.**

HEADLIGHTS

IMPORTANT NOTE: On Diesel models, with the air filter mounted behind the right-hand headlight unit, you will first have to remove the large hose, unscrew the clamp nut and take off the air filter assembly. See **Job 31D.** On later models, there is sometimes an air intake silencer in the same place.

7A. Pull off the headlight multi-plug (**B**) and peel the rubber cover (**A**) from the back of the headlight.

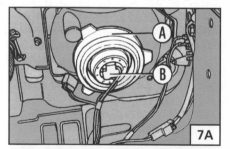

7B. Unhook the bulb securing spring (**C**) and withdraw the bulb.

Without touching the bulb glass, fit the new bulb. A locating tag ensures it only goes in in the correct position. Refit and reconnect in the reverse order.

making it easy! ● *If you touch a halogen headlight or driving light bulb with bare fingers you will shorten its life, so handle with a piece of tissue paper. If the bulb is touched, wipe it carefully with methylated spirit..*

FRONT SIDE LIGHTS

7C. The side light bulb holder (**A**) is under the main headlight bulb. The bayonet-type holder is pushed in slightly, turned anti-clockwise and removed. The bulb is a push-fit within it.

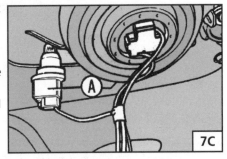

FRONT DIRECTION INDICATORS - EARLY MODELS

7D. Remove the two screws in the indicator light lens and remove the lens. The bayonet-type bulb is pushed slightly into its holder (**1**), turned anti-clockwise and removed. Check the lens seals and replace if leaky, or the bulb holder will corrode. Ensure the holes (**2**) are lined up with the lugs when refitting.

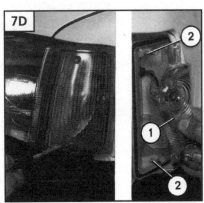

FRONT DIRECTION INDICATORS - LATER MODELS

7E. From inside the engine bay, press retaining tab (**A**) with a screwdriver and pull the light unit from the front of the car. Pull the bulb holder off the light unit.

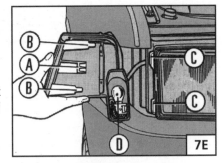

Remove bulb (**D**) and press in a new one. Ensure tabs (**B**) fit perfectly into slots (**C**) when replacing the lens.

INDICATOR SIDE REPEATERS

7F. From underneath the wing, unscrew and withdraw the plastic wheelarch liner. See *Chapter 6, PART I: BODYWORK AND INTERIOR, Job 6.*

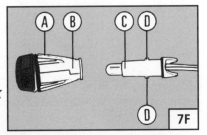

To replace the bulb, twist the bulb holder (**C**), from inside the wheel arch, until the pegs (**D**) line up with the slots in the lens body (**B**). Pull the bulb holder out, and replace the bulb. If you want to remove the lens and body, push in the tabs (**A**) and slide outwards.

REAR LIGHT UNIT

7G. Release retaining tabs (**A**) and (**B**) to free the light lens, then pull off the lens for access to the bulbs. All bulbs are of the bayonet type - push in slightly, turn anti-clockwise and withdraw.

7H. Ensure the pegs on the bulb are the right way round when attempting to refit - they only go one way. Bulb (**C**) is the direction indicator, (**D**) is the reversing light, (**E**) is the stop light, (**F**) is the tail light and (**G**) is the fog light.

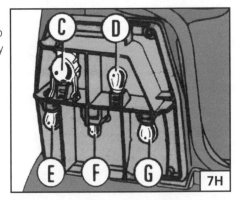

NUMBER PLATE LIGHT - EARLY MODELS

7I. Insert a screwdriver blade in the slot on the side of lens (**A**) and pull outwards to release it from holder (**B**).

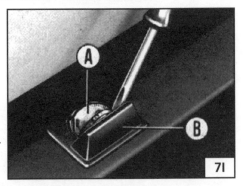

NUMBER PLATE LIGHT - LATER MODELS

7J. Press tabs (**A**) to remove the lens for access to the bulb holder and bulb.

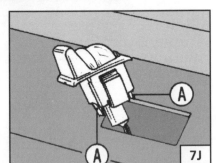

INTERIOR LIGHT - ALL MODELS

7K. Remove the interior light lens by placing a screwdriver in its side-notch. Replace the 10W cylindrical bulb (or the two 5W press-fit bulbs in versions with sunroof).

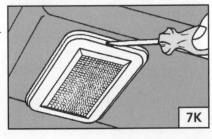

DASH BULBS

See *Chapter 6, Repairs and Replacements* for details of instrument panel removal for access to its light bulbs. The bulbs are a quarter-turn fit in the back of the panel.

FACT FILE: FUSES

● **7L.** The fuse box is found under the left-hand side of the dashboard. On some models, gain access by removing two knurled knobs, and lower the fuse box.

● A symbol above each fuse tells you which circuit it protects.

● The **amperage** is clearly marked on each fuse. ALWAYS replace a blown fuse with one of the correct amperage. NEVER 'fix' a fault by using a fuse of a higher amperage, nor 'bridge' a blown fuse - it could cause a fire!

● When a fuse is 'blown' its conductor wire (**L**) has a gap in it.

● If a fuse blows, find out why and put it right before fitting a new fuse.

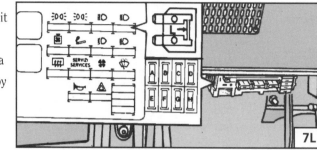

PART B: ENGINE AND COOLING SYSTEM

❑ Job 8. Change engine oil and filter.

SAFETY FIRST!

● *Refer to the section on ENGINE OILS and RAISING THE CAR SAFELY in **Chapter 1, Safety First!** before carrying out this work.*

● *You must wear plastic gloves when changing the oil. Used engine oil can severely irritate the skin and is carcinogenic. Used diesel engine oil is an even greater health hazard.*

● *Oil drain plugs are often over-tightened, so take care that the spanner does not slip.*

● *Take care that the effort needed to undo the drain plug doesn't tip the car off its supports - remember to use wheel chocks!*

8A. The sump drain plug is on the under-side of the sump on petrol engines, and on the side of the sump (timing belt end of engine) on the diesel. The plug has a recessed hexagonal head and you will need either a sump plug spanner, a large Allen key, or a 'Hex' headed socket fitted to a socket wrench.

IMPORTANT NOTE: The plug is a taper-fit and can become very tight, necessitating the use of a long drive-bar for its removal.

8B. Once the initial tightness of the plug has been released, unscrew the last few turns by hand, holding the plug in place until the threads have cleared, then withdrawing it smartly to allow oil to flow into the receptacle beneath.

ℹ INSIDE INFORMATION: On side-mounted drain holes, as the oil empties, the angle of 'spurt' will change, so be prepared to move the container. **ℹ**

making it easy! ● *Only drain the oil from a warm engine - but not so hot that the oil can scald!*

● *Allow the oil to drain for at least ten minutes before replacing the sump plug.*

● *You can use this time by renewing the oil filter.*

8C. The oil filter on OHV engines is located on the rearward-facing side of the engine. On all other engines, including diesel, it is mounted low on the front of the

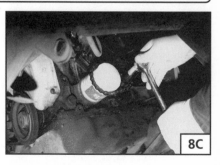

engine block, towards the timing belt. Use a chain wrench to unscrew the old filter. Note that there may be a lot of oil spilt as the filter seal is broken, so keep the drip tray beneath it.

8D. To prevent the rubber sealing ring on the new filter from buckling or twisting out of shape while tightening, smear it with clean oil.

8D

8E. Screw the new filter onto the stub by hand. When the rubber sealing ring contacts its seat, continue to turn the filter a further 3/4 of a turn, *by hand only*. Over-tightening the filter makes it difficult to remove at the next oil change and can buckle the seal, causing a leak.

8E

i INSIDE INFORMATION: It isn't necessary to use excessive force when refitting the sump plug. Simply grip the spanner so that the thumb rests on the spanner head, limiting the amount of leverage that can be applied. Use firm pressure only. Before refitting the plug, wipe around the drain hole with a piece of clean cloth to remove any dirt. *i*

8F. Pour in the correct quantity of **Selenia** engine oil (see *Chapter 3, Facts and Figures*) and check the level against the dipstick.

i INSIDE INFORMATION: FIRE engines fill *very* slowly! If you're impatient, oil will spill over the top. *i*

8F

Note that the empty oil filter will cause the level to drop slightly when the engine is started and the oil flows into it. Before using the car, run the engine for two minutes, turn off, leave to stand for a few minutes and then recheck and correct the oil level.

❑ **Job 9. Check/adjust valve clearances.**

There are two types of valve gear, and both need valve clearances to be checked at intervals when the engine is cold.

● OHV ENGINES have conventional valve rockers with screw-adjustable tappets. See *Job 9B.*

● 'FIRE' and OHC ENGINES have a belt-driven overhead camshaft with shim-and-bucket type tappets. See *Job 9F.*

OHV ENGINES

9A. Remove the air cleaner, disconnect the HT leads from the spark plugs, and remove the plugs. Remove the four bolts securing the rocker cover, and lift off the cover. If the cover sticks,

9A

jar it with the flat of your hand or a rubber mallet. Do not attempt to lever it off or it will distort.

FACT FILE: SETTING OHV VALVE CLEARANCES

● Valve clearances must be set when there is no pressure on the valve. The 'Rule of Nine' ensures that valves are always adjusted at the right time.

● **9B.** Number the valves, counting them from the timing cover end. With the gearbox in neutral and the spark plugs removed, turn the engine by hand so that number 8 valve is fully open (fully depressed by the rocker). You can

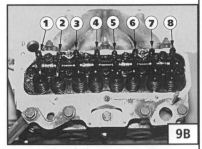

9B

now check or adjust the clearance for valve number 1. Following the chart below, you should now fully open valve number 6 while adjusting the clearance for valve number 3. (8 + 1 = 9; 6 + 3 = 9 - it works every time!)

IMPORTANT NOTE: Valve clearances for inlet and exhaust valves are different - see *Chapter 3, Facts and Figures.*

Valve Fully Open	Check and Adjust
8 - Exhaust	1 - Exhaust
6 - Inlet	3 - Inlet
4 - Exhaust	5 - Exhaust
7 - Inlet	2 - Inlet
1 - Exhaust	8 - Exhaust
3 - Inlet	6 - Inlet
5 - Exhaust	4 - Exhaust
2 - Inlet	7 - Inlet

● If you adjust the valves in the above order, you will have the minimum amount of engine-turning to carry out.

9C. Slide the end of the appropriate feeler gauge between the end of the valve stem and the rocker arm. It should just slide in but be in contact with both the valve and the rocker, giving a stiff, sliding fit.

9C

9D. To adjust the clearance put a ring spanner on the lock nut, slacken the nut and turn the adjuster screw with a small-ended or adjustable spanner.

Set the correct gap with the adjuster, then tighten the lock-nut without disturbing that setting.

- The lock nut will tend to tighten the adjuster screw as it is fastened down.

- You may need to ease the adjuster screw back a little so that it is pulled into its correct position as the nut is tightened.

It's a good idea to fit a new rocker cover gasket to avoid oil leaks.

ALL OHC AND DIESEL ENGINES

9E. Remove the air cleaner (where necessary), then remove the bolts holding the camshaft cover in place and lift the cover off.

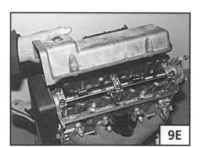

9F. The valve clearance is measured directly beneath the cam and must be checked when the high point of the cam is pointing directly upwards and away from the cam follower.

Try different feeler gauge thicknesses until you find one that's a tight sliding fit between cam and follower. Make a written note of each clearance starting with number 1 at the timing belt end of the engine.

ℹ INSIDE INFORMATION: Remember that clearances for inlet and exhaust valves differ. See *Chapter 3, Facts and Figures.* Counting from the timing belt end the valves are: 1, 3, 6, 8 - exhaust; 2, 4, 5, 7 - inlet. ℹ

If a clearance is outside the tolerances shown in *Chapter 3, Facts and Figures*, the relevant shim will have to be changed. New shims are available from your FIAT dealer. This work is fully described in *Chapter 6, Repairs and Replacements.*

☐ **Job 10. Check crankcase ventilation.**

10. Check the condition of the breather hose from the valve cover or cam cover to the air cleaner. The one shown has split lengthways because of oil contamination and needs replacing. If the pipe has become blocked or damaged, replace it, transferring the flame trap from inside the old pipe to the new one. On some models, you will have to remove the air filter housing to get at the crankcase ventilation pipe beneath.

☐ **Job 11. Check camshaft timing belt.**

ALL OHC AND DIESEL ENGINES

Remove the camshaft belt outer cover. See *Chapter 6, Repairs and Replacements, PART A: ENGINE, Jobs 8, 17* and *31.*

11. Examine the belt for wear. If there is any cracking, or if the toothed side appears worn, or any 'teeth' are missing, replace the belt straight away. If the belt breaks the valves may collide with the pistons, causing serious engine damage. Camshaft belt replacement is described in *Chapter 6, Repairs and Replacements,* or you may wish to have your FIAT dealer carry out the work for you.

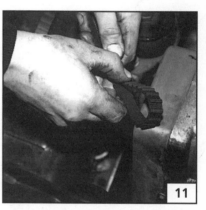

☐ **Job 12. Change camshaft timing belt.**

ALL OHC AND DIESEL ENGINES

It is ESSENTIAL that you renew the camshaft drive belt at the recommended interval. See the *Service Interval Chart* at the start of this chapter. *Chapter 6, Repairs and Replacements* explains how to carry out the work.

SAFETY FIRST!

- *The coolant level should be checked - and the cooling system worked on, ONLY WHEN THE COOLANT IS COLD. If you remove the pressure cap or bleed screws when the engine is hot, scalding coolant will spurt out.*
- *Keep anti-freeze away from children. If it is accidentally swallowed or contacts skin or eyes, rinse immediately with plenty of water and seek immediate medical help.*

☐ Job 13. Check cooling system.

13. Examine the cooling system hoses, looking for signs of splitting, chafing and perishing. Squeeze the top and bottom radiator hoses. Any hard, brittle areas or crackling sounds tell you that the hoses are decomposing from the inside - replacements needed!

Ensure that hose clips are secure and firm but not over-tightened.

SAFETY FIRST!

● See **SAFETY FIRST!** at the start of **Job 13.**

☐ Job 14. Change engine coolant.

Remove the expansion tank cap and, on early models only, the radiator filler cap.

Move the heater control to the red (open) position. Loosen the worm-drive clip and pull off the bottom radiator hose. Also open the drain plug or tap at the centre of the rear flank on the engine block on OHC and diesel engines. Drain the coolant into a container. On models with a separate expansion tank, detach the hose from the expansion tank and drain the tank.

i INSIDE INFORMATION: From time to time it's a good idea to flush the cooling system. With the bottom hose re-connected, disconnect and remove the top hose from the radiator. Insert the end of a garden hose first into the hose (packing the gap with a rag) and then the radiator inlet, flushing the system in both directions until the water comes out clear. *i*

IMPORTANT NOTE: Flush first with the heater control turned OFF until the engine and radiator are clear, so that you don't flush sediment into the heater. Then with the heater turned ON, flush the heater system out.

ALL LATER VEHICLES

14A. To prevent air-locks forming in the cooling system as it is refilled (all hoses and the drain plug reconnected, of course!), most models have two air-bleed screws

strategically positioned in the system. These should be opened before refilling. The first is located on the right-hand side of the radiator (models without separate expansion tank)...

14B. ... and the second (arrowed) is found on the left-hand heater hose in front of the bulkhead. Only undo the screws by two or three turns. Retighten both screws when air-free coolant emerges.

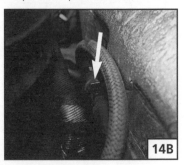

IMPORTANT NOTE: Don't worry if there is only one bleed screw, or if - as is the case with some diesels - there are no bleed screws. In the first case, just bleed from the one point. In the second, detach the small-diameter top-hose from the thermostat housing and bleed air from here point, reconnecting only when bubble-free coolant emerges.

14C. Refill the cooling system with a 50/50 mixture of clean water and fresh **Paraflu** anti-freeze. Tighten the bleed screws when coolant, and not air, comes out steadily. Run the engine for a few minutes and bleed again.

IMPORTANT NOTE: It is highly likely that more air will be dislodged when you first use the car. Keep your eye on the coolant level (See **Job 2**) - perhaps carrying some 50/50 diluted coolant with you for the first few journeys.

PART C: TRANSMISSION

☐ Job 15. Check manual gearbox oil level.

The combined oil level and filler plug is on the forward-facing side of the gearbox. Check the level with the car on level ground.

15. From beneath the car, wipe around the filler plug with a rag to prevent dirt contamination. Remove the plug - using either a 10 mm Allen key or a conventional spanner, depending on type - and top-up if necessary, using the specified **Tutela** transmission oil

(see **Chapter 3, Facts and Figures**), until oil just dribbles from the filler hole. Refit the plug.

☐ Job 16. Change manual gearbox oil.

16. The combined gearbox and final drive oil should be drained at the time shown in the Service Interval Chart. Do so only after the car has been used and the gearbox oil is warm, so that it flows well. Remove the drain plug (on the forward-face of the gearbox, accessed from beneath the car)

and drain the oil into a container. (See **page 8** on oil disposal.) Leave for 10 minutes to drain completely, and refill with the correct grade of **Tutela** transmission oil through the level/filler plug, as described in **Job 15.**

☐ Job 17. Check auto. transmission fluid level.

The automatic transmission fluid level should be checked with the car on level ground and the engine at normal running temperature - the car should have been driven for about 4 miles. The level is checked by means of a dipstick next to the battery.

IMPORTANT NOTE: i) It is especially important that the fluid is at the correct level. If the system needs regular topping up because of leaks, fix them as rapidly as possible or have your FIAT dealer check the system. ii) Wipe the dipstick only with a lint-free rag to avoid clogging up transmission valves. Keep dirt out!

17. Check the level with the engine idling and the gear selector in the 'P' (PARK) position. Pull out the dipstick, wipe it clean with paper kitchen towel, re-insert it and check the level. The upper and lower marks on the dipstick 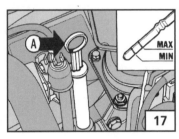 represent minimum and maximum acceptable fluid levels.

If necessary, fresh **Tutela CVT** should be poured in through the dipstick tube, using a funnel in the tube or by using ATF from a dispenser with a small spout. You may have to leave the fresh oil to clear the tube before seeing a clear dipstick reading.

☐ Job 18. Change auto. transmission fluid and filter.

As well as **Tutela CVT** fluid, you will need a new, sump gasket and a new gearbox oil filter, from your FIAT dealer. The filter should be changed every time the oil is replaced.

18A. Always drain the fluid when the transmission is warm, such as after a run. Raise the front of the car on ramps, so the fluid drains well from the drain hole (**C**) at the rear under-side of the 'box.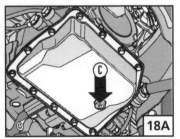

Remove the drain plug with an Allen key or hexagonal socket adaptor, and allow the fluid to drain into a container beneath the transmission - allow ten minutes for complete drainage.

Underneath the car, remove the 13 transmission sump bolts.

𝒊 INSIDE INFORMATION: The sump is easily distorted, so, when refitting, tighten all bolts progressively and evenly to the recommended torque - see **Chapter 3, Facts and Figures. 𝒊**

18B. The filter is secured by one central screw. Undo this and pull the filter down, detaching its upper fluid pipe in the process. Remove the filter, discard it and fit the replacement. Refit the sump, using a new gasket and non-setting gasket sealer.

Replace the drain plug and fill the gearbox through the dipstick tube. (See **Job 17.**)

IMPORTANT NOTE: Take care not to allow any dirt or grit to get into the gearbox.

☐ Job 19. Check driveshaft gaiters.

19. Grasp and turn the inner drive-shafts and gaiters, checking for signs of gaiter splitting or damage that could allow grease out or - worse still - water in. Ensure the gaiter clips are secure. Repeat for the outer gaiters.

IMPORTANT NOTE: Change any split, damaged or suspect gaiter as soon as possible - preferably before using the car again.

☐ Job 20. Check/adjust clutch pedal/cable.

The clutch mechanism is self-adjusting, although the cable linkage can stretch over a period of time and may need adjustment.

ADJUSTMENT - EARLY (PRE-FACELIFT) MODELS

Inside the car, measure the difference in height between clutch and brake pedals. The clutch pedal should be 8 to 12 mm lower than the brake pedal. If not, adjust the cable. The clutch adjuster can be reached from inside the engine bay; it's on top of the gearbox (shown here with battery removed).

20. Slacken the outer lock-nut from the inner adjusting nut using two spanners in opposition. Note that turning the adjusting nut inwards along the threaded rod will increase pedal travel. Tighten lock-nut against inner nut after adjustment.

ADJUSTMENT - LATER MODELS (EXCEPT HYDRAULIC CLUTCH VERSIONS)

'Work' the clutch pedal a few times, pull back the carpet from under the pedal, then measure the full travel of the pedal, which should be between 136 and 146 mm. If not, adjust as described above previously.

❏ Job 21. Check auto. transmission selector cable.

It should only be possible to start the engine when the gear selector is in the 'P' or 'N' position. Place it in each of the other positions and try to start the car. If it starts, the fault must be put right! Also check that, with the ignition off and the selector lever in 'D' (Drive), 'L' (Low), 'R' (Reverse) or 'N' (Neutral), the timed warning buzzer should sound. If it doesn't, the selector cable adjustment may be faulty.

See *Chapter 6, Repairs and Replacements, PART B: TRANSMISSION AND CLUTCH, Job 8* for adjustment details.

PART D: IGNITION AND ELECTRICS

See *FACT FILE DISCONNECTING THE BATTERY* on *page 36*.

SAFETY FIRST!

● *You may minimise the risk of shock when the engine is running by wearing thick rubber gloves and by NEVER working on the system in damp weather or when standing on damp ground. Read **Chapter 1, Safety First!** before carrying out any work on the ignition system.*

● *ELECTRONIC IGNITION SYSTEMS INVOLVE VERY HIGH VOLTAGES! All manufacturers recommend that only trained personnel should go near the high-tension circuit (coil, distributor and HT wiring) and it is ESSENTIAL that anyone wearing a medical pacemaker device does not go near the ignition system.*

● *Stroboscopic timing requires the engine to be running - take great care that parts of the timing light or parts of you don't get caught up in moving components!*

● *Don't have loose clothing or hair.*

❏ Job 22. Check/clean/gap spark plugs.

GENERAL. On OHV and non-FIRE OHC engines the spark plugs face forwards, allowing easy working access. On the FIRE OHC engines they are on the back of the engine.

ℹ️ INSIDE INFORMATION: On FIRE-engined cars removing the air cleaner provides better access. The (rectangular) air cleaner housing is released by undoing the single 10 mm nut on the top, and the rear, releasing the clips on the front, and unclipping the intake hose, which allows the housing to swivel to one side. ℹ️

22A. Carefully remove the spark plug caps, being careful to pull only on the cap and not the HT lead. If you can't be sure to remember which HT lead

belongs to which spark plug, number them from one end of the engine to the other.

22B. Unscrew the plug using the correct type of spark plug socket. Take care to keep the spanner strictly in line with the plug so as not to crack the electrode.

If the electrodes of the plugs look rounded and worn, replace the plugs. See *page 153* for plug fault details.

22C. It is essential that the plug is gapped correctly. See *Chapter 3, Facts and Figures.* Use a feeler blade of the correct thickness, sliding it between the electrodes. It should be a firm sliding fit. Use a gapping tool or carefully wielded pliers to bend the curved electrode towards or away from the centre electrode. Take GREAT CARE not to damage the insulator near the tip of the plug.

making it easy! ● *Leave the spark plug in the socket spanner while using the wire brush - this is kinder on the fingers and reduces the risk of dropping the plug and breaking it.*

ℹ️ INSIDE INFORMATION: With all Uno engines, the spark plugs screw into aluminium, which is easily damaged if the spark plugs do not engage their threads properly. It is important therefore to screw in the plugs by hand initially - by, say, two or three turns - before using the plug spanner. A light smear of copper grease on the plug threads will enable them to turn more freely and also make them easier to remove next time. Finally, don't over-tighten the plugs - firm hand-pressure on the spanner is sufficient. ℹ️

Job 23. Change spark plugs.

Spark plugs 'tire' and lose efficiency over a period of time, even if they look okay. See **Job 22** for information on their removal and replacement.

Job 24. Check/clean HT leads and distributor cap.

GENERAL. Refer to *Chapter 6, Repairs and Replacements,* for further information concerning ignition coil and distributor types and locations.

SAFETY FIRST!

● *See **SAFETY FIRST!** at the start of this section and Chapter 1, Safety First!*

Remove each plug lead from the spark plugs, pulling only on the plug caps, not on the HT cables. Also, remove the large HT lead from the coil and take off the distributor cap, either by popping off its spring retainers (see illustration **25A**)...

24A. ...or by undoing the two retaining screws. Clean the cap and cables with a clean rag, applying a little aerosol water-dispellant spray to help shift oil and grime.

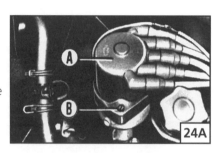

24B. Check each of the HT posts inside the cap for burning or damage, and the central carbon brush to ensure that it's not worn down and that the spring loading is okay.

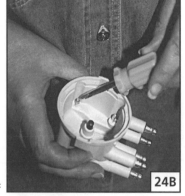

IMPORTANT NOTE: DO NOT spray water dispellant or apply lubricant to any part of an electronic ignition distributor. (It's okay to clean the cap, as described, however.)

Job 25. Check/adjust contact breaker points.

DISTRIBUTORS WITH CONTACT BREAKERS - POINTS INSPECTION

25A. Remove the distributor cap as described in **Job 24**, and pull off the rotor arm...

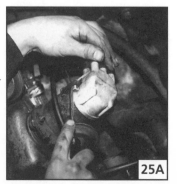

25B...the spark cover...

25C. ...and the bearing support, if fitted, by removing the two fixing screws.

25D. With the ignition turned off, push the contact breaker points apart with a screwdriver and examine the points faces (arrowed).

i INSIDE INFORMATION: Most FIAT mechanics take out the distributor - as shown here - for replacement or setting of points. See later in this Job. *i*

FACT FILE: CONTACT BREAKER POINTS FAULTS

● If a metal build-up or 'pip' is clearly visible on one of the points, they need replacing.

● If there is any visible burning on the face of the points, they should be replaced.

● If the faces or the points are badly burned or bluish in colour, the condenser unit is probably defective and should also be replaced.

● Points are cheap to replace and it isn't worth cleaning them up, as described in some manuals.

SAFETY FIRST!

● *See **SAFETY FIRST!** on page 44 at the start of this section and Chapter 1, Safety First!*

The size of the points gap is altered by the fixed contact plate in the distributor being moved away from or nearer to the cam in the centre of the distributor. The wider the gap, the earlier the points open (and the longer the points are open for), and so the size of the points gap has a direct bearing on the ignition timing.

i INSIDE INFORMATION: If the distributor shaft bearings are worn, the dwell angle/points gap, and thus the timing, will fluctuate as the engine runs. If this is the case, you will have to set the points to an 'average' of the various readings you will obtain. *i*

FACT FILE: DISTRIBUTOR TYPES

● Two basic types of conventional distributor have been fitted to FIAT Unos with contact breaker distributors.

● The earlier **Ducellier** distributor was fitted to Overhead Valve engines and is adjusted with a screwdriver, with the distributor cap removed.

● The later **Marelli** distributor was fitted to earlier non-FIRE Overhead Camshaft engines and has a hole in the side of the body through which the points gap can be adjusted (although the points cannot be examined without removing the cap).

● The **Marelli** unit has a bearing support over the points, easily seen with the cap removed.

making it easy!

● *The old-fashioned way of setting points, using a feeler gauge to set the gap, is not very accurate. Far better is to use a dwell meter, which sets the 'gap' by measuring the time for which the points are open.*

● *The use of a dwell meter is highly recommended when checking or adjusting the points on either engine type, but particularly on the FIRE OHC engine, where points access is awkward.*

● *Connect the dwell meter as described on its instructions and measure the points dwell - the amount of time for which the points are open in each rotation. See **Chapter 3, Facts and Figures** for your engine's setting.*

● *Checking and adjusting the points requires the engine to be turned slowly, by hand, in the normal direction of rotation. This can be done in one of two ways.*

● *Select a gear, jack one front wheel off the ground and turn it to rotate the engine.*

● *Or, remove a front wheel, detach the right-hand inner-wing panel and use a socket on the crankshaft pulley bolt to turn the engine.*

● *In both cases, it helps to remove the spark plugs first.*

SETTING THE POINTS GAP

In an emergency, or if you don't own a dwell meter, you could set the points gap using a feeler gauge. Follow the instructions given next for adjusting the points, but with these differences:

● Select a feeler gauge of the correct thickness. (See **Chapter 3, Facts and Figures.**)

● The points gap must be set when the heel of the points is on the highest part of the cam, so that the points are at maximum opening.

● Adjust the gap to make the feeler gauge a sliding fit, contacting both sides of the points as it goes in.

i INSIDE INFORMATION: Don't let the spring in the points fool you into thinking you have a tight sliding fit when you don't. But a loose fit is just as bad. Use an electric torch to help you to see what is going on. *i*

DUCELLIER (OHV ENGINE) DISTRIBUTORS

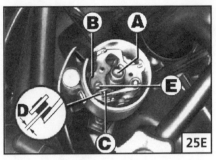

25E. Turn the ignition off. Before adjusting the points, remove the distributor cap and rotor arm as described previously. Slacken the contact breaker locking screw (**E**) and use a screwdriver inserted into the adjuster slot (**B**) to move the fixed contact in or out as necessary, adjusting the points gap (**C** and **D**). Turn the engine over by hand, as described in **MAKING IT EASY!** and adjust the position of the fixed contact until the dwell figure given in **Chapter 3, Facts and Figures** is achieved, with the engine being turned.

LUBRICATE DISTRIBUTOR: Apply a couple of drops of oil to the felt pad (**A**) to provide lubrication for the distributor shaft. Apply a tiny smear of grease to the side of the cam face, using the tip of a small screwdriver.

LATER OHV-ENGINE DISTRIBUTORS

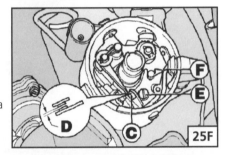

25F. Slacken the screw (**E**) and adjust the points gap (**C** and **D**) by inserting and carefully twisting a screwdriver in the slot (**F**).

MARELLI (FIRE OHC ENGINE) DISTRIBUTORS ONLY

25G. For the position and appearance of the Marelli distributor, see **Job 24A.** Make sure the ignition is turned off. The points gap (**1**) on this distributor can be set by connecting a dwell meter and adjusting the gap with a 3 mm Allen key (**2**), inserted through the body of the distributor. See **Job 26** for more details.

25H. This is the adjuster screw (arrowed) on the points, inside the distributor.

❏ **Job 26. Replace contact breaker points.**

DISTRIBUTORS WITH CONTACT BREAKERS ONLY

It is important to correctly identify the type of distributor fitted to your Uno. See *FACT FILE: DISTRIBUTOR TYPES* in *Job 25*. You should wipe both faces of the new contact breaker points with a cloth dipped in methylated spirits or cellulose thinners.

DUCELLIER (OHV ENGINE) DISTRIBUTORS ONLY

26A. Remove the low tension (**1**) and condenser (**2**) cables - remove the terminal screw and washer. Unscrew and remove the contact breaker locking screw (**25F, part E**) and lift off the points.

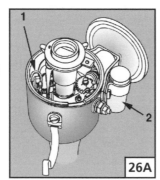

MARELLI (OHC ENGINE) DISTRIBUTORS ONLY

After removing the distributor cap, lift off the rotor arm and remove the bearing support.

26B. The distributor points are replaced as a unit with the entire base plate - they are not separable. The two leads (arrowed) will have to be disconnected from their terminals inside the body.

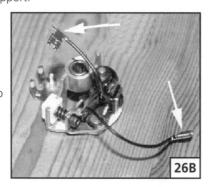

ℹ️ INSIDE INFORMATION: FIAT dealers recommend that these points are replaced with the distributor out of the car. Disconnect the low tension lead from the condenser at the coil, take off the distributor cap. ℹ️

26C. Remove the vacuum advance pipe from its stub (arrowed). So that the distributor can be replaced without 'losing' the ignition timing, put a dab of typists' correction fluid across the base of the distributor and onto its mounting, as shown. Take off the two nuts and washers securing the distributor, and withdraw it from the engine.

IMPORTANT NOTE: If the ignition timing is 'lost' *for* any reason, or you are not sure that it is correct, see *Job 27*.

26D. On the bench (vice jaws protected), lift off the rotor arm and cover, remove the two screws and clips (**C**) holding the bearing support (**D**) in place, and lift away.

26E. Take out the two screws (**1**) holding the vacuum advance unit (**2**) in place and lift it away. Remove the clip (**3**), detach the two leads (see **26B**) and lift the points out.

IMPORTANT NOTE: There may be shim washers beneath the plate. Leave them in place or retrieve for refitting later.

LUBRICATE DISTRIBUTOR: When fitting a new contact breaker assembly, and whenever inspecting the condition of the points, put a couple of drops of oil on the bush in the middle of the assembly

CHECK DISTRIBUTOR SHAFT - ALL TYPES

While replacing the points, try moving the distributor shaft (**26E, part 4**) from side to side. If there is any noticeable movement, the points gap and timing will fluctuate as the engine runs, leading to inefficiency in the ignition system. The only solution is distributor replacement.

❏ **Job 27. Check ignition timing.**

GENERAL. Ignition timing can be adjusted only on engines with conventional contact breaker ignition, and on the 903cc OHV, 1116cc and 1299cc non-FIRE OHC engines with Marelli breakerless electronic ignition. The timing of engines fitted with Digiplex or Microplex ignition (Turbo i.e. models are an example) cannot be altered.

On the OHV and FIRE OHC engines the static timing marks are located in a 'window' on the clutch bell-housing. Some later non-FIRE OHC engines may also have 'window' located timing marks.

27A. A plastic plug may first have to be removed from the window in order to see the marks...

27B. ...which consist of three or four pointers with their corresponding timing positions marked against them - e.g. 0 degrees (Top Dead Centre), 5 degrees

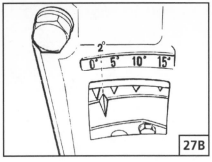

Before TDC, 10 degrees BTDC etc. A timing mark - an engraved line - is also provided on the flywheel rim.

27C. On most non-FIRE OHC, engines the static timing marks are located at the crankshaft pulley, accessed by removing the off-side inner wing panel. All have a groove on the pulley (**B**). Depending on the car's age, the fixed timing marks may consist of:

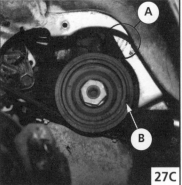

● a notched metal plate alongside the pulley, corresponding with a groove on the pulley edge;

● or three marks (**A**) moulded on the plastic belt cover, alongside the pulley.

---

making it easy! ● Use typists' correction fluid to highlight the timing marks and make them easier to see in the timing light beam.

27D. Connect a timing light according to the maker's instructions, making sure none of the wires can come into contact

with any hot or moving parts of the engine. Disconnect and block the vacuum pipe to the distributor advance mechanism. (The distributor cap has been removed here, so that you can see the position of the timing marks. You have to carry out this job with everything connected up, of course!)

Check the timing by directing the flashing beam of the timing light at the timing marks on the engine, which will appear 'frozen'. If the timing is not as specified in *Chapter 3, Facts and Figures,* adjust it as follows:

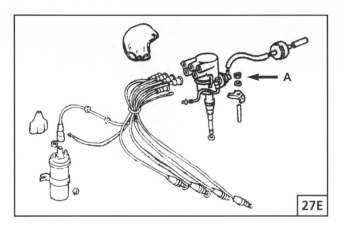

27E. On OHV and OHC (non-FIRE) engines, slacken the distributor clamp nut (**A**) enough for the distributor to turn under firm hand pressure.

27F. On FIRE OHC engines and some later non-FIRE OHC units with the horizontally-mounted distributor, the top clamp nut is situated here. Its partner/s is (or are) immediately opposite or symmetrically,

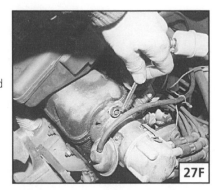

beneath. Slacken all, but initially just retighten the top one when the ignition timing is correct. Retighten the lower one/s when you have finished.

ON BOTH TYPES: As the distributor is turned (clockwise to advance, anti-clockwise to retard) so the timing mark on the flywheel will be seen to move relative to the pointers. Move the distributor so the timing marks are aligned correctly, and retighten the clamp nut or bolts.

☐ Job 28. Check/adjust alternator drive belt.

28A. Depending on your Uno model, access to the alternator belt and adjustment fixings may be difficult from the engine bay. If this is the case, raise and support the

off-side wheel, remove the wheel and detach the access panel by tapping the pins out from the centres of the plastic expansion plugs which secure it. Some models may have screws securing the panel.

28B. Check the belt, and if there is any sign of cracking, 'polishing', fraying or severe wear on the inner face, replace it.

28C. The alternator drive belt should deflect no more than 10 mm when firm thumb pressure is applied to the belt between the

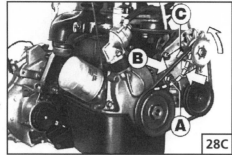

pulleys in the direction of the arrow (**A**), with the dotted line showing the direction of deflection in exaggerated form. This is the early OHV engine.

28D. If adjustment is necessary, slacken the upper pivot bolt (**B**) and the lower bolt (**C**), on all models. This is the later, FIRE engine.

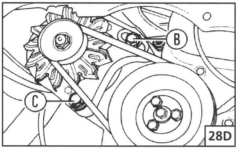

Use a length of wood to pivot the alternator away from the engine block but take great care not to damage the alternator casing. Tighten the bolts when the tension is correct.

IMPORTANT NOTE: The alternator/belt installations vary across the range of engines and ages of Uno in use, and OHV models have the alternator mounted in front of the engine. Most alternators, however, are mounted behind the engine. Suffice it to say that the principle of belt adjustment is the same on all models.

❏ **Job 29. Check electric fan operation.**

Drive the car until it is at normal operating temperature. Park outdoors and, with the gearbox in neutral (or 'P' in the case of an automatic) leave the engine running. At just above normal temperature the electric cooling fan should come on, and then go off again when the temperature drops. Refer to your gauge, if fitted. If it doesn't behave, you will need to check the thermo-switch on the radiator, along with all connections and wires in its circuit with the fan motor. See **Chapter 6, Repairs and Replacements.**

PART E: FUEL AND EXHAUST

SAFETY FIRST!

● *Always wear impervious gloves so that fuel cannot come in contact with your skin. It can induce cancer.*

❏ **Job 30. Check fuel pipes for leaks.**

Check the fuel lines in the engine compartment, looking for signs of chafing, splits and perishing of the rubber and plastic parts. Ensure any worm-drive hose clips used on the connections are firm and secure.

❏ **Job 31. Change air filter.**

OHV AND EARLY, NON-FIRE OHC ENGINES

31A. Start by unscrewing the three or four nuts (wing-nuts on early OHV engines) and lifting off the cover followed by the filter element. Wipe out the inside of the housing, to remove any oil or debris before fitting the new element. Take care to seat the

filter properly in the housing and to replace any sealing washers beneath the cover nuts.

IMPORTANT NOTE: On early OHV engines the air intake has a SUMMER and a WINTER setting. The latter takes air from over the hot, manifold part of the engine. Set yours to the correct position for the time of the year.

LATER NON-FIRE OHC ENGINES

31B. These have a large rectangular filter casing over the camshaft cover. Undo the two spring clips (**A**) - one at either front corner of the casing, and the

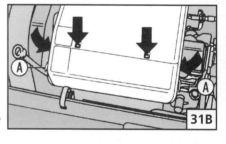

two filter casing screws (arrowed). Pull off the smaller, front section of the casing, and remove the element from within it. Fit the new element with the pleats facing downwards.

FIRE OHC ENGINES

31C. Release the two plastic spring clips (**A**), one on each side of the air cleaner housing, by pulling outwards, and disconnect spring clip (**B**) at

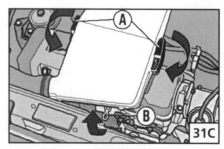

the front of the housing. Pull the front part of the housing forwards so that the filter element can be pulled out and replaced. When you push the new element into position, make sure the outer seal is properly fitted to the channel. Replace the front of the housing and secure the clips.

DIESEL AND TURBO I.E. ENGINES

31D. On early models, the air filter may be found behind the right-hand headlight. To remove the element, undo outer wing nut

(**A**), cover plate (**B**), inner wing nut (**C**) and slide out the filter. The clamp plate (**E**) is retained by the bolt (**D**). To remove the assembly, you must also take off the hose and clip (**F**).

31E. On most vehicles, the diesel's filter casing (**A**) is located at the back of the engine, and forms half of the intake air chamber. Flip

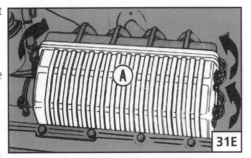

the four over-centre catches (as arrowed), pull the filter lid away from the air chamber/manifold, lift out the filter element, clean out the casing then fit the new element - pleats upwards - into the chamber. Refit the lid.

31F. The Turbo i.e.'s filter assembly is similar to the diesel's, but located against the near-side inner wing. The filter element is fitted with the pleats facing downwards.

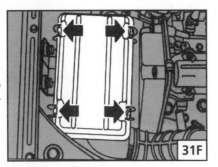

❑ **Job 32. Change petrol fuel filter.**

WEBER CARBURETTOR ENGINES ONLY

32A. If your engine is fitted with a Weber carburettor (see **Job 35**), you may find a filter plug at the fuel inlet. Disconnect the earth battery lead,

detach the fuel supply hose from the carburettor and mop up spilt fuel with a rag. Unscrew the filter plug, take out the gauze, clean and replace it. Refit/reconnect in the reverse order. If the original hose clips had to be cut off, fit new worm-drive clips.

32B. If your (carburettor) engine's fuel supply hose to the carburettor is equipped with a disposable in-line fuel filter, renew it by disconnecting the battery earth lead, undoing the fuel hose clips at either side of the filter unit, and removing the filter. Absorb spilt fuel with a rag. Discard the filter, and fit the new one with its arrow pointing in the

direction of fuel flow. Refit/reconnect in the reverse order. If the original hose clips have to be cut off, fit new worm-drive clips.

FUEL INJECTION MODELS

SAFETY FIRST!

● *The high pressure pipework on a fuel injection system can retain its pressure for days even after the engine has been switched off.*

● *When you disconnect the pipework, a jet of fuel can be emitted under very high pressure - strong enough to penetrate the skin or damage the eyes.*

● *NEVER work on the fuel pipework when the engine is running (except when bleeding Diesel injectors - see* **Job 34. BLEEDING THE SYSTEM***.*

● *ALWAYS place a rag over a union while it is being undone until all the pressure has been let out of the system.*

● *You are recommended to wear strong rubber gloves and goggles when disconnecting the fuel injection system's high pressure pipework. Always disconnect VERY slowly, letting pressure out progressively. See* **Chapter 6, PART F: Job 8** *for details of how to depressurise the system.*

● *Disconnect the battery negative earth before working on the fuel system.*

● *Work outdoors and away from sources of flame or ignition.*

● *ALWAYS wear rubber gloves - don't let your skin come into contact with fuel.*

IMPORTANT NOTES:
● Wear plastic gloves and goggles and have a large rag and a suitable fire extinguisher ready.
● Place a container beneath the filter to catch fuel spillage.

32C. The filter, on the right-hand side inner wing, near the timing belt cover, must be renewed at the specified service interval to prevent damaging sediment from getting into the injection mechanism. On all types it

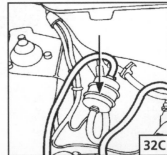

should be released from its mounting bracket. On non-Turbo engines the inlet and outlet hose clips should be removed (cut them off, if they are the original FIAT crimped type) and the new filter fitted with its arrow in the direction of fuel flow.

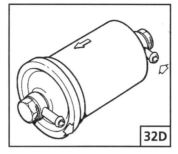

32D. The Turbo i.e. filter has banjo-type fuel unions - undone with a spanner. You must take care not to lose the copper washers of these unions! Fit the new filter with its arrow in the direction of fuel flow.

IMPORTANT NOTE: After clamping the new filter in place, refit the hoses, tighten the unions, ensure no traces of fuel are left in the engine bay, reconnect the battery and restart the engine. Check carefully to ensure there are no leaks.

On all petrol-injected cars there is also a low pressure filter to be renewed at the same time. It is fitted under the body, close to the fuel tank, along the fuel supply pipe. Renew it in the same manner as the main filter, taking the same precautions.

❏ Job 33. Drain diesel fuel filter.

The fuel filter is located in the right-hand rear corner of the engine compartment. Water carried in the fuel accumulates in the bottom of the filter, and should not be allowed to build up. To drain it...

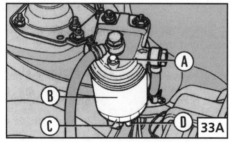

33A. ...position a receptacle under the filter, then unscrew the knurled tap (**D**) at the bottom of the filter. Now undo the air bleed screw (**A**). (On older diesels this is (**B**) in illustration **33B**.) Note that this bleed point may instead be a nipple on the filter head fuel union.

Drain a teacupful of fluid to ensure that all water is removed, then retighten the tap and the bleed screw. Remove the fluid receptacle.

33B. If your Uno Diesel is equipped with a primer pump (**C**) at the filter head, pump the button repeatedly until resistance is felt.

Whether or not there is a primer, start the engine and allow it to idle for a while to chase air from the system. If there are any engine-running problems after this, refer to **Job 34A** for details of system bleeding.

❏ Job 34. Change diesel fuel filter.

Drain the fuel filter. Unscrew the complete filter canister from its head, in the same way that you would an engine oil filter. If it is too tight, use an oil filter wrench on the lower, flatted zone (**C**) in illustration **33A.** Wipe the underside of the filter head, fill the new filter with fuel, lightly lubricate its seal with fuel, then screw it onto the filter head. Once it is 'nipped up', tighten it as far as possible by hand, without 'murdering' it.

Each time the diesel fuel system is opened - such as when replacing the fuel filter, air is admitted to the system, and it must be chased out otherwise the engine will not run properly. After filter replacement, it may be possible to bleed the system as described in **Job 33A.** If this is insufficient to achieve smooth, consistent engine running, bleed fully as follows.

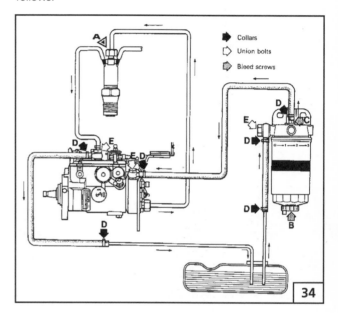

34. BLEEDING THE SYSTEM: Very carefully slacken each injector pipe union (only one at a time) at the injector end (**A**) using a split ring spanner, while the engine is idling. If the engine will not idle, do this while an assistant cranks it using the starter motor. Do not undo the union, merely loosen it slightly. Tighten the union progressively only when the engine is running by itself and when fuel, free of air bubbles, emerges continuously from the open union. Repeat this procedure at each injector union until idling is smooth and consistent.

IMPORTANT NOTE: If the engine does not eventually start, check all the unions (**D**) for the fuel inlet pipe and the other unions (**E**), replacing the sealing washers if necessary to eliminate any air leaks.

❏ Job 35. Check/adjust petrol engine idle and emissions.

Setting the idle speed and mixture is not just a matter of making the car run smoothly and economically; it's also a question of allowing it to run within the legal hydrocarbon (HC), Nitrous Oxide (NO) and carbon monoxide (CO) emission limits. If it is outside limits, the car will fail the annual test. (However, a worn engine will fail even if the carburettor or injection system is correctly set up.)

i INSIDE INFORMATION: These jobs require the use of a tachometer (rev-counter) and an exhaust gas analyser to achieve any degree of accuracy. If you don't own them - and relatively inexpensive tools are now available - you may wish to have the work carried out by your local FIAT dealer. *i*

ROUGH GUIDE: Within each section is a description of how you can get the car running tolerably well without any specialist equipment, so that you can take it to your FIAT dealership for accurate (and MoT-able!) tuning.

CARBURETTOR MODELS ONLY.

TAMPER PROOFING: All Uno carburettors originally had a tamper-proof seal (some plastic, some aluminium) placed over the mixture adjustment screw. These seals are to prevent anyone unauthorised from altering the mixture and exhaust emissions. In certain countries these seals must be retained by law.

If the seal is a plastic cap placed over the adjuster screw, it can be broken off with pliers. If it is a plug within the screw recess, force it out with a sharp object.

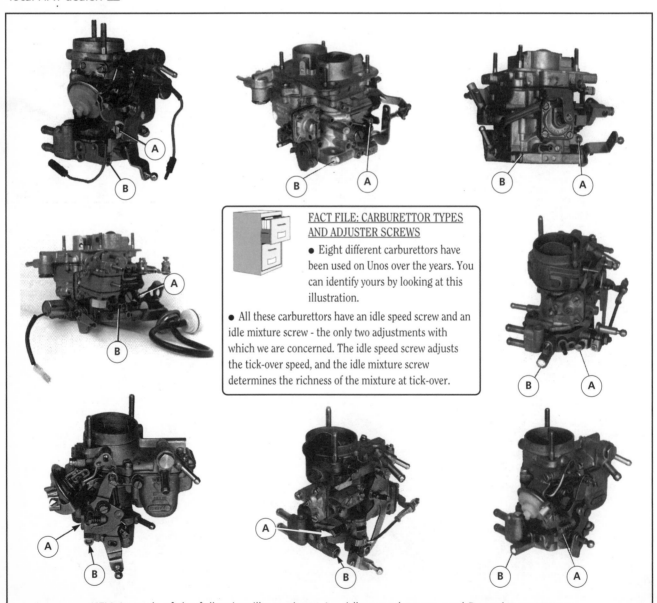

KEY: In each of the following illustrations: A = idle speed screw, and B = mixture screw (probably covered with a plug - see above).

35A. IDLE SPEED
ADJUSTMENT: Connect a rev-counter according to the maker's instructions, and check the idle speed. Turning screw (**A**) clockwise increases the idle speed, anti-clockwise reduces it. Set the idle speed in accordance with *Chapter 3, Facts and Figures.*

ROUGH GUIDE: Turn the screw until the engine is running at the slowest speed at which it runs smoothly and evenly.

MIXTURE ADJUSTMENT: Check that the idle speed is correct and make sure that the engine is at full operating temperature. Connect an exhaust gas analyser as instructed by the maker. If the CO reading is outside the range shown in *Chapter 3, Facts and Figures*, adjustment is required as follows:

Use a narrow-blade screwdriver and turn the screw clockwise to weaken (reduce) or anti-clockwise to richen (increase) the reading.

ROUGH GUIDE: Turn the mixture screw inwards (clockwise). As you do so, the tick-over speed will increase, until the point comes where the engine starts to run 'lumpily'. Back off the screw until the engine runs smoothly again, and then some more until the speed just starts to drop. At this point, screw the adjuster back in by a quarter-turn and you'll be somewhere near the optimum setting for smooth running.

IMPORTANT NOTE: After setting the mixture adjustment, re-check and, if necessary, re-adjust the idle speed.

TURBO I.E. FUEL INJECTION MODELS ONLY

35B. Check and adjust the idle speed and mixture in the same way as for the carburettors detailed earlier, but with these differences:

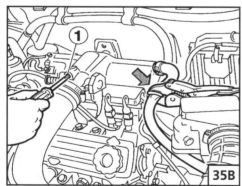

● carry out settings immediately after running the engine at a fast idle for twenty seconds or so.
● constrict the supplementary air pipe (arrowed) with a self-grip wrench to prevent false readings.
● on both Turbo i.e. models, the idle speed screw (**1**) is on the throttle valve body (secured by a lock-nut on 1.3 Turbo i.e.)...

35C. ...and the idle mixture screw (arrowed) is on the airflow sensor. The airflow sensor of the 1.3 Turbo i.e. is slightly different from the 1.4 Turbo i.e. version shown.

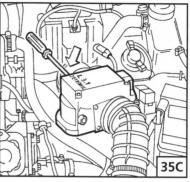

NON-TURBO FUEL INJECTION MODELS ONLY

The idle speed and mixture settings are controlled by the Electronic Control Unit (ECU) which is 'self-learning' and is programmed to adjust itself to give the ideal settings under all conditions. No manual adjustment is possible, nor provided for. If there is a problem, you will need to take your car to a FIAT dealer, with the appropriate diagnostic equipment.

☐ Job 36. Check emission control systems.

PETROL INJECTION MODELS ONLY

36. On petrol-injected Unos, sophisticated emission control equipment is fitted.

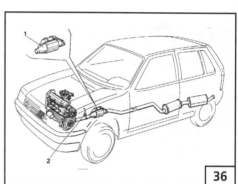

FACT FILE: EMISSION CONTROL SYSTEM

● The main features of the system are:
an **Electronic Control Module Unit or (ECU)** - the 'computer brain', which is programmed to alter the car's fuel and ignition settings according to information received from various sensors.

● a **catalytic converter** in the exhaust system, to convert CO and other gases to less harmful gases.

● a **Lambda sensor** in the exhaust manifold or front pipe (according to model) to detect the 'tune' of the exhaust gases and give a signal to the ECU.

● a petrol **evaporation control system**, to cut down on petrol vapour emissions from the fuel tank.

ELECTRONIC CONTROL MODULE: This is not an item that requires any servicing. If you think it might be faulty, ask your FIAT dealer or fuel injection specialist to check it for you. This must be done by someone with the correct FIAT plug-in diagnostic equipment and data.

CATALYTIC CONVERTER: The CAT (*illustration 36, part 1*) is not serviceable. If it fails, you will be told at the MoT test. Replacement is expensive, so we recommend you obtain a second opinion before replacing the 'cat'.

LAMBDA SENSOR: For information concerning the sensor (illustration **36, part 2**). See **Job 37**.

CHARCOAL CANISTER: This unit is located behind the cars' front panel, and does not need regular servicing. Check the canister one-way valve (see **Chapter 6, Repairs and Replacements, Part F, FUEL AND EXHAUST** for illustration) by disconnecting it and trying to blow through both ends. You should only be able to blow air towards the canister, not away from it. If the valve is faulty, renew it, making sure that it is fitted the right way round.

🅘 INSIDE INFORMATION: If the canister is flooded with petrol, it is probable that one of the **purge valves** or **purge valve floats** is faulty. Get this investigated and rectified by a FIAT dealer. If the engine cuts out and then restarts after a while, it could be the **breather hose valve**, fitted under the fuel filler neck. This one-way valve allows air to enter the tank as the fuel level falls, otherwise an air lock can prevent fuel reaching the engine. To test the valve, take off the pipe clips, remove the valve and test it as for the canister one-way valve, above. It should allow air to pass into the tank, but not the other way. 🅘

❑ **Job 37. Check lambda sensor.**

PETROL INJECTION MODELS ONLY

For a description of how the sensor works, see **Job 36, FACT FILE: EMISSION CONTROL SYSTEM**. It should be checked at the recommended interval - the cost of checking and replacing the sensor is far less than that of having to replace the catalytic converter because it has been polluted due to a sensor fault.

making it easy • *Replacement of the sensor is a simple job, but it can only be tested by your FIAT dealer with the correct equipment.*

• *If the sensor is faulty, have it renewed by your dealer.*

• *Lambda sensors are very delicate and easily damaged. It is not likely that you would be able to return one to the supplier if you fitted it yourself.*

• *Lambda sensors are only fitted to cars with a catalytic converter.*

❑ **Job 38. Check/adjust diesel idle speed.**

To accurately check and adjust the diesel's idle speed you need a diesel-specific rev-counter. If you're happy with the idle speed, leave well alone. But if you're convinced the idle is incorrect, it's best to take the car to a FIAT dealer. If you wish to adjust the speed yourself, get the engine to normal operating temperature, and check there is some free play in the accelerator cable before proceeding.

ADJUSTMENT - BOSCH PUMP

38A. Adjust the idle speed, which should be approximately 800 rpm, by slackening the lock-nut of the adjuster screw (**1**) then turning the screw inwards to increase the speed - or outwards to decrease. Retighten the lock-nut when the speed is correct.

ADJUSTMENT - LUCAS/ROTODIESEL/CAV PUMP

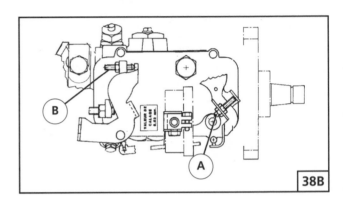

38B. Adjust the idle speed, which should be approximately 800 rpm, by slackening the lock-nut of the adjuster screw (**A**) and turning the screw to give the desired speed. Retighten the lock-nut, then rev the engine high and allow it to return to idle. If it goes below idle speed (i.e. it threatens to stall, or does stall), or if it decelerates too slowly, slacken the lock-nut of the adjuster screw (**B**), adjust it and check the deceleration again. Repeat as necessary to achieve comfortable deceleration without stalling, then tighten the lock-nut.

❑ **Job 39. Check/adjust diesel injection timing.**

Although a check of the injection timing is scheduled as a service item, there is no reason why the timing should have altered if the pump mounting bolts are tight and the pump has not been disturbed. Injection timing is best checked dynamically by a FIAT dealer or diesel specialist using specialised equipment. If you want to check the timing statically, and you have access to a dial gauge and the necessary adaptor to fit it to the pump, proceed as follows:

39A. Slacken the injection pump flange nuts - one can be seen (**A**) in illustration **39B** - and rear support bracket lower bolt. Make sure that the manual cold start control lever (at the dashboard, where fitted) is fully off.

BOSCH PUMP ONLY

39B. Unscrew the plug (*illustration 39A, part B*) at the rear of the injection pump, and screw in a Bosch pump dial gauge and adaptor. (The FIAT tool number for this is no. 1865090000.) With the tool fully screwed in, turn the engine in the opposite direction to normal rotation until the plunger inside the pump reaches its lowest position - as indicated by gauge movement. In this position, zero the gauge. Now turn the engine in normal direction until engine piston No. 1 is at Top Dead Centre. The dial gauge should read 1 mm if the timing is correct. If it isn't, gently turn the injection pump housing relative to its mounting until the correct measurement is shown on the gauge. Now lock up the pump flange nuts and rear support bracket bolt. Remove the tool and refit the blanking plug to the back of the pump. Adjust the idle speed if need be. See *Job 38*.

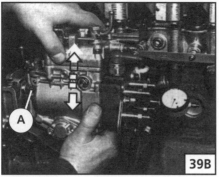

LUCAS/ROTODIESEL/CAV PUMP ONLY

39C. You will find a label attached to the top of the injection pump (see illustration **38B**), quoting the correct timing measurement in millimetres: e.g. 8.52 mm. Slacken the pump flange nuts (as in, *illustration 39B, part A*) and the rear support bolt (as in, *illustration 39A, part A*). Remove the plastic cap from the pump top. Now turn the engine crankshaft in the opposite direction to normal rotation by about 20 degrees. Using either FIAT tool No. 1865091000 or, with the necessary Lucas dial gauge (**A**), the holder (**B**) and the

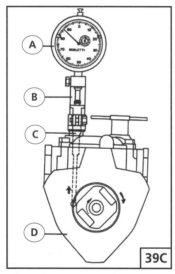

probe (**C**) threaded into position in place of the plastic cap, position the engine crankshaft at Top Dead Centre. Ensure that the dial gauge is fitted to its holder and the pump (**D**) with a pre-loading of 10-15 mm, then zero it. Slowly turn the pump body, turning the upper part away from engine block. Now, slowly turn the engine crankshaft in the normal direction of rotation until the dial gauge indicates the measurement you read off the pump label (that's the correct timing point). Tighten the pump nuts/bolt. Turn the crankshaft by two complete revolutions in the normal direction of rotation, then re-check the timing. If incorrect, repeat the timing procedure. Remove the tool and refit the plastic plug. Adjust the idle speed if need be. See *Job 38*.

❏ Job 40. Check inlet and exhaust manifold fixings.

Check that the inlet and exhaust manifold nuts and bolts are tightened to the correct torque. See *Chapter 3, Facts and Figures.*

❏ Job 41. Check exhaust system.

41. Examine the silencer and exhaust pipes and joints for corrosion and signs of leaking, indicated by a 'sooty' deposit at the point of the leak. Also check the

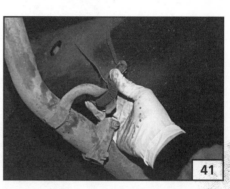

condition of the rubber 'hangers' that hold the system to the car. If any are missing or broken, the exhaust system can fracture due to extra stresses. Stretch the rubber, and look for cracks.

making it easy!
• *If you suspect a leak but its location isn't obvious, start the engine and pressurise the system by holding a piece of board against the tailpipe. Under pressure, the leak should be more noisy and obvious. Don't burn yourself on the exhaust!*

PART F: STEERING AND SUSPENSION

❏ Job 42. Check front wheel bearings.

In order to check for wear:
• raise the front of the car on axle stands (see *Chapter 1, Safety First!*)
• place the gearbox in neutral
• pull the handbrake securely on and chock the rear wheels

Try spinning each wheel (as far as possible with a front-drive car), feeling for rough rotation. Rock the wheel about its centre, feeling for excess bearing play.

i INSIDE INFORMATION: If a wheel bearing is worn, you will normally hear a noise on the outer, loaded bearing when cornering. *i*

❏ Job 43. Check front suspension.

BOTTOM BALL JOINT

Jack up the car underneath the suspension lower arm (wishbone), so that the wheel is two inches off the ground. See *Chapter 1, Safety First.*

43A. Place a long, rigid bar between the ground and the bottom of the tyre tread, and gently 'jog' the wheel upwards repeatedly while a helper looks at and feels the lower balljoint for vertical movement. The helper should NOT lie under the car, and you should be careful not to rock the car off the jack. Also examine the ball joint gaiter for any damage or leakage of grease - a

simple, visual examination. You will have to replace the wishbone assembly if the gaiter is damaged. See **Chapter 6, Repairs and Replacements** for information.

TRACK CONTROL ARM INNER BUSHES

43B. Further raise the car and support it on an axle stand under the subframe so that the suspension on the side being checked can hang free. Lever between the arm and subframe, looking for excessive movement of the bushes. Some cushioned flexing is normal. See **Chapter 6, Repairs and Replacements** for bush replacement information.

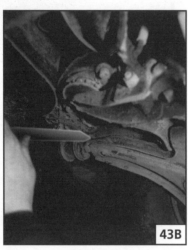

SUSPENSION STRUT/SHOCK ABSORBER

43C. Examine the shock absorber, which is enclosed inside the coil spring, for leaks, looking for signs of a 'damp' oil stain seeping from underneath the top half of the shock absorber body.

The top of the strut/shock absorber is mounted in a rubber bush which can be checked for softness, cracking or deterioration from inside the engine bay.

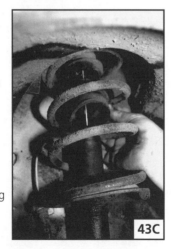

BOUNCE TEST: Try 'bouncing' each front corner of the car in a rhythmical motion, pressing down as hard as you can. When you let go, the movement should continue for no more than one-and-a-half rebounds. If it does so, this is a sure indication that the shock absorber is worn and should be replaced. If one of the front shock absorbers needs replacing, replace both, for safety reasons.

❏ **Job 44. Check track rod ends.**

44. Drive the car on to car ramps, firmly apply the handbrake and chock the rear wheels. Get your helper to sit inside the car, turn the ignition key to the 'MAR' (ON) position to release the steering column lock. Now, move the steering wheel repeatedly about 100 mm (4 in.) each way while someone checks for free movement in each track rod end (TRE). Also, look out for a split gaiter. Replace the TRE if the gaiter is split, or it will rapidly fail.

ℹ INSIDE INFORMATION: Try placing your hand over the TRE as the steering is moved. If there are any signs of wear, replace the TRE. ℹ

❏ **Job 45. Check steering column and rack.**

STEERING COLUMN

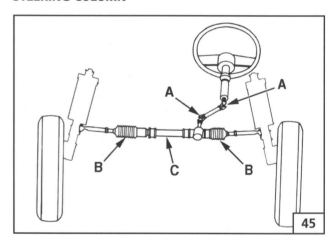

45. The steering column has two universal joints (**A**) which need to be checked for wear. While your assistant is turning the steering wheel, check to see if there is any movement in the universal joints.

ℹ INSIDE INFORMATION: Place your hand over the joint - you can usually feel the movement better than you can see it. If there is ANY movement at all, play at the steering wheel will be greatly exaggerated - replace the faulty universal joint. ℹ

STEERING RACK GAITERS

Turn the ignition key to the 'MAR' (ON) position but take care not to start the engine. Turn the steering wheel to full right lock. From underneath the bonnet, examine the gaiter (**B**) on the left-hand side, which will now be fully extended. Check visually for splits or oil leakage. Turn the steering wheel to the opposite lock and examine the gaiter (**B**) on the other side of the rack. If necessary, replace IMMEDIATELY - the rack will rapidly be ruined if the gaiter is split.

Also, watch the steering rack body (**C**) to see if it is firmly attached. If there is any movement between the rack and its mountings, check the securing bolts for tightness.

❏ Job 46. Check rear wheel bearings.

46. Uno rear wheel bearings are sealed in their hubs and are usually very long lived. See the checking procedures described in **Job 42**, but

remember not to apply the handbrake! Also note that the rear wheels will be easier to spin than the fronts.

❏ Job 47. Check rear suspension.

Chock the front wheels, jack the rear of the car, and place stands under the axle, as close to the wheels as possible. Lower the car onto the axle stands.

47A. Check the axle forward bush pivots and the shock absorber lower mounting bolts for tightness. Check the condition of the axle mounting bushes by levering them with a screwdriver.

Replace if excessive movement or bush deterioration are noticed. See **Chapter 6, Repairs and Replacements.**

REAR SHOCK ABSORBERS

47B. Look for signs of leaks coming from underneath the top part of each rear shock absorber (at position **A**) and replace if necessary. Check the top and bottom rubber mounting bushes. If any are soft or split they must be replaced. Check that the bump stops are present and correct.

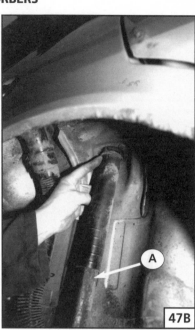

BOUNCE TEST: Bounce-test the shock absorbers as in **Job 43.**

❏ Job 48. Check wheel bolts for tightness.

Remove each wheel bolt in turn and ensure that they run smoothly. Clean the threads, if necessary. Refit and check that all are tightened to the correct torque - see **Chapter 3, Facts and Figures** - using a torque wrench.

PART G: THE BRAKING SYSTEM

SAFETY FIRST!

● *Before raising the car, see **Chapter 1, Safety First!***

● *Also, be sure to read the section on **BRAKES AND ASBESTOS** in **Chapter 1, Safety First!** for further important information.*

● *Your car's brakes are its most important safety-related items. Do NOT attempt any work on the braking system unless you are fully competent to do so.*

● *If you have not been trained in this work, but wish to carry it out, we strongly recommend you have a garage or qualified mechanic check your work before using the car on the road.*

● *Always start by washing the brakes with a proprietary brand of brake cleaner - brake drums removed where appropriate - and never use compressed air to clean off brake dust.*

● *Always replace brake pads and/or shoes in complete 'axle' sets of four - never replace them on one wheel only.*

● *After fitting new brake shoes or pads, avoid heavy braking for the first 150 to 200 miles (250 to 300 km), except in an emergency.*

● *Start by raising the wheel to be worked on and supporting it on an axle stand. Remove the road wheel - see **Chapter 1, Safety First!***

❏ Job 49. Check front brakes, change pads.

Checking the brake pads of most Uno models involves the same amount of work as changing them. For that reason, brake pad replacement for the most commonly found front caliper type (the caliper with no inspection opening) is covered here in detail rather than in *Chapter 6, Repairs and Replacements*.

CALIPER WITH NO INSPECTION OPENING

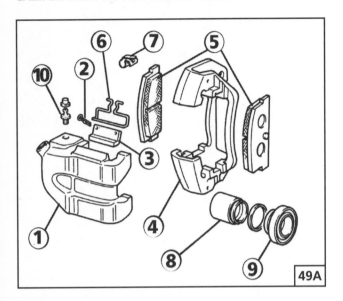

49A. This drawing illustrates the various components of the front brake assembly.

49B. You can't see the pads without first removing the caliper. Start by removing the two spring clips (*49A, part 2* - only the top one is shown here) one at the top of the caliper assembly, and one at the bottom. Some models may have four such spring clips. Grasp the outer eyes and pull.

49C. You can now drive the TWO tapered locking plates (*49A, part 3* - start with the top one, shown here) from between caliper and caliper support bracket. Because they are tapered, start by pushing the caliper towards the support bracket, to help relieve pressure. With both upper and lower locking plates removed, the caliper (*49A, part 1*) can be lifted away.

IMPORTANT NOTE: DO NOT allow the weight of the caliper to hang from the flexible hose - position it to rest on the driveshaft, or support it from the road spring using a length of wire.

Compare the thickness of the two pads - there should be no significant difference. The minimum recommended thickness of lining material is 1.5 mm, but bearing in mind the amount of time before the next service, you may wish to replace the pads before they get to this stage.

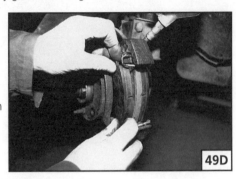

49D. Having got this far, you'll want to remove the pads (*49A, parts 5*), which lift away. The two large springs (*49A, part 6*) are NOT removed. Wash all parts of the assembly with a proprietary brake cleaner.

You can now check the thickness of the brake disc, which should not be below 9 mm at any point.

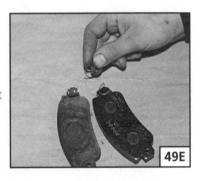

49E. Before refitting, don't forget the two anti-rattle springs (*49A, part 7*), one at the top and bottom of each pad. The pad on the left has the old-style bent-steel spring clips; the new FIAT ones on the right come complete with the correct spring clips. We STRONGLY recommend the use of FIAT original-equipment brake components.

> ### FACT FILE: BRAKE DISC WEAR SYMPTOMS
>
> ● There are certain essential checks you should carry out for yourself, with brake pads removed:
>
> ● Look for any obvious grooves worn into the disc. Slight undulations are acceptable, but anything worse and the disc should be replaced.
>
> ● Look and feel for any wear-ridge on the outer edges of the disc.
>
> ● The depth will give an indication of wear.
>
> ● Check for corrosion of the disc surface. If any is found, the brake caliper is probably faulty, and needs checking.
>
> ● If any surface flaking is found on either side of the disc, replace them both.
>
> ● If you are not certain whether any wear is acceptable, ask your specialist or FIAT dealer to check.

Before reassembling the brake, check the condition of the brake caliper. Have an assistant VERY SLOWLY AND GENTLY apply pressure to the brake pedal while you watch the piston (*49A, part 8*), which should move outwards. If it doesn't easily move, it is seized and the caliper should be replaced. DO NOT allow the piston to project more than 10 mm or it may be forced from the caliper - use a G-clamp as an 'end stop'.

49F. Check inside the caliper housing for signs of corrosion. If any is found, or the seal is damaged, the caliper should be exchanged for a new or overhauled unit from your FIAT dealership. Examine the piston's protective gaiter (*49A, part 9*) for splitting and fluid leaks. This one is in poor condition and the caliper requires immediate replacement.

49F

making it easy!
● *In order to fit new pads, the caliper piston must be pushed back into the bore.*

● *Use an old battery hydrometer to draw about half of the fluid from the master cylinder.*

● *Push the piston back into the caliper, using a G-clamp.*

● *Keep an eye on the master cylinder so that it doesn't overflow as fluid is pushed back up the pipe.*

49G. Before fitting the pads, put a light smear of lithium brake grease (NOT ordinary grease) on the pads' metal backplates at the points shown.

49G

IMPORTANT NOTE: Be very sparing or grease could migrate to the friction linings!

49H. When refitting the locking plates, start with the lower one. Lever the caliper up with a screwdriver while pushing, then tapping if need be, until they are fully home. Don't forget the retaining clips (*49A, part 2*), one at the top and one at the bottom.

49H

IMPORTANT NOTE: After fitting the pads, apply the brakes firmly several times to adjust them.

CALIPERS WITH INSPECTION WINDOW

All of the above information on the caliper type with no inspection window must be read and followed carefully.

With this type of caliper it is possible to inspect the pads through the caliper frontal aperture. For details of checking and replacement See *Chapter 6, Repairs and Replacements, PART H: BRAKES, Job 2*.

❏ **Job 50. Check rear brakes.**

SAFETY FIRST!

● *Read SAFETY FIRST at the start of **Job 49** before proceeding!*

GENERAL. The vast majority of Uno models are fitted with drum-type rear brakes, but Turbo i.e. models have a disc-and-caliper arrangement instead.

Slacken the wheel bolts, raise the wheel, remove it and support the car with an axle stand. Make sure that the wheels remaining on the ground are chocked in both directions and that the handbrake is off.

DRUM REAR BRAKES

making it easy!
● *If the drum sticks, try: disconnecting the handbrake cable from beneath the car.*

● *screw a pair of bolts into the two threaded holes in the drum. Evenly tightening the bolts will force the drum off the shoes.*

● *tap carefully around the drum with a hide mallet to help loosen it.*

50A. Remove the two bolts (one of them the wheel positioning stud) and remove the drum. Clean the inside of the drum and the brake with aerosol brake cleaner. If the drum is badly scored or cracked, replace it.

50A

Examine the brake shoes for wear or oil contamination. If the latter, the wheel cylinder is probably leaking (see *50B*) and the shoes will have to be scrapped. FIAT recommend a **minimum** 1.5 mm shoe lining thickness, but it's advisable to replace shoes well before they're this thin.

50B. Fold back each of the two rubbers on the wheel cylinder. Any fluid found inside requires a new cylinder.

IMPORTANT NOTE: For information on replacing missing or damaged springs, rear brake shoes or wheel cylinders, see *Chapter 6, Repairs and Replacements.*

50B

DISC REAR BRAKES (TURBO i.e.)

With the rear of the car raised and safely supported (see **Chapter 1, Safety First**) and the rear wheels removed, brake pad inspection can be carried out by looking through the aperture in the caliper body. The pads should be replaced as detailed in **Chapter 6 , Repairs and Replacements**. Minimum thickness is 1.5 mm - but don't let them get this low!

SAFETY FIRST!

● *Raise the rear of the car to adjust the handbrake. It is ESSENTIAL to ensure the front wheels are securely chocked in both directions, and that axle stands or ramps are used to support the car*

☐ Job 51. Check/adjust handbrake.

The handbrake is intended to 'set' itself in use as the rear brake self-adjusters operate. If the handbrake seems not to work, even though lever travel is not excessive, remove the rear drums and examine the brake shoes (see **Job 50B**) rather than over-tighten the handbrake cable. The handbrake may need adjusting when, after a time, the handbrake cable stretches or if the rear brake friction materials are replaced.

51. Apply the handbrake lever by three to five 'clicks' of the ratchet. From underneath the car, slacken the lock-nut (**b**) and turn the adjusting nut (**a**) until the cable (**c**) is drawn

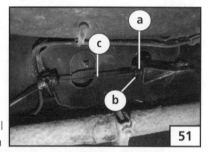

taut. Check that both rear wheels are 'locked' when the handbrake is ON, and that both rear wheels are completely free when it is fully OFF. When everything works properly, tighten lock-nut (**b**) and grease the adjuster mechanism and cable ends. Lower the car to the ground, and check again that moving the handbrake through three to five notches is sufficient to hold the car stationary. A proper check of handbrake efficiency can only be carried out by a garage with a 'rolling road' brake tester.

☐ Job 52. Check brake pipes.

FLEXIBLE HOSES

Check the flexible brake pipes that connect the calipers to the metal pipes on the body. Try bending back on themselves those that are not contained in a protective coil, and look for any signs of cracking, particularly at the bends. Check them all for signs of rubbing, splitting, kinks and perishing of the rubber. Check hoses for 'ballooning' with the brake pedal pressed.

RIGID PIPES

Check all rigid pipes for signs of damage or corrosion and check that all of the locating clips are sound and in place.

☐ Job 53. Change brake hydraulic fluid.

Change the brake fluid at the recommended interval. See **Chapter 6, Repairs and Replacements PART H: BRAKES, Job 15.**

i INSIDE INFORMATION: Brake fluid absorbs water from the air. This corrodes brake components and can cause total brake failure. With brakes applied heavily, the fluid can heat to above 100 degrees Celsius, the water vaporises, and the pedal goes to the floor! *i*

PART H: BODYWORK AND INTERIOR

☐ Job 54. Lubricate hinges and locks.

54. Apply a few drops of light oil (from either an aerosol or oil can) to the hinges of the bonnet, doors and tailgate. Dip the door/tailgate key in graphite powder and insert the key to lubricate the lock barrels. Grease the door and tailgate latch mechanism (aerosol grease is handy), the bonnet release

mechanism (and the tailgate's, if applicable) and the cable end.

☐ Job 55. Check windscreen.

Clean the windscreen with a proprietary glass cleaner and examine it for stone chips, cracks and scoring. While some degree of damage is acceptable, the strict MoT Test regulations limit the amount and position of such defects.

Some screen chips can be repaired and made invisible.

☐ Job 56. Check seat and seat belt mountings.

Your car's seat and safety belt mountings and backrest adjustment locking mechanism will be checked as part of the annual test, but it pays to check them beforehand. Also, regularly check that the seat belts: a) retract easily and smoothly, and b) 'hold' when you snatch them, or under sharp braking.

☐ Job 57. Check headlight alignment.

Have the headlight alignment checked by your FIAT dealer, who will have the necessary beam-setting equipment to carry out the work accurately. This job will also be carried out as part of the MoT Test.

57A. On early cars, ensure that the beam correction knurled knobs (at the bottom corner of each headlight, inside the engine bay) are in the light-load position before headlight alignment is carried out. Otherwise the beams will aim too high if unladen. Don't confuse the beam correctors with vertical alignment - screw (**A**) and horizontal - screw (**B**).

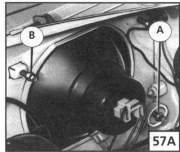

57B. On later cars the beam correction adjuster is a small lever (**c**) just beneath the headlight vertical alignment

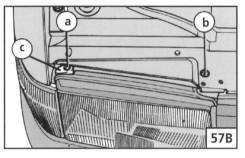

screw (**a**) at the headlight top. Vertical alignment is adjusted with screw (**a**) and horizontal with (**b**). Some later cars have a beam adjuster on the dash. Set it to position '0' before the beams are aligned.

☐ Job 58. Check underbody.

Check the condition of the underbody for damage and corrosion. Take a tin of waxy underbody seal and a brush under the car and replace any missing underbody seal.

☐ Job 59. Check spare tyre.

This job should ideally be carried out every month or two - you never know when you're going to need that spare! But if you haven't remembered, do it at the time shown on the *Service Interval Chart* at the latest.

i INSIDE INFORMATION: Put in the maximum recommended pressure for heavy-duty use - it's always easier to let some air out if necessary, than to put some in. Lift the spare out check the 'hidden' lower side wall (see *Job 6*) for cracking. *i*

☐ Job 60. Change pollen filter.

When fitted to the fresh air intake, replace it at the scheduled mileage interval

PART I: ROAD TEST

☐ Job 61. Road test and specialist check - after every service.

Before you can claim to have 'finished' working on your car, you must check it, test it, and, if necessary, have a qualified mechanic check it over for you.

If you are not a qualified mechanic, we strongly recommend having someone who is a properly qualified mechanic - your FIAT dealership perhaps - inspect all of the car's safety-related items after they have been worked on at home and before using the car on the road.

● Before setting out, check that the lights, indicators and in-car controls, as well as seat belts and seat adjustments, all work correctly.

● Run the car for several minutes before setting out then turn off, check fluid levels and check underneath for leaks.

● Check that the steering moves freely in both directions and that the car does not 'pull' one way or the other when driving in a straight line - but do bear in mind the effect of the camber on the road.

● Make sure that the brakes work effectively, smoothly and without the need for 'pumping'. There should be no juddering or squealing.

● Check that the car does not 'pull' from one side to the other when you brake firmly from around 40 mph. (Don't cause a skid and don't try this if there is any following traffic.)

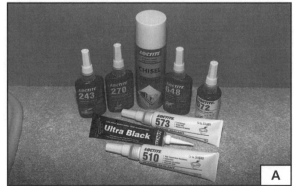

A. FIAT sell and recommend Loctite products. There is a range of gasket sealants and 'CHISEL' aerosol gasket shifter...

B. ...as well as bio-degradable spray-on engine degreaser.

CHAPTER 6
REPAIRS AND REPLACEMENT

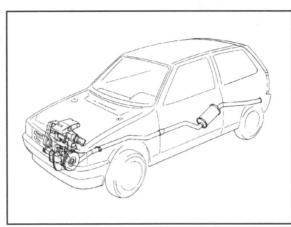

This chapter shows you how to remove and overhaul all the major 'wearing' parts of the car. We deliberately *don't* show how to rebuild major components, such as the gearbox, or differential. You are much better off, in terms of time, cost and the provision of a guarantee, to buy a replacement unit.

The same applies to major electrical components, such as alternator and starter motor. If as we recommend you stick to 'original' FIAT replacement parts, you will maintain the original quality of your car.

Chapter Contents

Illustration and Section Numbers

● In this chapter, each area of the car is dealt with in a different PART of the chapter, such as, *PART A: ENGINE*.

● Each Job in each PART has a separate identifying number. For example *Job 4. OHC Cylinder Head Removal.*

● Every Job is broken down into easy-to-follow Steps, numbered from 1-on.

● Illustrations are numbered so that you can see at a glance where they belong!

● The illustration *Job 1-4* (in PART A) for example, relates to the text in *Job 1, Step 4.*

FACT FILE: UNO ENGINE TYPES

FIAT Unos used four different main engine types.

The OHV (Overhead Valve) engine can be recognised by the fact that the carburettor is mounted almost directly onto the cylinder head with no inlet manifold. See illustration *PART A: Job 1-1.*

The OHC 'FIRE' (Fully Integrated Robotised Engine) Overhead Camshaft unit has a rectangular oil filler cap and a distributor mounted horizontally on the end of the cylinder head. See illustration *PART A: Job 18-1.*

The non-'FIRE' 1116/1299/1301/1372cc OHC (Overhead Camshaft) engine has a sloping cam cover and (usually) a cylinder block mounted distributor. See illustration *PART A: Job 9-1*, although appearances can vary greatly! For instance, **the non-'FIRE' 1372 OHC** engine has a sloping, cast alloy cam cover and a distributor on the end of the head.

The DIESEL engine is dealt with in *Jobs 28 to 35*. See illustration in the *FACT FILE* before *Job 28*.

PART A: ENGINE

PART A: Contents

FACT FILE: PISTON/CONROD ASSEMBLIES

● On all Uno Petrol engines, the piston and conrod have to be assembled with the offset the right way round. (We recommend that your FIAT dealer assembles the pistons onto the conrods for you.)

● Although the amount of offset differs, this is the direction of offset on all Petrol engines.

● There is no offset on Uno 1697cc Diesel engines.

a - direction of rotation

b - bore no. stamp (all OHC engines)

c - bore no. stamp (OHV engines)

d - piston centre-line

e - conrod centre-line

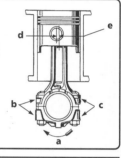

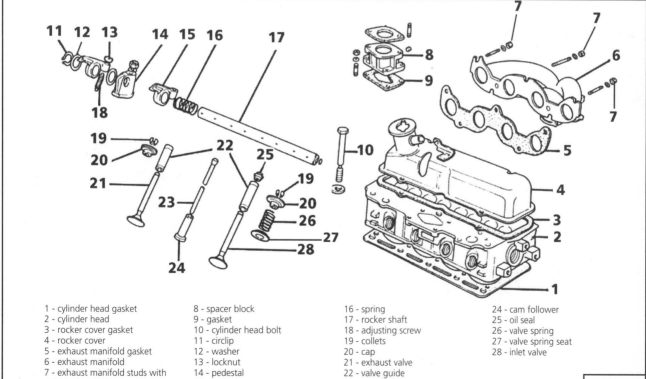

1 - cylinder head gasket	8 - spacer block	16 - spring	24 - cam follower
2 - cylinder head	9 - gasket	17 - rocker shaft	25 - oil seal
3 - rocker cover gasket	10 - cylinder head bolt	18 - adjusting screw	26 - valve spring
4 - rocker cover	11 - circlip	19 - collets	27 - valve spring seat
5 - exhaust manifold gasket	12 - washer	20 - cap	28 - inlet valve
6 - exhaust manifold	13 - locknut	21 - exhaust valve	
7 - exhaust manifold studs with nuts and washers	14 - pedestal	22 - valve guide	
	15 - rocker	23 - push rod	

Job 1-1

Job 1. OHV cylinder head - removal.

☐ **Step 1:** Familiarise yourself with illustration **Job 1-1**, showing the cylinder head components referred to in the following text.

ℹ INSIDE INFORMATION: Allow the engine to cool right down before starting work, or you will run the risk of causing cylinder head distortion. **ℹ**

SAFETY FIRST!

● *Disconnect both battery leads, negative terminal first.*

☐ **Step 2:** Drain the cooling system. See **PART C: COOLING SYSTEM.**

☐ **Step 3:** Remove the air cleaner, carburettor and spacer block and gasket. See **PART F: FUEL AND EXHAUST SYSTEM.**

☐ **Step 4:** Remove all five nuts and washer holding the exhaust manifold and ducting to the cylinder head. The rocker cover has already been removed from this engine.

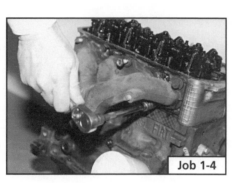

Job 1-4

☐ **Step 5:** Remove the distributor and leads, paying particular attention to **PART D: IGNITION.**

☐ **Step 6:** Remove the water temperature sender unit cable from the sender unit in the cylinder head. (See illustration **Job 1-15 (b)** for position on head.)

☐ **Step 7:** Remove the thermostat housing from the cylinder head. (See illustration **Job 1-15, (a)** for position on head.)

☐ **Step 8:** Disconnect all water hoses from the cylinder head.

☐ **Step 9:** Note alternator cable positions and disconnect. Remove the alternator after undoing the three nuts and bolts.

☐ **Step 10:** Undo and remove the rocker cover securing nuts, spring washers and packers. Then lift off the rocker cover and gasket.

☐ **Step 11:** Unscrew the four rocker post nuts evenly a few turns at a time until all are loose. Remove the nuts and spring washers and pull the rocker shaft assembly clear of the studs.

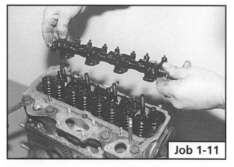

Job 1-11

☐ **Step 12:** Remove the pushrods one at a time, keeping them in the correct order.

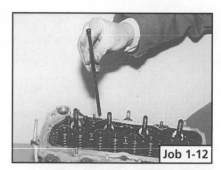

Job 1-12

Job 1-13

making it easy ☐ **Step 13:** So that you don't confuse the order in which the pushrods were fitted, put masking tape around the end of each one as it is removed and number it. No. 1 is at the timing chain end.

Step 14: Unscrew the cylinder head bolts half a turn at a time and in the order shown.

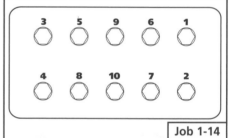

3 5 9 6 1

4 8 10 7 2

Job 1-14

ℹ Step 15: INSIDE INFORMATION: Don't forget the bolt hidden inside the inlet manifold. When free, remove all bolts and washers. **ℹ**

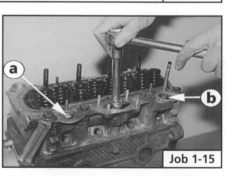

a   b

Job 1-15

☐ **Step 16:** You will also have to remove the water pipe bracket previously held by two of the bolts.

Job 1-16

Step 17: The cylinder head is now ready to be removed.

Job 1-17

making it easy!
● If the head is stuck, use a wooden hammer shaft or something similar, as a lever in one of the exhaust ports to break the seal.

Protect the bores and main waterways by plugging with clean rag. (For cylinder head overhaul, see **Job 3.**

Job 2. OHV cylinder head - refitting.

Step 1: Make sure you have all the gaskets you will need, from your FIAT dealership. All the gaskets should be renewed.

Step 2: Ensure that cylinder head and block surfaces are thoroughly cleaned. Remove the rag from the cylinder bores and ensure that the bores and piston crowns are perfectly clean. Apply a coating of new engine oil to the cylinder walls.

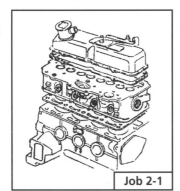
Job 2-1

Step 3: Make sure that the two cylinder head locating dowels are properly fitted in the recessed bolt holes at the front and rear of the cylinder block.

Job 2-3

Step 4: Correctly locate a new gasket over the dowels with the word "ALTO" facing upwards. **IMPORTANT NOTE:** The cylinder head gasket should be fitted dry, with no oil or grease being applied to any of the mating surfaces.

Job 2-4

Step 5: Carefully lower the cylinder head into position.

Step 6: The securing bolts may now be loosely fitted to the cylinder head.

8	6	2	5	10
○	○	○	○	○
7	3	1	4	9
○	○	○	○	○

Job 2-6

ℹ INSIDE INFORMATION: Don't forget the cylinder head bolt inside the inlet manifold. (See **Job 1, Step 15**.) Also note that two of the bolts, next to the temperature sender unit position, also secure the water pipe bracket. (See **Job 1, Step 16**.) ℹ

You can now refit the sender unit.

Step 7: Using a torque wrench tighten the cylinder head bolts a little at a time in the order shown above until all reach their specified torque requirement. See **Chapter 3, Facts and Figures**.

Step 8: Fit the pushrods in the same order as removed, lubricating the ends beforehand.

Step 9: Fully unscrew the rocker arm adjusters and lower the rocker gear carefully onto the four studs in the cylinder head, ensuring that all the rocker ball ends are located in the pushrod cups.

ℹ INSIDE INFORMATION: Spinning the pushrods between your fingers helps to ensure proper location in the tappets. ℹ

Step 10: Refit the nuts and washers to the studs and tighten progressively to the specified torque. See **Chapter 3, Facts and Figures**.

Step 11: Adjust the valve clearances. See **Chapter 5, Servicing Your Car, Job 9**.

Job 2-12

Step 12: Refit the exhaust manifold and ducting, the alternator and the thermostat housing.

Step 13: Refit the distributor. See **PART D: IGNITION**.

Step 14: Refit the rocker cover, using a new gasket.

Job 2-14

ℹ INSIDE INFORMATION: Avoid distortion of the rocker cover by not over-tightening the bolts. Over-tightening distorts the pressed-steel cover and causes leaks! ℹ

Step 15: Refit the carburettor and the air cleaner. See **PART F: FUEL AND EXHAUST**.

Step 16: Reconnect all the water hoses, remake the electrical connections and connect the battery.

Step 17: Refill the cooling system, using the correct **FL Paraflu** anti-freeze solution. See **Chapter 3, Facts and Figures**.

Job 3. OHV cylinder head - dismantling and overhauling.

Step 1: The most important items to note here are the valves themselves (**1**), valve guides (**2**), caps (or valve retainers) (**3**)

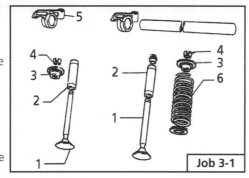

Job 3-1

and collets (**4**), the rocker arms (**5**) and valve springs (**6**) - sometimes two fitted, one inside the other.

Step 2: Use a suitable valve spring compressor to compress each spring in turn to allow the removal of

Job 3-2

the split collets from the valve stems. Take care not to lose the collets when releasing the spring compressor.

making it easy
- *Keep the valves in their correct order by pushing their stems through some cardboard and numbering them, number one being at the timing chain end.*
- *Another means of identification is to label each valve with masking tape which you can write on with a biro or felt pen.*

Step 3: The valve spring caps, springs and spring seats can all be lifted clear and the valves withdrawn from their guides.

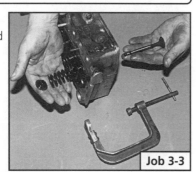

Job 3-3

ℹ Step 4: INSIDE INFORMATION: The valves should slide freely out of their guides. Any resistance may be caused by a build-up of carbon, or a slight burr on the stem where the collets engage. This can

Job 3-4

usually be removed by careful use of fine wet-or-dry paper, allowing you to withdraw the valves without scoring their guides. ℹ

Keep the valves in their correct order.

Step 5: Re-insert each valve into its guide, keeping hold of the valve end. Try to move the valve from side to side. Try again from the other end of the valve guide. If *any* movement can be felt, the guide is worn and must be replaced by your FIAT dealer or specialist workshop.

Step 6: The cylinder head is made of light alloy and is easily damaged when being cleaned. Use a rotary wire brush from the combustion chambers and ports, but no sharp objects such as screwdrivers should be used. The machined surfaces must have all traces of old gasket removed by use of a straight edge - take great care not to dig it in! Then wash down with paraffin to remove old oil and dirt, and dry off with a clean rag.

At *all* costs, avoid gouging the cylinder head. This can be very expensive to put right!

making it easy
- *Try using a proprietary gasket remover, such as Loctite 'Chisel', to loosen old gasket material.*

Step 7: Clean the carbon from the valves with a rotary wire brush and wash them in paraffin. This is a cleaned-up valve next to a typically carboned-up one. Wash the valve springs, caps, seats and collets and dry.

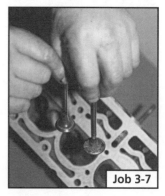

Job 3-7

making it easy
- *Clean the flat ends of the valve heads back to the shiny metal! Now the sucker on the end of your valve grinding stick won't keep falling off when you grind-in the valves!*

Step 8: The cylinder head should be checked for distortion by use of a straight edge and feeler gauge. At the same time check for excessive corrosion. If you are in doubt, or if

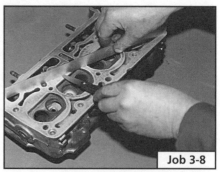

Job 3-8

the old gasket has blown, have the cylinder head refaced by your FIAT agent or engine specialist.

Step 9: Examine the valve seats for pitting or burning. Also, check the valve seats in the cylinder head. Small pits can be removed by grinding the valves onto their seats. The seats in the cylinder head will have to be recut (again, by your local FIAT agent if the pitting is too deep), and new valves fitted.

FACT FILE: VALVE GRINDING

□ **Step 10:** Apply a small quantity of coarse grinding paste evenly round the valve seat. A valve grinding stick with a suction pad slightly smaller than the valve head should be selected. Put a

Job 3-10

dab of moisture onto the suction pad and press the grinding stick to the first valve.

□ **Step 11:** Lower the valve stem into its guide and, holding the grinding stick between the palms of your hands, rub your hands together (like a bushman making a fire), rotating the valve and grinding the two seats together. Lift the valve regularly, say every ten or so turns, to allow the grinding paste to be redistributed. When you can feel the paste wearing smooth, remove the valve and wipe all the surfaces clean.

Job 3-11

IMPORTANT NOTE: Make sure that no paste is allowed to enter the guide. This would cause a lot of wear to the valve stem and guide.

● A complete ring of grey contact area should be visible on the valve head and its seat in the cylinder head. If necessary, start off with coarse paste to remove the deeper pits, and finally use fine paste to obtain a smooth finish. If pitting is too bad, you could have the valve face and the valve seats resurfaced or, in worst cases, the valve and/or valve seat (in the cylinder head) will have to be replaced. Consult your FIAT dealer or engine specialist if in doubt.

i INSIDE INFORMATION: A narrow contact band means more seat pressure and longer life. A wide band allows rapid valve burning. *i*

Now repeat this operation on the remaining seven valves.

□ **Step 12:** Wash the whole cylinder head again using paraffin and an old brush, making sure that all traces of grinding paste are removed, then dry off. Use compressed air if available.

SAFETY FIRST!

● *Treat compressed air with respect. Always wear goggles to protect your eyes.*
● *Never allow the airline nozzle near any of the body apertures.*

□ **Step 13:** The valve stems must be amply lubricated with clean engine oil and then located in their respective guides, after pushing new oil seals onto the tops of the guides. Temporarily wrap sellotape around the tops of the valve stems so that the seal slides over the collets groove.

i **Step 14:** INSIDE INFORMATION: Check the valve springs' heights against new ones if possible, but if not, check them against each other. If any are shorter than the others, play safe and replace the complete set. After a long time in use, they are bound to have suffered fatigue which could cause complete valve failure. *i*

□ **Step 15:** Place the valve spring seat over the guide, and then position the spring, with the tighter coils towards the seat, followed by the cap. Compress the spring enough to allow you to engage the split cotters with the valve stem.

i INSIDE INFORMATION: Use a little grease to keep the collets in place, see **Job 20, Step 16**. Slowly release the compressor, checking that the collets are correctly located. Tap the end of each valve stem with a soft hammer to bed the collets in. With all the valves in place, the cylinder head is ready for refitting as described in **Job 2**. *i*

Job 4. OHV engine - timing chain and sprockets - removal.

□ **Step 1:** Take note that on early OHV Unos, there was no timing chain tensioner fitted (arrowed). On these engines, the tensioners are incorporated in the chain links.

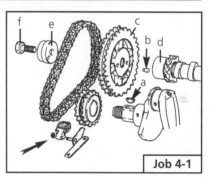

Job 4-1

□ **Step 2:** If yours is a later OHV-engined Uno, a timing chain tensioner will have been added. See illustration **Job 4-1**, arrowed.

i INSIDE INFORMATION: When an early-type of chain needs replacement, you may wish to convert to the later type. See illustration **Job 4-16** for the tensioner mounting points. *i*

□ **Step 3:** Slacken the alternator mounting bolts and remove the drive belt.

□ **Step 4:** Unscrew the crankshaft pulley bolt.

i INSIDE INFORMATION: Prevent the engine turning by engaging a low gear and asking a helper to apply the foot brake firmly. If this fails, remove the starter motor and prevent the flywheel ring gear from turning with a large screwdriver. *i*

□ **Step 5:** Disconnect the fuel pump hoses and blank off with a bolt of suitable size, unbolt the pump and remove it together with the spacer and pushrod. The left hand is

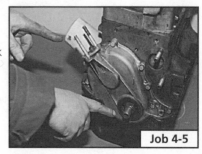

Job 4-5

pointing out the fuel pump mounting bolts; the right hand is pointing to the crankshaft pulley position.

Step 6: With the aid of suitable lifting apparatus, raise the engine just enough to take the weight off the right hand mounting. Undo and remove the mounting. Loosen the timing cover bolts.

Job 4-6

Step 7: After draining the oil, slacken the sump bolts removing all but the back four or five bolts.

Job 4-7

Step 8: Carefully lower the sump enough to clear the timing cover. Avoid damaging the sump gasket.

Job 4-8

Step 9: The timing cover bolts can now be removed and the cover lifted away.

Job 4-9

Step 10: Note the timing marks on both chain sprockets - a 'dot' on the camshaft pulley and a line on the crankshaft pulley.

Job 4-10

Step 11: Later engines are fitted with a separate chain tensioner which is mounted on the No. 1 main bearing cap and secured by the cap bolts. Before proceeding to *Step 13*,

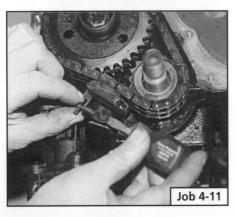

Job 4-11

release the tension by pushing on the plunger to compress the spring and turn the lever on the end in an anti-clockwise direction, looking from the left in this illustration.

Step 12: Undo the camshaft securing bolt. This also releases the fuel pump drive cam.

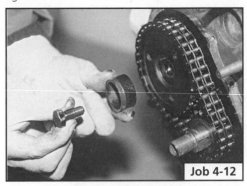

Job 4-12

Step 13: Use two large screwdrivers as levers to release the sprockets, then carefully pull the sprockets off their shafts. Lift the chain and sprockets clear.

Job 4-13

Step 14: Remove the woodruff key from the crankshaft (see illustration *Job 4-1, a*) and put in a safe place. The camshaft uses a dowel peg (*Job 4-1, b*) for sprocket location.

Step 15: You can now examine the tensioner for wear on its slipper surface.

Job 4-15

Step 16: If badly grooved, the tensioner is removed by undoing the two front main bearing cap bolts. The sump will have to be completely removed first.

Job 4-16

Step 17: Unlock the tensioner by turning the lever on the end in a clockwise direction.

Job 5. OHV engine - timing chain and sprockets - refitting.

FACT FILE: TIMING CHAIN TENSIONER

● Where the separate type of tensioner is fitted, check the chain contact pad for signs of wear.

● It is usually best to replace the tensioner when the chain is renewed.

Step 1: Turn the crankshaft until the woodruff key slot is uppermost. Insert the key and lightly tap fully home if it is a tight fit, leaving the forward edge slightly lower than the back.

Step 2: Tap the crankshaft sprocket into position, making sure that the groove locates properly with the woodruff key.

Step 3: Turn the camshaft so that the timing dimple on its sprocket will align correctly, when fitted, with the straight line on the crankshaft sprocket. See *Job 4, Step 10.*

Step 4: To replace the tensioner (where fitted, and when necessary) see *Job 4, Steps 15, 16 and 17.* Release the new or replacement tensioner before fitting. See illustration *Job 4-11.*

Step 5: Fit the chain to the crankshaft sprocket. If it's the early type, without a separate tensioner, make sure that the chain is held with the self-tensioning links facing the cylinder block.

Step 6: Locate the camshaft sprocket teeth with the upper chain loop, still retaining correct alignment of the two timing marks.

Step 7: Locate the camshaft sprocket (see illustration *Job 4-1, c*) with the camshaft (*Job 4-1, d*) and secure it by fitting the fuel pump (*Job 4-1, e*) cam on its locating dowel (*Job 4-1, b*). Fit the fuel pump drive cam (*Job 4-1, e*) and the retaining bolt (*Job 4-1, f*) and tighten to the specified torque. See *Chapter 3, Facts and Figures.*

Step 8: Where a separate tensioner is fitted, unlock the tensioner by turning the lever on the end in a clockwise direction.

Step 9: Rotate the engine two full turns clockwise and check that the timing marks on the sprockets are exactly aligned. See *Job 4, Step 10.* No. 4 piston should now be at Top-Dead-Centre on the compression stroke.

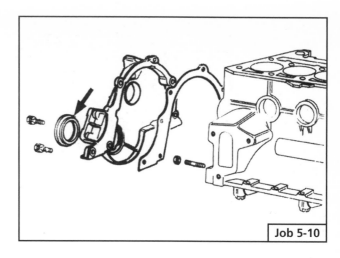

Job 5-10

Step 10: Remove the old seal (arrowed) from the timing cover by levering it out from the inside. Clean off all traces of old gasket and sealant from the cover.

Step 11: Fit the new seal squarely into its hold and tap home.

Step 12: Clean the mating surface on the cylinder block.

Step 13: Smear a little grease on the timing cover to locate the gasket and fit the timing cover to the block, ensuring that the fuel pump pushrod bush is in place. Screw

Job 5-14

the bolts in finger-tight.

Step 14: Clean the pulley hub and coat with clean engine oil. Push the pulley onto the crankshaft end and carefully locate its groove over the woodruff key (location slot, arrowed).

Step 15: Centralise the cover seal on the pulley and tighten the cover securing bolts.

Step 16: Tighten the crankshaft pulley nut to the correct torque. See *Chapter 3, Facts and Figures.*

Step 17: Refit the sump and refill with oil.

Step 18: Refit the alternator drive belt and fuel pump.

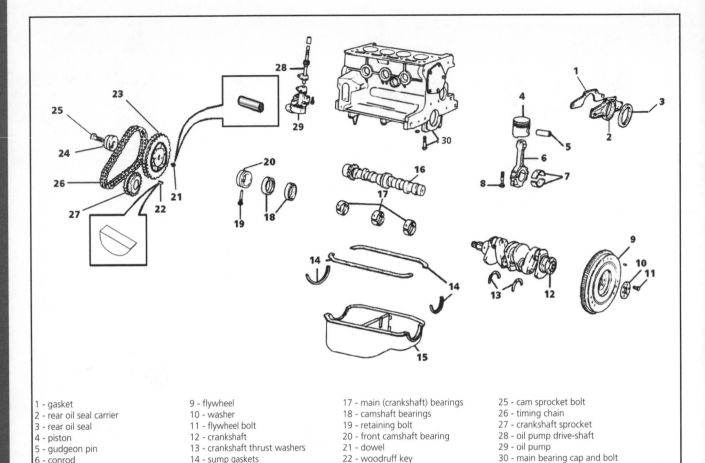

1 - gasket
2 - rear oil seal carrier
3 - rear oil seal
4 - piston
5 - gudgeon pin
6 - conrod
7 - big-end bearings
8 - big-end bolts

9 - flywheel
10 - washer
11 - flywheel bolt
12 - crankshaft
13 - crankshaft thrust washers
14 - sump gaskets
15 - sump
16 - camshaft

17 - main (crankshaft) bearings
18 - camshaft bearings
19 - retaining bolt
20 - front camshaft bearing
21 - dowel
22 - woodruff key
23 - camshaft sprocket
24 - fuel pump cam

25 - cam sprocket bolt
26 - timing chain
27 - crankshaft sprocket
28 - oil pump drive-shaft
29 - oil pump
30 - main bearing cap and bolt

Job 6-1

Job 6. OHV engine - dismantling.

☐ **Step 1:** Familiarise yourself with the major bottom-end engine components shown in illustration *Job 6-1*.

☐ **Step 2:** Remove the water pump. See *PART C: COOLING SYSTEM.*

☐ **Step 3:** Unbolt and remove the clutch from the flywheel.

☐ **Step 4:** Remove the cylinder head as described in *Job 1. Steps 2 to 13.*

☐ **Step 5:** Remove the dipstick and guide tube.

☐ **Step 6:** With the engine lying on one side, unbolt and remove the sump.

☐ **Step 7:** Check the connecting rods (see illustration *Job 6-1, part 6*) and their big end bearing caps to make sure that each is marked with matching numbers or punch marks, starting with No. 1 at the timing cover end. Mark if necessary. Undo the big-end bolts and remove the caps, loosen them if stubborn with a soft faced mallet. Keep the caps in their original order.

☐ **Step 8:** INSIDE INFORMATION: Remove shell bearings by pressing on the side opposite the location slot in the connecting rod and cap. Keep them in their correct order if they are to be reused. *i*

☐ **Step 9:** Withdraw the piston/conrod assemblies from the top of their bores, keeping them in order.

☐ **Step 10:** Position a block of wood inside the crankcase to stop crankshaft movement. Undo the crankshaft pulley nut and remove the pulley.

☐ **Step 11:** Remove the timing chain and sprockets. See *Job 4*.

☐ **Step 12:** Unbolt the oil pump and remove.

☐ **Step 13:** Remove the locking screw from the camshaft front bearing and withdraw the camshaft. Take care that the cam lobes do not damage the bearings as the camshaft is pulled through.

☐ **Step 14:** Remove the cam followers, keeping them in their correct order.

☐ **Step 15:** Undo the securing bolts, remove the flywheel and the rear engine plate.

☐ **Step 16:** Stand the block in the upside down position, unbolt and remove the crankshaft rear oil seal carrier.

☐ **Step 17:** Make sure the main bearing caps are numbered and note which way round they are fitted, then undo their bolts and remove them. Keep the bearing shells with their caps and the centre thrust washers in their correct positions.

☐ **Step 18**: Lift the crankshaft away from the cylinder block and recover the other halves of the main bearing shells.

Job 7. OHV engine - reassembly.

i INSIDE INFORMATION: It is good policy to change the oil pump when carrying out an engine overhaul. An engine supplied by your FIAT agent would include a new pump. *i*

IMPORTANT NOTE: All bearings, shells, piston rings and ALL seals that bear on moving parts MUST be copiously lubricated with fresh engine oil as the engine is being reassembled. Work ONLY in clean conditions, with clean components and clean hands.

CHECKING FOR WEAR

GENERAL

All parts must be thoroughly cleaned for inspection - still keeping them in the right order for reassembly in case they are to be re used. Check each component as follows:

CYLINDER BLOCK

Look for any cracks in the casting, particularly at bolt holes and between cylinders. Check the bores for score marks, caused by burned pistons or broken rings. Check for a wear ridge just below the top of the bore where the top piston ring ends its travel. If any of these defects are present in any of the cylinders, they will have to be rebored. Ask your FIAT agent or engine specialist to inspect and measure the bores for wear if you are unsure. It is sometimes possible to 'glaze bust' the bores and fit new piston rings, assuming the pistons to be in good condition. All of this work can be carried out by your FIAT agent, who will supply the pistons when reboring and who should also fit the pistons to your connecting rods as the gudgeon pins are a press fit into the connecting rod small ends - which have to be heated - not a DIY job.

CRANKSHAFT

Check all the mains journals and crankpins for any signs of wear ridges round the circumference or scoring of the surface. Check for ovality with a suitable micrometer, 0.025 mm being the maximum permissible amount. Check the shell bearings, which should have an even, dull grey finish. If this has worn through to the copper coloured backing, or if the crankshaft has any of the previously mentioned faults, the crankshaft should be reground by your specialist who will also supply the new shell bearings and thrust washers.

CAMSHAFT

Check the bearings in the cylinder block and replace if there are excessive wear signs. Once installed, the centre and rear bearings should be reamed out to size by your FIAT agent. The front bearing is already reamed. Check each cam lobe for wear, which can be quite rapid once started. The cam followers should also be checked, particularly where they contact the cam lobe. If you are replacing the camshaft, fit new followers as well.

TIMING CHAIN AND SPROCKETS

The timing chain should be changed as a matter of course during a complete overhaul but check the sprockets for tooth wear at the same time and renew as necessary.

i INSIDE INFORMATION: If your timing chain is one of the self tensioning type (early engines), fit the later type with a separate tensioner. See **Job 4.** *i*

CYLINDER HEAD

See **Job 3.**

ROCKER SHAFT AND ROCKERS

Check the shaft for wear at the rocker pivot points.

i INSIDE INFORMATION: Check the rocker bushes for wear by positioning the rockers on a 'new' part of the shaft and rocking sideways. *i*

Check the rocker ends for damage to the case hardening, where they contact the valve stem. Check the adjusting screw ball and thread. Check the pushrods for straightness and the ball and sockets for wear.

OIL PUMP

Unscrew the four bolts holding the two parts of the pump body together. Wash all the parts in paraffin and dry them. Check the gear teeth for wear, visually and by rocking the gears together. By using a feeler gauge, check that the clearance between the gear teeth and the pump body does not exceed 0.14 mm. And with a straight edge across the top of the body, check that the gear end float does not exceed 0.105 mm. If either is the case, fit a new pump

i INSIDE INFORMATION: It is good policy to change the oil pump when carrying out an engine overhaul. An engine supplied by your FIAT agent would include a new pump. *i*

ENGINE REASSEMBLY

SECTION A - CRANKSHAFT

☐ **Step A1:** Make sure the bearing seats in the block are perfectly clean and locate the shells so that their tabs engage with the slots.

☐ **Step A2:** Apply some grease to the smooth side of the thrust washers (see illustration **Job 6-1, part 13**) and stick them in position either side of the centre main bearing.

☐ **Step A3:** Oil the shells liberally with fresh engine oil and lower the crankshaft into position.

☐ **Step A4:** Fit the remaining halves of the shells into the bearing caps and position the remaining halves of the thrust washers on either side of the centre main cap with grease.

☐ **Step A5:** Oil the crank journals and position the caps the right way round and in the correct order.

☐ **Step A6:** Screw the bolts in finger tight and check that the crankshaft rotates freely and smoothly.

☐ **Step A7:** Tighten the bolts evenly and progressively until the specified torque setting is reached. See **Chapter 3, Facts and Figures.** Check again that the crankshaft rotates smoothly.

Step A8: Check the crankshaft end float by using a feeler gauge between the thrust washer and the crankshaft. Thicker washers are available if required, see *Chapter 3, Facts and Figures.*

Step A9: Fit the rear oil seal carrier (with its new seal), using a new gasket. Lubricate the seal.

Step A10: Fit the rear engine plate.

i **Step A11:** INSIDE INFORMATION: Check the flywheel for score marks or micro cracking on the clutch contact surface. Deep score marks or cracking would be too much to machine out, making a new flywheel necessary. *i*

Position Nos. 1 and 4 big-end crankpins at TDC, then fit the flywheel with the TDC mark facing upwards. Tighten the bolts to their specified torque, see *Chapter 3, Facts and Figures.*

SECTION B - CAMSHAFT

Step B1: Oil the cam followers and refit in their original positions.

Step B2: Oil the camshaft bearings (see illustration *Job 6-1, parts 18* and *20*) and install the camshaft with care, avoiding damage to the bearings by the cam lobes.

Step B3: Fit the front bearing (see illustration *Job 6-1, part 18*), chamfer first, and secure with the locking bolt. Lubricate the cam lobes.

SECTION C - OIL PUMP

Step C1: Position the gasket on the crankcase mounting.

Step C2: Locate the drive-shaft in the pump and offer the assembly to the crankcase allowing the drive-shaft and camshaft gears to mesh. Fit the mounting bolts.

Step C3: Fit the oil return pipe.

i INSIDE INFORMATION: The sump cannot be fitted until the timing cover is in place and the pistons and connecting rods fitted. *i*

SECTION D - TIMING CHAIN AND SPROCKETS

See *Job 5.*

SECTION E - PISTON/CONNECTING ROD ASSEMBLIES

IMPORTANT NOTE: The pistons and connecting rods are to be fitted as assemblies. Their dismantling and reassembly is a job for your FIAT agent - not a DIY job.

Step E1: Make sure the bores and pistons are clean. Position the piston ring gaps at equal intervals round the pistons circumference and lubricate well. Make sure the rings are fitted with the word TOP upwards.

Step E2: Locate the upper half of the big end shell bearing in the conrod, making sure that the mating surfaces are clean.

Step E3: Locate a ring clamp over the piston rings and tighten enough to close the ring gaps, but not too tight! Lubricate the rings so that they compress and slide easily within the clamp.

Job 7-E3

Step E4: Position the assembly in its correct bore with the piston arrow pointing towards the timing cover and the connecting rod number facing away from the camshaft.

Step E5: With the ring clamp touching the cylinder block, use a hammer shaft to carefully tap the piston through and into the bore.

Job 7-E5

Step E6: Lubricate the crankpin and the big-end shell and draw the conrod down the bore so that the big end locates with the crankpin.

Step E7: Fit the other half of the big-end shell to the bearing cap and lubricate. Offer the cap to the connecting rod and make sure that the numbers match. Screw in the fixing bolts and tighten progressively to the correct torque. See *Chapter 3, Facts and Figures.*

Step E8: Fit the remaining piston/conrod assemblies.

Step E9: Prepare the sump for refitting by positioning the cork strips (see illustration *6-1, part 14*) in each end and trimming them just proud of the flange.

Step E10: Position the side gaskets and apply gasket cement where they contact the cork strips.

Step E11: Position the sump and screw in the bolts and nuts. Tighten progressively. Check that the drain plug is tight.

SECTION F - CYLINDER HEAD

Step F1: Stand the engine on its sump and fit the cylinder head, see *Job 2, Steps 2 to 8.*

SECTION G - ANCILLARY COMPONENTS

Step G1: Refit the exhaust manifold and ducting, the alternator and the thermostat housing.

Step G2: Refit the distributor. See *PART D: IGNITION.*

Step G3: Refit the carburettor and the air cleaner, see *PART F: FUEL AND EXHAUST.*

Step G4: Fit a new oil filter.

Step G5: Refit the coolant pump. Check for play in the bearings and for any sign of leaking.

Step G6: Refit the dipstick tube.

Step G7: Fit the clutch. See **PART B: TRANSMISSION.**

SECTION H - INSTALLATION AND INITIAL START UP

Step H1: Reconnect the engine to the transmission. See **Job 26.**

Step H2: Refit the complete unit to the car. See **Job 23.**

ℹ Step H3: INSIDE INFORMATION: Before fitting the spark plugs and with a fully charged battery, turn the engine on the starter until the oil warning light goes out. This primes the lubrication system and gives more immediate oil pressure on initial start up after overhaul - a critical time in the life of an engine. **ℹ**

Step H4: Fit the spark plugs and speed up the slow running adjustment screw on the carburettor by a complete turn before starting the engine.

Step H5: Allow the engine to warm up on fast idle until it reaches working temperature and then slow it down to its normal speed.

Step H6: Stop the engine and allow it to cool, check the oil and coolant levels and look for any leaks.

Step H7: Avoid over-revving or overloading the engine during its settling down period of 600 miles, then retighten the head as follows: Using the correct sequence, slacken each head bolt by one quarter of a turn and immediately retighten it to the specified torque. Adjust the tappets. See **Chapter 3, Facts and Figures**.

IMPORTANT NOTE: Some FIAT cylinder head gaskets do NOT need re-torquing after a bedding-down interval. Check with your supplier.

Job 8. Non-Fire OHC engine - timing belt removal/replacement

IMPORTANT NOTE: It is false economy to refit a used timing belt. If the belt breaks, it will cause complete engine failure so always fit a new one when replacing it.

Step 1: Disconnect the battery and remove the alternator drivebelt as described in **PART C: COOLING SYSTEM.**

Step 2: Take off the timing belt cover. This is held by a total of four bolts (arrowed).

Job 8-2

making it easy • The crankshaft pulley nut will be difficult to turn.
• If the engine is in the car, engage a gear (or 'Park' in the case of an automatic) and have an assistant hold the footbrake down very firmly. This will stop the engine from turning.
• Alternatively, with the starter motor removed, you can have a helper prevent the flywheel ring gear from turning with a large screwdriver.

Step 3: Take off the crankshaft pulley nut and remove the pulley.

Step 4: Before removing the belt, put the pulley nut back onto the crankshaft, take the car out of gear (if the engine is still in the car) and remove the spark plugs. You can now turn the engine in a clockwise direction using the refitted crank pulley nut - without the pulley, of course!

Job 8-3

Step 5A: With the timing belt still in place, turn the engine so that the timing mark on the sprocket lines up with the one on the front cover. On some engines, the front cover looks like this...

Job 8-5A

Step 5B: ...while on the majority, it looks like this. The top part of the cover backplate slides out so that the plastic pip (arrowed) is level with the camshaft

Job 8-5B

drivegear. Turn the gear so that the timing mark (arrowed) lines up with this pip.

Step 6A: You must also check that the mark (**a**) on the timing belt pulley lines up with the reference mark (**b**) on the oil seal housing. It will be **essential** that all of these marks align when the new belt is fitted!

Job 8-6A

Job 8-6B

Job 8-7

Job 8-8

Step 8: ...and remove the camshaft timing belt.

Step 9: When fitting a new belt, it will have to be tensioned correctly. See **Job 17** for details. HOWEVER, you will not be able to lever against plastic cover backplate to put pressure on the tensioner.

i INSIDE INFORMATION: Use a piece of cranked rod (or a screwdriver with a cranked end) in one of the holes in the adjuster. You will be able to lever against the socket of your spanner, tensioning and tightening at the same time. *i*

Step 6B: On earlier engines rotate the crankshaft so that the reference mark on the driving pulley is in line with the TDC reference mark on the front cover. If the engine is in the vehicle, position the crankshaft at TDC using the reference marks on the flywheel and bellhousing window.

Step 7: Slacken off the belt tensioner...

Job 9. Non-Fire OHC cylinder head - removal

Step 1: Take note of the parts shown in this drawing - which is also referred to in several other jobs on the non-FIRE OHC engine.

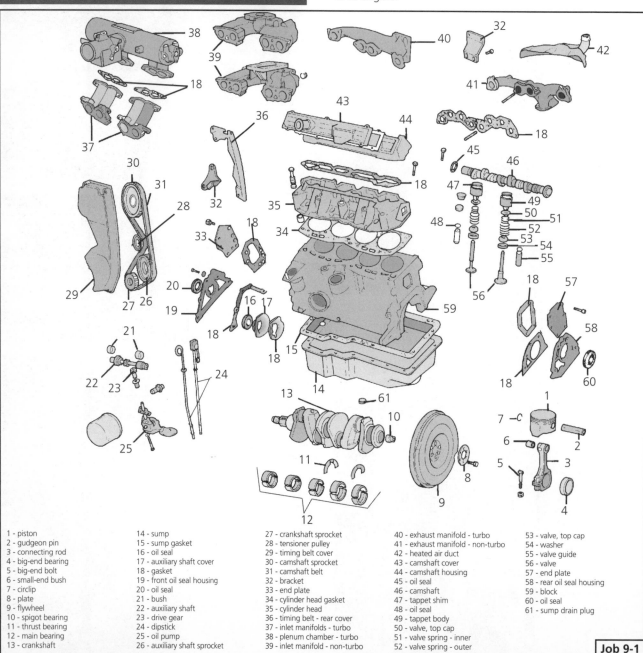

1 - piston	14 - sump	27 - crankshaft sprocket	40 - exhaust manifold - turbo	53 - valve, top cap
2 - gudgeon pin	15 - sump gasket	28 - tensioner pulley	41 - exhaust manifold - non-turbo	54 - washer
3 - connecting rod	16 - oil seal	29 - timing belt cover	42 - heated air duct	55 - valve guide
4 - big-end bearing	17 - auxiliary shaft cover	30 - camshaft sprocket	43 - camshaft cover	56 - valve
5 - big-end bolt	18 - gasket	31 - camshaft belt	44 - camshaft housing	57 - end plate
6 - small-end bush	19 - front oil seal housing	32 - bracket	45 - oil seal	58 - rear oil seal housing
7 - circlip	20 - oil seal	33 - end plate	46 - camshaft	59 - block
8 - plate	21 - bush	34 - cylinder head gasket	47 - tappet shim	60 - oil seal
9 - flywheel	22 - auxiliary shaft	35 - cylinder head	48 - oil seal	61 - sump drain plug
10 - spigot bearing	23 - drive gear	36 - timing belt - rear cover	49 - tappet body	
11 - thrust bearing	24 - dipstick	37 - inlet manifolds - turbo	50 - valve, top cap	
12 - main bearing	25 - oil pump	38 - plenum chamber - turbo	51 - valve spring - inner	
13 - crankshaft	26 - auxiliary shaft sprocket	39 - inlet manifold - non-turbo	52 - valve spring - outer	**Job 9-1**

INSIDE INFORMATION: Allow the engine to cool right down before starting work, or you will run the risk of causing cylinder head distortion. **ℹ**

☐ **Step 2**: Disconnect the battery earth lead.

☐ **Step 3:** Drain the cooling system and depressurise the fuel system, if yours is a fuel injection engine - see *PART F: FUEL AND EXHAUST*.

☐ **Step 4:**
Remove the air cleaner by releasing the spring clips at the front of the unit (arrowed) and the screw or screws on the top face (arrowed) and remove the oil vapour recovery pipe.

Job 9-4

☐ **Step 5:** Disconnect the crankcase vent hose from the cylinder head and the inlet tract or the SPI injector unit, as appropriate and blank off with a bolt of suitable size.

☐ **Step 6:**
Disconnect the engine end of the accelerator cable (**a**), the idle speed check actuator (**b**) and the injector supply (**c**).

Job 9-6

☐ **Step 7:**
Disconnect the electrical leads from the following: the inlet manifold vacuum sensor (arrowed), the manifold coolant temperature sensors (arrowed) and the throttle position switch.

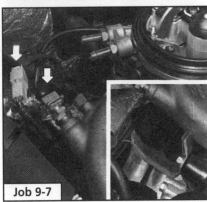
Job 9-7

☐ **Step 8:** Detach the exhaust downpipe from the manifold. (See illustration *Job 9-7,*-inset.)

☐ **Step 9:**
Remove the dipstick (arrowed) and the cylinder head coolant temperature sensor (arrowed).

Job 9-9

☐ **Step 10:** Also remove all the HT leads (with the distributor cap). Place them to one side.

☐ **Step 11:** Undo the brake servo hose from the manifold.

☐ **Step 12:** Undo the hoses connected to the inlet manifold and thermostat.

☐ **Step 13:**
Disconnect the fuel supply and return hoses from the injector unit housing (**a**). Plug the ends.

☐ **Step 14:**
Disconnect the butterfly valve opening sensor connector (see illustration *Job 13-b*) and the earth cables (*Job 13-c*).

Job 9-13

☐ **Step 15:** Remove the timing belt. See *Job 8.*

☐ **Step 16:** Unbolt and remove the camshaft sprocket. If necessary, use a screwdriver held through the sprocket against a mounting bolt behind it, to stop it from turning.

Job 9-16

☐ **Step 17:** Remove the timing belt tensioner but note that it is in three parts - see *Job 17*.

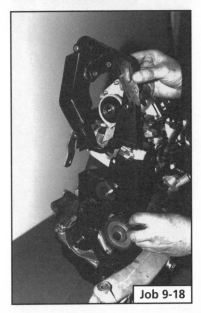
Job 9-17

☐ **Step 18:** Unbolt and remove the timing belt backplate. You could leave the bottom half in place, if you are going no further than removing the cylinder head.

Job 9-18

Step 19:
Take off the six nuts and washers holding the cam cover in place and remove it.

Job 9-19

Step 20:
The camshaft housing must now be removed in order to access the cylinder head bolts. Slacken the 12 housing bolts progressively,

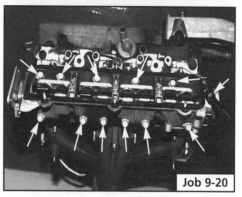

Job 9-20

so that no strain is put on the housing through the valve springs.

Step 21: The camshaft housing can now be lifted away. Note the gasket positioning and fit a new one on reassembly.

Job 9-21

ℹ Step 22:
INSIDE INFORMATION: If the cam followers are loose, you may wish to remove them now so that they don't fall out and lose their position. Keep them in the correct order so that they can go back where they came from on reassembly. ℹ

Job 9-22

Job 9-23

Job 9-24

Step 23: The camshaft end plates - or the distributor, which is fitted here on some models - must be removed...

Step 24: ...in order to remove the camshaft. Take care to ensure that the tappets are either removed or pushed clear and that you don't damage the bearings inside the camshaft

housing by knocking them with the cams on the camshaft as you withdraw it.

Step 25: Start by removing the 4 or 5 small cylinder head bolts (according to model)...

Job 9-25

Step 26:
...numbered 1 to 4 or 5, in the order shown.

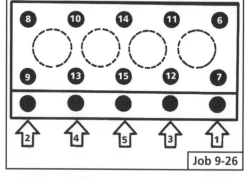

Job 9-26

Step 27:
Now slacken the remaining 10 bolts half a turn at a time, in the order shown in *Step 26*, until all are loose, and then remove them with their washers.

Job 9-27

Step 28:
Check that nothing remains attached to, or obstructs the cylinder head and lift it clear of the block. If stuck, it is permissible to tap the head lightly with a soft mallet to free it. Never use a wedge between the joint faces and remember that the head will not slide off as it is located on dowels.

Job 9-28

Step 29: Remove the old gasket.

Job 10. Non-Fire OHC cylinder head - refitting.

Refer to illustration *Job 9-1* for the components covered in this Job.

i INSIDE INFORMATION: FIAT recommend that you should not re-use cylinder head bolts which have been refitted more than three times before. Fit new ones if in doubt, so that you can ensure reliability. **i**

☐ **Step 1:** Clean the block and cylinder head mating surfaces with a straight edge, taking particular care with the light alloy head. Any gouging of the metal could prove very expensive to have put right!

---

making it easy • Carburettor cleaner - or the purpose-made Loctite 'Chisel' aerosol spray, available from your FIAT dealer, will help to remove pieces of stuck-on gasket.

Make sure that all the holes and coolant passages are clear of any foreign matter, particularly the cylinder head bolt holes which must be clear right down to the bottom.

☐ **Step 2:** With the block face perfectly clean, remove the cylinder head gasket from its wrapping and, keeping it away from

Job 10-2

oil or grease, place it on the block with (on FIAT gaskets) this copper-ringed hole above the correct water passage. The gasket only fits correctly one way round.

☐ **Step 3:** Lower the cylinder head into position and locate it on the two dowels (see illustration *Job 10-2*, arrowed).

☐ **Step 4:** The 10 main cylinder head securing bolts and washers can now be screwed in by hand. Don't fit the smaller ones (arrowed) yet.

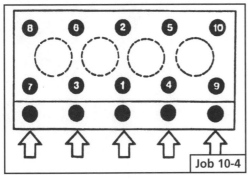

Job 10-4

☐ **Step 5A:** Tighten the 10 larger bolts in their correct sequence as shown in illustration *Job 10-4.* All of the settings are shown in *Chapter 3, Facts and Figures*.

☐ **Step 5B:** Tighten the head down to the first torque setting, following the correct tightening order.

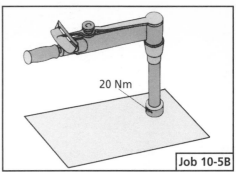

20 Nm

Job 10-5B

☐ **Step 5C:** In the same order, tighten the bolts to their second torque setting.

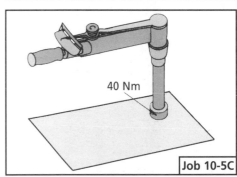

40 Nm

Job 10-5C

☐ **Step 5D:** Tighten each bolt, once again in the correct order, by a further 90 degrees. You could use an angle gauge (available from auto-accessory stores) in order to be precise.

Job 10-5D

☐ **Step 5E:** Tighten by another 90 degrees, bolt-by-bolt, again in the correct order.

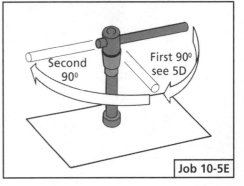

Second 90º

First 90º see 5D

Job 10-5E

☐ **Step 6:** Fit the four or five smaller bolts, according to model (see illustration *Job 10-4*, arrowed) close to the spark plug holes, and tighten to their specified torque. See *Chapter 3, Facts and Figures.*

☐ **Step 7:** All items previously removed in *Job 9* can now be fitted in reverse order. When connecting the exhaust always use a new flange gasket.

☐ **Step 8:** Ensure that all connections are sound and secure.

☐ **Step 9:** Top up the cooling system with the correct 50/50 solution of **Tutela** anti-freeze solution. Check the oil level.

Job 11. Non-Fire OHC Turbo - cylinder head - removal.

Refer to illustration **Job 9-1** for the components covered in this Job. The model illustrated is the 1372cc version. The general principles remain the same for earlier Turbo i.e. models.

ℹ INSIDE INFORMATION: It is necessary to remove the inlet manifold, the turbo charger and the exhaust manifold before removing the head. Disconnect the HT leads from the spark plugs, leaving the cap and leads on the distributor. **ℹ**

☐ **Step 1:** Disconnect the battery earth lead.

☐ **Step 2:** Remove the air flow switch unit (**a**) and its reinforced pipe (**b**).

Job 11-2

☐ **Step 3:** Disconnect the throttle cable from the butterfly casing linkage (**a**) and withdraw the air supply pipe (**b**).

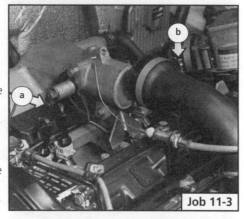

Job 11-3

☐ **Step 4:** Disconnect the air cooling supply pipe (arrowed) and the pipe to the idle supplementary air solenoid valve and the injectors (arrowed).

Job 11-4

☐ **Step 5:** Disconnect all four vacuum pick up pipes (arrowed).

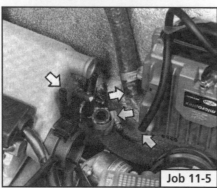

Job 11-5

☐ **Step 6:** Disconnect the electrical supply from the butterfly opening sensor (arrowed), and undo the bolt securing the inlet manifold bracket to the cylinder head, as shown.

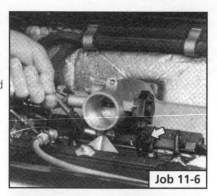

Job 11-6

☐ **Step 7:** Undo the cable shield fixing screws. Unplug the connectors from the injectors (arrowed).

Job 11-7

☐ **Step 8:** Disconnect the earth cable or cables (**a**) and unplug the cable from the temperature sensor (**b**).

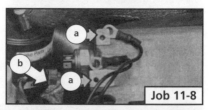

Job 11-8

☐ **Step 9:** Remove the injector cable shield.

Job 11-9

☐ **Step 10:** Undo the union connecting the fuel pressure regulator pipe (**a**) located on the inlet manifold and disconnect the injector fuel supply pipe (**b**).

Job 11-10

☐ **Step 11:** Unplug the connector for the injector cooling fan thermostatic switch (arrowed).

Job 11-11

Step 12: Undo the front bolts (arrowed) securing the heat shield to the inlet manifold...

Job 11-12

Step 13: ...and undo the rear bolts...

Job 11-13

Job 11-14

Step 14: ...before removing the heat shield.

Step 15: Unbolt and remove the fuel pressure regulator.

Job 11-15

Step 16: Remove the bolts...

Job 11-16

Step 17: ...and the nuts, holding the inlet manifold in place and remove it.

Job 11-17

Step 18: From under the car, undo the fixing nuts (arrowed) and remove the exhaust front section.

Job 11-18

Step 19: Undo the turbo mounting bolts (arrowed).

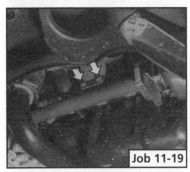

Job 11-19

Step 20: Drain the cooling system after disconnecting the supply and return pipes (arrowed).

Job 11-20

Step 21: Disconnect the oil supply pipe (arrowed)...

Job 11-21

Step 22: ... and the air intake pipe (arrowed).

Job 11-22

Step 23: From under the car, disconnect the oil return pipe (arrowed) from turbo to sump and the heat exchanger air pressure pipe (arrowed).

Job 11-23

❑ **Step 24:** Remove the bolts securing the turbo mounting bracket.

Job 11-24

❑ **Step 25:** Unbolt the coolant collection pipe (arrowed) from the pump.

Job 11-25

❑ **Step 26:** You can now remove the exhaust manifold/turbocharger assembly upwards.

❑ **Step 27:** To complete the cylinder head removal, refer to *Job 18, Steps 16 to 18.*

Job 11-26

Job 12. Non-Fire OHC Turbo - cylinder head - refitting.

Follow the procedure described in *Job 10*, which describes the refitting of the non-Turbo cylinder head. Take special note of the INSIDE INFORMATION: at the start of *Job 10*.

Job 13. Non-Fire OHC cylinder head - dismantling and servicing.

Refer to the illustration *Job 9-1* for the components covered in this Job.

_i_ INSIDE INFORMATION: These cylinder heads use hardened valves and seats for use with unleaded petrol. We advise you to consult your FIAT agent or engine specialist for valve grinding or machining of these components. **_i_**

❑ **Step 1:** Remove the camshaft housing from the cylinder head. See *Job 9*.

❑ **Step 2:** Remove the camshaft housing end plate (or the distributor mounted in the same place on certain models).

Job 13-2

❑ **Step 3:** Remove the cam followers and shims from the housing, keeping them in the correct order for refitting in the same positions.

Job 13-3

❑ **Step 4:** Slide the camshaft out, taking care not to damage the camshaft bearings with the cam lobes.

Job 13-4

❑ **Step 5:** Follow *Job 20,* for information on removing and refitting the valves.

❑ **Step 6:** Fit the camshaft housing to the cylinder head and adjust the valve clearances. See *Job 16*.

Job 14. Non-Fire OHC engine - dismantling.

❑ **Step 1:** Familiarise yourself with the layout of the engine. Refer to illustration *Job 9-1* for an exploded view of the engine components.

❑ **Step 2:** Remove the cylinder head. See *Job 9, if non-Turbo* or *Job 11, if Turbo*.

❑ **Step 3:** Remove the distributor. See *PART D: IGNITION, Job 2.*

❑ **Step 4:** Remove the petrol pump and spacer block, if fitted to the engine.

❑ **Step 5:** Remove and discard the oil filter and remove the crankcase breather with its pipe.

❑ **Step 6:** Remove the water pump complete with its distribution pipe and the power steering pump, if fitted.

❑ **Step 7:** Remove the alternator, the crankshaft pulley, the crankshaft and auxiliary shaft sprockets, the cam belt tensioner and the cam belt cover backplate.

❑ **Step 8:** Remove the auxiliary shaft sprocket...

Job 14-8

Step 9: ...the end plate and seal, and remove the shaft.

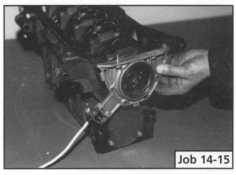

Job 14-9

Step 10: Undo and remove the clutch, and then the flywheel.

Job 14-10

Job 14-11

Job 14-12

Step 11: Turn the engine assembly over and remove the sump.

Step 12: Take off the oil pump (the three larger bolts)...

Job 14-13

Job 14-14

Step 13: ...and the return pipe.

Step 14: Undo and remove the front crankshaft seal carrier (5 bolts)...

Step 15: ...and the rear crankshaft seal carrier (6 bolts).

Job 14-15

Step 16: Check that all the connecting rods and their big-end bearing caps are marked with matching numbers, starting from the timing cover end. Make sure that the markings tell you which way round they go!

Job 14-16

Step 17: Undo the securing bolts and remove the caps, keeping them in their correct order.

Job 14-17

making it easy! ● Use a hammer handle to tap the pistons carefully up and out of the bores.

Step 18: Withdraw the piston/connecting rod assemblies from the tops of their bores...

Job 14-18

Step 19: ...and keep them in the correct order.

Job 14-19

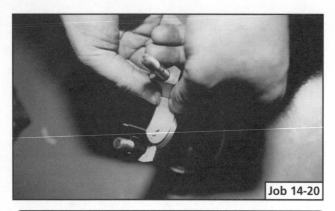

Job 14-20

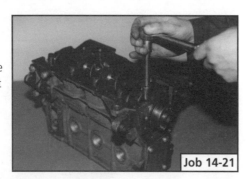

making it easy / ☐ **Step 20:** *Bearing shells are best removed by sliding them out, pushing the tab-end out first.*

☐ **Step 21:** Check that the five crankshaft main bearing caps are correctly marked, starting from the timing cover end.

Job 14-21

☐ **Step 22:** Undo and remove them, keeping them in order.

Job 14-22

☐ **Step 23:** Lift the crankshaft clear of the cylinder block.

Job 14-23

☐ **Step 24:** Remember to retrieve the two thrust washers from the end main bearing in the block. There are none in the cap.

Job 14-24

Job 15. Non-Fire OHC engine - reassembly.

CHECKING FOR WEAR

GENERAL

As the checks carried out on the cylinder block are common to most engines, read the opening paragraphs of **Job 7**, under the Section headings GENERAL and CYLINDER BLOCK.

ℹ️ INSIDE INFORMATION: It is good policy to change the oil pump when carrying out an engine overhaul. An engine supplied by your FIAT agent would include a new pump. **ℹ️**

IMPORTANT NOTE: All bearings, shells, piston rings and ALL seals that bear on moving parts MUST be copiously lubricated with fresh engine oil as the engine is being reassembled. Work ONLY in clean conditions, with clean components and clean hands.

CRANKSHAFT

☐ **Step 1:** Refer to **Job 7**, and carry out **Steps A1** to **A9**.

Step 2: Refit the front oil seal carrier, using a new seal and gasket. Prise out the old and drift in the new one evenly. Apply Loctite 510 to the joint, across the sump flange seating face.

PISTON/CONNECTING ROD ASSEMBLIES

Job 15-3

☐ **Step 3:** Refer to **Job 7**, and follow **Steps E1** to **E8**.

making it easy / • *Fitting new piston rings is tricky! They're brittle and break easily.*
• *Use a feeler gauge to 'spiral' each ring over the upper grooves, starting with the bottom ring and working each one down one groove at a time.*

CYLINDER HEAD

Step 4: Fit the cylinder head. Refer to **Job 10**, for non-Turbo or **Job 12** for Turbo engines.

COMPLETE THE ENGINE ASSEMBLY:

☐ **Step 5:** Position the auxiliary shaft in the cylinder block and fit the end plate complete with a new seal.

☐ **Step 6:** Fit the oil pump and fit the return pipe, tightening the bolts to their specified torque. See **Chapter 3, Facts and Figures**.

IMPORTANT NOTE: Fill the pump with fresh engine oil, to prime it, before refitting with a new gasket.

☐ **Step 7:** Refit the sump using a new gasket.

☐ **Step 8:**
Refit the cam belt tensioner and lock in the non-tensioning position with Locktite.

Job 15-8

ℹ INSIDE INFORMATION: Before finally tightening the tensioner nut, remove it, clean the thread and apply Loctite Threadlocker to help stop the nut and washer shaking loose. ℹ

☐ **Step 9:** Fit the crankshaft and auxiliary shaft sprockets, and tighten to their correct torques. See *Chapter 3, Facts and Figures.*

IMPORTANT NOTE: When refitting the crankshaft pulley nut, note that the stepped side must face the engine.

☐ **Step 10:** Fit the crankshaft pulley and tighten. See *Chapter 3, Facts and Figures*.

☐ **Step 11:** Fit the water pump and distribution pipe.

☐ **Step 12:** Refit the flywheel and tighten the six bolts to their correct torque. See *Chapter 3, Facts and Figures*.

☐ **Step 13:** Refit the clutch. See *PART B: TRANSMISSION, Job 4*.

---

making it easy

- *When reinserting the camshaft, it can be difficult to get the camshaft fully in to its end seal.*
- *DON'T try hammering it in - all you'll do is damage the seal.*
- *Lubricate the seal with fresh engine oil, insert the camshaft and put the housing on its end. Push down with a little pressure while revolving the camshaft until it eases its way into the seal.*

☐ **Step 14:** Refit the fuel pump and pushrod using new gaskets on both sides of the spacer block, 0.3 mm thick between the spacer and the engine and 0.7 mm between the spacer and the pump. See *PART F: FUEL AND EXHAUST SYSTEMS* for information on setting the pump position.

☐ **Step 15:** Lubricate the sealing ring and screw on a new oil filter.

☐ **Step 16:** Refit the distributor. See *PART D: IGNITION, Job 2*.

☐ **Step 17:** Refit the cylinder head. See *Job 10* if non-Turbo, or *Job 12*, if Turbo.

☐ **Step 18:** Follow *Job 7, Steps H1* to *H6*, to complete the installation and initial start up.

Job 16. Fire and Non-Fire OHC - cylinder heads, valve clearance adjustment.

ℹ INSIDE INFORMATION: Adjustment should always be made with the engine cold. ℹ

☐ **Step 1:** Remove the camshaft cover and the spark plugs. Jack up a front wheel and engage top gear. Turning the wheel will rotate the engine and therefore the camshaft. (If the cylinder head is detached and on the bench, turn the camshaft by gripping the camshaft sprocket.)

☐ **Step 2:** The inlet and exhaust valves use different clearances which are checked when each cam lobe is pointing directly away from its follower. See *Chapter 3, Facts and Figures.*

☐ **Step 3:** The order in which the valves are fitted in the cylinder head is:

Inlet: 2-3-6-7
Exhaust: 1-4-5-8

from the timing cover end.

☐ **Step 4:**
Select a feeler blade which is about the thickness of the correct valve clearance and insert it between the heel of the cam

Job 16-4

and the cam follower shim when the cam lobe is uppermost. If necessary, select different thicknesses of feeler blade until a small amount of drag can be felt as the blade is pushed in and out. Record the total blade thickness. This is the valve clearance for this valve.

☐ **Step 5:** Rotate the camshaft and repeat this operation on each of the remaining seven valves, noting their respective clearances. Those which have clearances within limits obviously don't need any further attention.

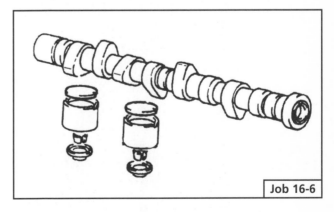
Job 16-6

☐ **Step 6:** The remaining valves will now need to have their shims changed for thicker or thinner ones, bringing their clearances to within the specifications shown in *Chapter 3, Facts and Figures.*

❑ **Step 7:** In theory, a special tool is needed to depress the cam follower and allow extraction of the shim. This is available to your FIAT dealer, or you will have to make a lever with a fork that locates nicely on the rim of a cam follower allowing removal of the shim by prising it from the follower.

ℹ️ INSIDE INFORMATION: In practice, you would probably spend longer making the tool than removing and refitting the camshaft a couple of times, after first measuring and noting all of the valve clearances, so that you can calculate the amount of increase or decrease in shim thickness needed. You should also note that some shims can be *extremely* awkward to shift, even with the camshaft removed. And far more awkward with it in place! We recommend camshaft removal! ℹ️

❑ **Step 8:** The thickness of a shim is engraved on it in 'mm'. If this is worn away, you will have to measure the thickness with a metric micrometer - or have your FIAT dealer do it for you.

❑ **Step 9:** Where a clearance is too small with the thinnest shim in position, the valves should be removed and the stem ground just sufficiently to make the correction. Your FIAT dealer can do this, keeping the end square and retaining a smooth finish.

Job 17. Fire OHC engine - timing belt, removal and replacement.

❑ **Step 1:** These are the principal components concerned with timing belt removal and replacement.

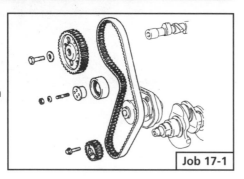

Job 17-1

IMPORTANT NOTE: FIAT strongly recommend that you should NEVER re-use a timing belt. Removal and re-application of the belt's tension can lead to premature failure. ALWAYS fit a new one!

❑ **Step 2:** Disconnect the battery earth. Remove the air cleaner, remove the spark plugs and take off the alternator drive belt.

❑ **Step 3A:** Remove the timing cover, not forgetting the bolt at the bottom.

Job 17-3A

❑ **Step 3B:** Take note of the different cover types used on different models.

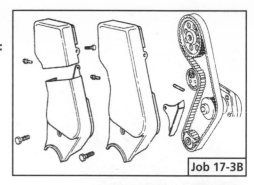

Job 17-3B

❑ **Step 4:** Unbolt and remove the crankshaft pulley.

Job 17-4

❑ **Step 5:** Using a spanner on the crankshaft bolt, turn clockwise until the camshaft sprocket timing mark (arrowed) is aligned with the mark on the cylinder head.

Job 17-5

❑ **Step 6:** Also, make sure that the timing mark on the crankshaft pulley is aligned with the mark on the oil pump cover (see arrows).

Job 17-6

❑ **Step 7:** Slacken the timing belt tensioner nut...

Job 17-7

INSIDE INFORMATION: Retighten the nut to temporarily retain the 'slackened' position, to make it easier to refit the belt, later.

Job 17-8

Job 17-9

Step 8: ...and move the pulley away from the belt by turning it.

Step 9: Remove the old belt.

Step 10: The new belt must be fitted with the arrows, printed on the outside of the belt, pointing in the direction of engine rotation. Ensure that the timing marks are still aligned.

Job 17-11

Step 11: Engage the belt with the crankshaft sprocket first, then in turn, the coolant and camshaft sprockets. Finally, feed it round the tensioner pulley. Also, as a double-check that the belt is not 'out', ensure that the yellow lines on the belt align exactly with the timing marks on the camshaft sprocket and crankshaft sprocket.

Step 12: Slacken the tensioner nut and push the pulley onto the belt until taut. Check that the timing marks are still correctly aligned. Still pressing the pulley against the belt, tighten its locking nut.

INSIDE INFORMATION: If you can't put enough pressure on the tensioner with your fingers, carefully use a long screwdriver as a lever. Alternatively, push a pair of bolts into the two holes in the tensioner and lever between them to turn the tensioner.

Job 17-12

Step 13: Turn the engine through two complete turns clockwise. If correctly tensioned, you should just be able to twist the belt

Job 17-13

through a quarter of a complete turn (i.e. through 90 degrees) with your thumb and finger at the centre of its longest run. Re-adjust if necessary.

Job 18. Fire OHC cylinder head - removal.

INSIDE INFORMATION: Allow the engine to cool right down before starting work, or you will run the risk of causing cylinder head distortion.

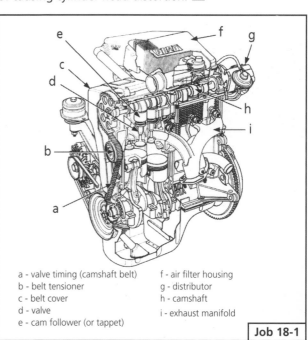

a - valve timing (camshaft belt)
b - belt tensioner
c - belt cover
d - valve
e - cam follower (or tappet)
f - air filter housing
g - distributor
h - camshaft
i - exhaust manifold

Job 18-1

Step 1: Shown in illustration *Job 18-1* is the layout of the major components of the FIRE Overhead Camshaft (OHC) engine.

Step 2: Disconnect the battery earth lead. Remove the air cleaner and disconnect the accelerator and choke controls.

Step 3: Drain the cooling system (engine COLD) and disconnect the coolant hoses from the head.

Step 4: Disconnect the hoses from the fuel pump and carburettor.

Step 5: Disconnect the vacuum and coolant hoses from the inlet manifold and cylinder head.

Step 6: Disconnect the leads from the fuel cut off solenoid (when fitted), the coolant temperature switch and the (smaller) low tension leads from the coil.

Step 7: Remove the distributor cap and leads and place to one side.

Step 8: Unbolt the timing belt cover and remove. See **Job 17.** Remove the distributor. See **PART D: IGNITION**.

Step 9: Put number one piston at TDC as described in **Job 17, Steps 5** and **6**.

Step 10: Slacken the timing belt tensioner and remove the belt from the sprockets.

Step 11: Unbolt the inlet manifold and, if you prefer, remove it complete with the carburettor.

Job 18-11

Job 18-12 Job 18-13

Step 12: On the opposite side of the engine, take off the hot air ducting from the exhaust manifold studs - two locknuts.

Step 13: Disconnect the exhaust downpipe bracket. Unbolt the manifold from the cylinder head and tie to one side (in the engine bay), or remove if you prefer.

Step 14: Unscrew the cylinder head bolts half a turn at a time in the order shown, until all are loose.

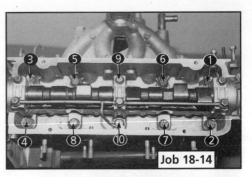

Job 18-14

Step 15: Now remove the bolts and their washers from the cylinder head.

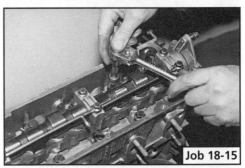

Job 18-15

Step 16: The cylinder head is now ready for removal. Never attempt to use a wedge between the cylinder head and block. This causes a lot of damage.

Job 18-16

making it easy • If the head is stuck, use a wooden hammer shaft or something similar, as a lever in the exhaust ports to break the seal.

Job 19. Fire OHC cylinder head - refitting.

Step 1: The illustration below shows the layout of the cylinder head components. The valve cover gasket is reusable unless damaged, in which case it must be replaced.

1 - camshaft belt cover
2 - oil seal
3 - camshaft
4 - shim
5 - collets
6 - valve spring
7 - bottom valve spring cap
8 - valve guide
9 - tappet
10 - top valve spring cap
11 - oil seal
12 - valve
13 - camshaft cover
14 - cover gasket
15 - oil pipe
16 - inlet manifold
17 - inlet manifold gasket
18 - exhaust manifold gasket
19 - exhaust manifold
20 - cylinder head
21 - gasket
22 - thermostat housing
23 - cylinder head gasket
24 - camshaft pulley
25 - bearing
26 - crankshaft pulley
27 - camshaft drivebelt
28 - hub

Job 19-1

Step 2: Before refitting, make sure that the cylinder head and block surfaces have been thoroughly cleaned and that the bolt holes in the cylinder block are clear to their bottoms.

Step 3: Align the camshaft sprocket timing mark (arrowed) with the one on the cylinder head.

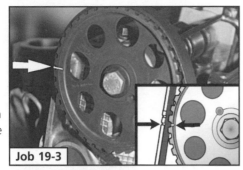

Job 19-3

Step 4: Make sure that the two aligning dowels are in place, at opposite ends of the block.

Job 19-4

Step 5: The new cylinder head gasket must be fitted dry. Any gasket sealer, oil or grease could cause it to blow. Place it over the dowels on the cylinder block with the word 'ALTO' facing upwards.

Job 19-5

Step 6: Place the cylinder head carefully on the block, locating it with the positioning dowels.

Job 19-6

SAFETY FIRST!

● *Make sure you don't trap your fingers between the cylinder head and block!*

ⓘ Step 7: INSIDE INFORMATION: The cylinder head bolts must be cleaned, dipped in engine oil and drained for thirty minutes before fitting. This stops them 'hydraulicing' when being screwed home and allows them to be 'torqued' down evenly. **ⓘ**

Step 8: Fit the cylinder head bolts and their washers finger tight, then tighten them in the sequence shown here using the following procedure:

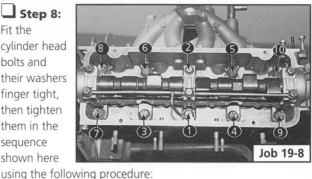

Job 19-8

Step 9: First, tighten the bolts to the torque figure shown in *Chapter 3*.

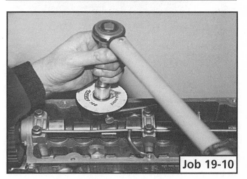

Job 19-9

Step 10: Then use an angle gauge to turn each bolt the number of degrees given in *Chapter 3, Facts and Figures.*

Job 19-10

Step 11: Refit the inlet manifold using a new gasket and be careful to position the accelerator cable bracket 14 to 16 mm from the alternator terminal clamp. Before the manifold nuts are tightened, insert the large serrated washer (if one is fitted) between the bracket and the manifold. Tighten the manifold nuts evenly to the correct torque. See *Chapter 3, Facts and Figures.*

Step 12: Refit the exhaust manifold with a new gasket and tighten to the correct torque. The downpipe bracket can now be reconnected.

Step 13: Making sure the timing marks are aligned, follow the instructions in *Job 17* for fitting a new timing belt. DON'T re-use the old one!

Job 19-13

Step 14: Refit the camshaft cover, timing belt cover and distributor cap and leads.

Step 15: Reconnect the controls, all hoses and remaining leads.

Step 16: Fill the cooling system (see *Chapter 5 Servicing Your Car, Job 14*) with the correct dilution of new **FL Paraflu** anti-freeze solution. See *Chapter 3, Facts and Figures*.

Step 17: Refit the air cleaner.

Job 20. Fire OHC cylinder head - dismantling and overhauling.

Step 1:
The cylinder head has to be partly stripped as it is being removed from the engine. See *Job 18*. Only the

camshaft and valves remain to be dismantled at this stage.

Step 2:
This is the general layout of the valve gear. Take careful note of the tappet shims (**A**) and valve collets (**B**).

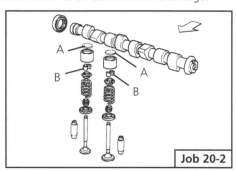

Step 3:
Undo the camshaft sprocket fixing bolt and remove the sprocket.

making it easy • Pass a steel bar through one of the sprocket holes to prevent rotation when undoing the camshaft sprocket bolt.

• Avoid damage to the cylinder head by putting a piece of wood under the end of the bar.

Step 4:
Mark the camshaft bearing caps, so that you can refit them in the same positions.

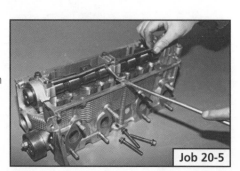

Step 5:
Unbolt and remove the oil feed pipe - carefully prise out the stub using a screwdriver, as shown after removing the relevant bolts.

Step 6:
Undo the remaining bolts and remove the bearing caps. Carefully remove the camshaft from the cylinder head, without

disturbing the shims and cam followers beneath.

ℹ️ INSIDE INFORMATION: 1) Note that the oil in the engine will tend to make the cam followers tricky to lift. Try prising carefully with a pair of screwdrivers, one each side and lift evenly.

2) If valve grinding or seat cutting has taken place, or the valves, camshaft or cam followers have been changed the original shims will no longer give the correct clearances. See *Job 16* for adjustments. ℹ️

Step 7:
Now remove cam followers (or tappets), keeping them in the correct order for refitting. They will be complete with their shims at this stage.

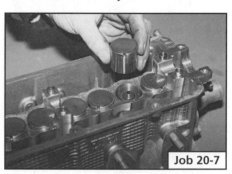

Step 8: The shims can each be removed, if necessary, but be sure to keep them with their correct 'partners'. Each shim is marked with its thickness (arrowed).

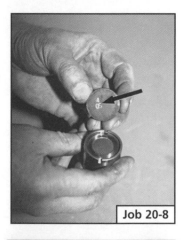

Step 9: Use a suitable valve spring compressor to compress each spring in turn to allow the removal of the split collets from the valve stems. Take care not to lose the collets when releasing the spring compressor.

Step 10: The valve spring caps, springs and spring seats can all be lifted clear and the valves withdrawn from their guides. Keep the valves in their correct order.

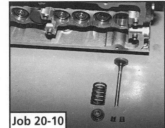

Job 20-10

making it easy / ● Keep the valves in their correct order by pushing their stems through some cardboard and numbering them, number one being at the timing belt end.

● An alternative means of identification is to label each valve with masking tape.

Step 11: INSIDE INFORMATION: The valves should slide freely out of their guides. Any resistance may be caused by a build up of carbon, or a slight burr on the stem where the collets engage. This can usually be removed by careful use of fine wet-or-dry paper, allowing you to withdraw the valves without scoring their guides. *i*

Step 12: The cylinder head is made of light alloy and is easily damaged when being cleaned. Use a rotary wire brush for the combustion chambers and ports, but no sharp objects such as a screwdriver should be used. The machined surfaces must have all traces of old gasket removed by use of a straight edge. Then wash down with paraffin to remove old oil and dirt and dry with clean rag. **At all costs**, avoid gouging the cylinder head. This can be very expensive to put right.

making it easy / ● Try using carburettor cleaner or proprietary gasket remover, to loosen old gasket material.

Step 13: The cylinder head must be checked for distortion by use of a straight edge and feeler gauge. At the same time check for excessive corrosion. If you are in doubt, or if the old gasket had blown, have the cylinder head refaced by your FIAT agent or engine specialist.

The valve should be checked for side movement in their guides. Anything but the very slightest tells you that the valve guides are in need of replacement. Your local FIAT agent or engine specialist should do this job. Examine the valve seats for pitting or burning, and also check their mating seats in the cylinder head. Small pits can be removed by grinding the valves onto their seats. The seats in the cylinder head will have to be recut, again, by your local agent if the pitting is too deep, and new valves fitted.

IMPORTANT NOTE: 'Unleaded' engine valve seats are too hard for hand 'powered' valve grinding to make much impression on them. You can only grind out the smallest of blemishes by hand.

Step 14: Clean the carbon from the valves with a rotary wire brush and wash them in paraffin. Wash the valve springs, caps, seats and collets and dry them.

making it easy / ● Clean the valve heads back to shiny metal.

● Now the sucker on the end of your valve grinding stick won't keep falling off!

Step 15: Grind in the valves. The process is the same as on OHV cylinder heads. See **Job 3, Step 10-on**.

Step 16: INSIDE INFORMATION: It can be tricky to re-fit the collets. Put a dab of grease on the collet, put a dab on the end of your screwdriver, pick up the collet and 'stick' it in place on the stem of the valve. *i*

Job 20-16

Step 17: Reassemble the rest of the cylinder head in the reverse order. Remember to oil the camshaft bearings and use a new camshaft oil seal. See your FIAT agent if there is any pitting or burning visible on the valve faces or seat.

Job 21. Fire OHC engine - dismantling.

Step 1: Familiarise yourself with the layout of the FIRE engine components, shown on the opposite page.

Step 2: Remove the cylinder head. See **Job 18**.

Step 3: Remove the distributor. See **PART D: IGNITION, Job 2**.

Step 4: Remove the thermostat housing.

Step 5: Remove the distribution pipe from the coolant pump and remove the pump. Discard the oil filter.

Step 6: Remove the fuel pump (when a mechanical pump is fitted), its spacer block and pushrod. See **PART F: FUEL AND EXHAUST SYSTEMS**.

Step 7: Remove the alternator and drive belt.

Step 8: Lock the flywheel and undo the crankshaft nut. Pull off the crank pulley.

Step 9: Remove the clutch and then the flywheel.

Step 10: Unbolt and remove the sump.

Step 11: Remove the oil pump and pickup assembly.

Step 12: Remove the engine back plate and timing index plate.

Step 13: Lay the engine on its side and undo the big-end bolts.

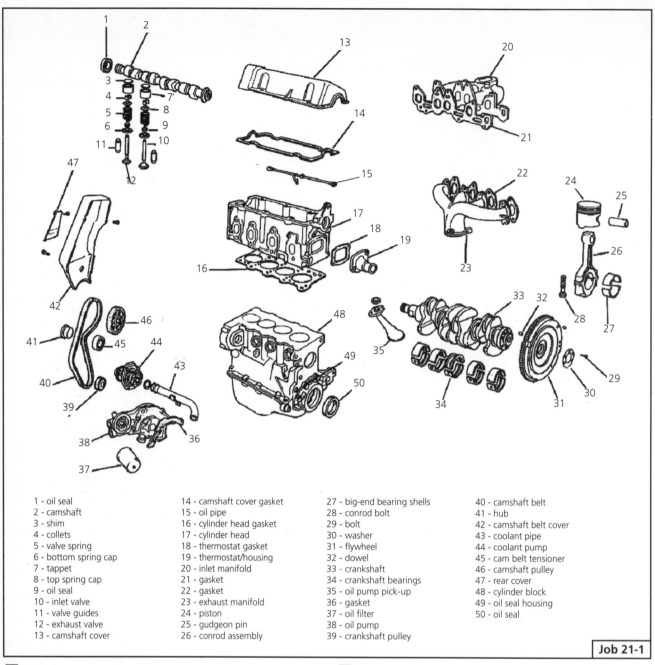

1 - oil seal	14 - camshaft cover gasket	27 - big-end bearing shells	40 - camshaft belt
2 - camshaft	15 - oil pipe	28 - conrod bolt	41 - hub
3 - shim	16 - cylinder head gasket	29 - bolt	42 - camshaft belt cover
4 - collets	17 - cylinder head	30 - washer	43 - coolant pipe
5 - valve spring	18 - thermostat gasket	31 - flywheel	44 - coolant pump
6 - bottom spring cap	19 - thermostat/housing	32 - dowel	45 - cam belt tensioner
7 - tappet	20 - inlet manifold	33 - crankshaft	46 - camshaft pulley
8 - top spring cap	21 - gasket	34 - crankshaft bearings	47 - rear cover
9 - oil seal	22 - gasket	35 - oil pump pick-up	48 - cylinder block
10 - inlet valve	23 - exhaust manifold	36 - gasket	49 - oil seal housing
11 - valve guides	24 - piston	37 - oil filter	50 - oil seal
12 - exhaust valve	25 - gudgeon pin	38 - oil pump	
13 - camshaft cover	26 - conrod assembly	39 - crankshaft pulley	

Job 21-1

☐ **Step 14:** Remove the bearing caps and half shells and keep them in order.

ℹ INSIDE INFORMATION: Make sure the caps have numbers matching those on their mating conrods. It is essential they are kept together. ℹ

☐ **Step 15:** Withdraw the piston/conrod assemblies from their bores and keep them strictly in the order they were fitted in.

☐ **Step 16:** Turn the cylinder block upside down and remove the rear crankshaft seal and carrier.

☐ **Step 17:** Undo the main bearing cap bolts and remove the caps. They are numbered from the front (timing belt end), the centre one being identified by the letter 'C'.

☐ **Step 18:** Lift out the crankshaft and retrieve the bearing shells and thrusts, keeping them in order in case they are re-used.

Job 22. Fire OHC engine reassembly.

CHECKING FOR WEAR

GENERAL

As the checks carried out on the cylinder block and crankshaft are common to most engines, read *Job 7, Checking for Wear*. Whenever rebuilding an engine, it is best to fit a new fuel pump. Fuel pump overhaul, in practice, is restricted to washing out the pump, checking the relief valve and changing the seal.

ENGINE REASSEMBLY

SECTION A - CRANKSHAFT

☐ **Step A1:** Make sure the bearing seals in the block are perfectly clean and locate the main bearing shells so that their tabs engage with the slots.

☐ **Step A2:** Position the thrust washers either side of the centre web - they are held in place by the bearing shell. Then carry out *Steps A3* to *A8* of *Job 7, PART A*.

Step A3: Fit the rear oil seal carrier (with its new seal - see illustration *Job 21-1, 49* and *50*), using RTV instant silicone gasket. Lubricate the 'bearing' surfaces of the oil seal with fresh engine oil.

SECTION B - PISTON/CONNECTING ROD ASSEMBLIES

Refer to *Job 7, PART E* and carry out *Steps E1* to *E3*, noting that the arrow on the piston crown must point to the camshaft drivebelt end. Continue with *Steps E5* to *E8*.

SECTION C - COMPLETE THE REASSEMBLY

Step C1: Fit a new seal to the oil pump and fit the pump, using a new gasket.

Step C2: Fit the pump pickup/filter assembly using a new sealing washer.

Step C3: Fit the engine backplate and fit the flywheel. Use a locking fluid on the flywheel bolts and tighten them to their correct torque. See *Chapter 3, Facts and Figures*.

Step C4: Refit the sump using a smear of Loctite RTV silicone on the gasket and refit the flywheel housing cover plate.

Step C5: Fit the crankshaft sprocket, locating it on its integral key. Tighten the securing bolt to its specified torque. See *Chapter 3, Facts and Figures*.

Step C6: Fit the new clutch. See *PART B: TRANSMISSION, Job 3.*

Step C7: Refit the cylinder head. See *Job 19*.

Step C8: Refit the coolant pump using Loctite RTV silicone gasket.

Step C9: Refit the timing belt rear cover. Refit the tensioner and lock it away from the tensioned position.

Step C10: Fit the new timing belt. See *Job 17*.

Step C11: Refit the crankshaft pulley.

Step C12: Refit the alternator and a new drive belt.

Step C13: Refit the oil dipstick.

Step C14: Refit the fuel pump and pushrod, using a new gasket on both sides of the spacer block. See *PART F: FUEL AND EXHAUST SYSTEMS*.

Step C15: Refit the thermostat housing, use a new gasket.

Step C16: Using a new seal, fit the coolant pipe to the back of the coolant pump.

Step C17: Lubricate the sealing ring and screw on a new oil filter cartridge.

Step C18: Follow *Job 7, INSTALLATION AND INITIAL START-UP, Steps 1* to *6*, to complete the installation and initial start up.

IMPORTANT NOTE: Some FIAT cylinder head gaskets do NOT need the head bolts re-torquing after a bedding-down interval. Check with your supplier.

Job 23. Petrol engine and transmission, all types - removal

IMPORTANT NOTE: 1. See *PART B: TRANSMISSION* for gearbox removal by itself. 2. See *FACT FILE: LATER GEARBOXES* on *page 102* for latest FIRE-engined cars.

i INSIDE INFORMATION: The complete engine/transmission unit is removed and replaced from under the car - and this applies to all types. Make sure you can raise the front of the car high enough (and support it safely and securely!) to allow the power unit to be pulled clear from underneath, before starting work! *i*

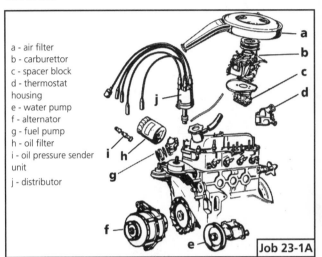

a - air filter
b - carburettor
c - spacer block
d - thermostat housing
e - water pump
f - alternator
g - fuel pump
h - oil filter
i - oil pressure sender unit
j - distributor

Job 23-1A

Step 1A: OHV ENGINES ONLY. Illustration *Job 23-1A* shows the components to be removed from the OHV 903cc engines. Later OHV engines have rectangular air filter housings and other detail differences.

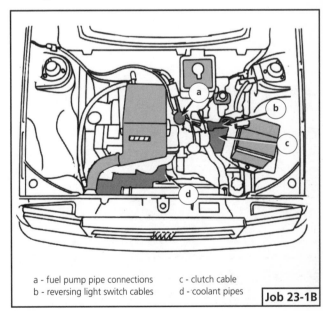

a - fuel pump pipe connections
b - reversing light switch cables
c - clutch cable
d - coolant pipes

Job 23-1B

Step 1B: FIRE OHC ENGINES ONLY. Illustration *23-1B* shows the position of components to be disconnected on this engine type.

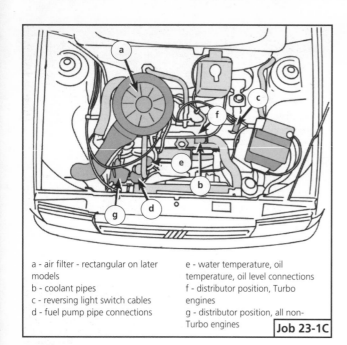

a - air filter - rectangular on later models
b - coolant pipes
c - reversing light switch cables
d - fuel pump pipe connections
e - water temperature, oil temperature, oil level connections
f - distributor position, Turbo engines
g - distributor position, all non-Turbo engines

Job 23-1C

☐ **Step 1C: NON-FIRE OHC ENGINES ONLY.** Illustration *Job 23-1C* shows the position of components to be disconnected on the 1116, 1299, 1301 and 1372cc engines.

ALL TYPES

☐ **Step 2:** Open the bonnet and disconnect the windscreen washer tube.

> *making it easy* ☐ **Step 3:** *Mark the bonnet hinge positions with masking tape round the edge of the hinges, for easy alignment when refitting.*
>
> • *With someone helping you to support the bonnet's weight, undo the hinge bolts and remove the bonnet from the car.*

☐ **Step 4:** Disconnect the battery earth lead.

☐ **Step 5:** Drain the cooling system and the engine oil.

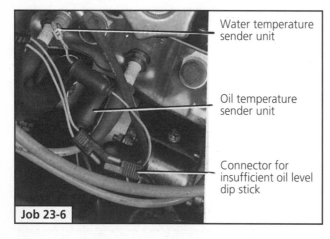

Water temperature sender unit

Oil temperature sender unit

Connector for insufficient oil level dip stick

Job 23-6

☐ **Step 6:** Disconnect the leads from the oil pressure switch, oil level indicator and oil temperature sender unit (when fitted), the starter motor, the alternator and the coolant temperature sender unit.

☐ **Step 7:** Undo the earth strap from the transmission. Disconnect the HT lead from the ignition coil and the LT lead from the distributor.

☐ **Step 8:** Remove the air cleaner.

☐ **Step 9:** Disconnect the clutch cable at the transmission end.

☐ **Step 10:** Unscrew the speedometer cable from the transmission.

☐ **Step 11:** Disconnect the reversing lamp switch.

☐ **Step 12:** Disconnect the coolant pump and cylinder head hoses.

☐ **Step 13:** Disconnect the hoses from the fuel pump and plug the ends.

☐ **Step 14:** Undo the controls from the carburettor.

☐ **Step 15:** Disconnect the heater hoses from the engine.

☐ **Step 16:** Disconnect the carburettor fuel return hose.

☐ **Step 17:** Slacken the drive-shaft to hub nuts but don't remove them until the front of the car has been raised.

> *making it easy* • *As the drive-shaft nuts are very tight, use a long bar to give extra leverage and ask a helper to plant his or her foot firmly on the brake pedal to prevent hub rotation.*

☐ **Step 18:** Raise the front of the car and support on axle stands. Remove the front wheels.

☐ **Step 19:** From under the car, remove the wheelarch liners (bolts arrowed) from both sides of the car.

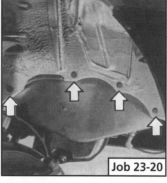

Job 23-20

☐ **Step 20:** Uncouple the exhaust downpipe from the manifold. Undo the exhaust mounting and move the exhaust system to the rear, out of the way.

☐ **Step 21:** Lever the gearchange rod balljoints apart at their forward ends.

☐ **Step 22:** Undo the track rod end balljoint nuts on each side of the car and part the joints from the steering arms with a 'splitter' tool.

☐ **Step 23:** Unbolt the brake calipers and tie them clear.

☐ **Step 24:** Remove the securing bolts from the hub carriers at the clamps at the bases of the suspension struts.

Job 23-25A

Step 25A: ALL NON-TURBO ENGINES. Remove the previously loosened hub nuts. Pull the tops of the hub carriers clear of the suspension strut clamps and release the drive-shafts from the carriers. One option is to tie the drive-shafts in the horizontal position as shown, holding them back so that they don't come out of the differential housing. Alternatively, the drive-shafts from the differential housing, after releasing the gaiters. See *PART B: TRANSMISSION, Job 9.* Place containers ready to catch the inevitable oil leaks.

Step 25B(i): TURBO ENGINES ONLY. The drive-shafts are unbolted from their flanges at their inboard, gearbox-ends.

Job 23-25B(i)

Step 25B(ii): The bases of the struts DON'T have to be removed from the hubs on Turbo engines, but on the right-hand side, you have to remove the upper bolt (arrowed) to provide enough clearance for the drive-shaft to be removed.

Job 23-25B(ii)

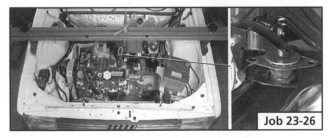

Job 23-26

Step 26: Support the weight of the power unit from above or from beneath with a trolley jack. Disconnect the bottom mounting (inset)...

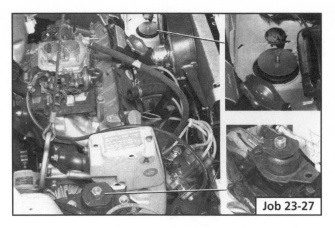

Job 23-27

Step 27: ...and the upper left and right hand mountings (insets).

Step 28: Carefully lower the unit to the ground and remove from under the car.

Job 23-28

Job 24. Petrol engine and transmission, all types - refitting.

This is a reversal of *Job 23. Removal*, plus these extra points:

Step 1: Lower the car to the ground before fully tightening the front suspension, drive-shaft and engine mounting bolts.

Step 2: Fill the cooling system, using the correct 50/50 **Paraflu** anti-freeze solution.

Step 3: Put fresh **Selenia** oil in the engine.

Step 4: Top up the transmission oil.

Step 5: Adjust the clutch free travel. See *PART B: TRANSMISSION.*

Step 6: Reconnect the battery.

For *Steps 1* to *4*, see *Chapter 3, Facts and Figures* for correct torque settings and quantities.

Job 25. Petrol engine/transmission, (removed from car), all types - separation.

making it easy / **Step 1:** Clean the whole unit with a proprietary degreaser - and dry off before starting work. This makes these heavy components easier and safer to handle and greatly reduces the risk of contamination when you strip them down.

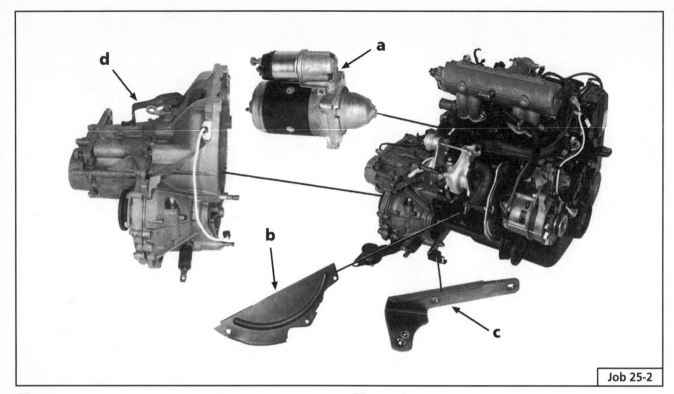

Job 25-2

☐ **Step 2:** Undo and remove the engine mounting brackets and starter motor (**a**).

☐ **Step 3:** Unbolt and remove the pressed steel cover plate (see illustration **Job 25-2, part b**) from the lower face of the flywheel housing and remove the gearchange mechanism bracket (**Job 25-2, part c**).

☐ **Step 4:** Undo the flywheel housing connecting bolts and note the position of the engine and transmission mounting brackets and lifting eyes.

☐ **Step 5:** Supporting the weight of the transmission (see illustration **Job 25-2, part d**) and, withdraw it from the engine in a straight line.

Job 26. Petrol engine/transmission, all types - reconnection.

Refer to **Job 25** for the location of components referred to here.

☐ **Step 1:** Offer the transmission to the engine. The input shaft should slide easily through the splined hub of the driven plate, as long as this is still centralised. See **PART B: TRANSMISSION, Job 4**. Re-centre the clutch if necessary.

making it easy ! ● *If the input shaft and hub splines are not aligned, ask a helper to turn the crankshaft pulley nut while you apply gentle pressure to bring the two units together.*

☐ **Step 2:** Once the input shaft is properly engaged, use two bolts, tightened evenly to draw the units together. DON'T force it! If the units don't come together easily, separate them, check clutch centring and try again. Fit the remaining bolts, not forgetting the lifting eyes and brackets.

☐ **Step 3:** Refit the flywheel housing cover plate and mounting brackets.

☐ **Step 4:** Refit the starter motor.

Job 27. Petrol and diesel engine mountings, all types - replacement.

making it easy ! ● *Change one mounting at a time. The others will help you keep the power unit correctly positioned.*

☐ **Step 1:** Support the weight of the power unit with a jack until there is no upward or downward pressure on the mounting to be changed.

Job 27-2

☐ **Step 2:** Undo the securing bolts and fit the new mounting. Remove the supporting jack.

FACT FILE: DIESEL ENGINES AND
SPECIAL TOOLS

● As the construction and assembly of the diesel
engine is, for the best part, the same as the petrol
engines, this section details only those procedures
which are specific to the diesel.

● Major differences lie in the areas of the cylinder head and camshaft
drive belt.

● Where inspection of components such as crankshaft, camshaft,
pistons, conrods, cylinder head face, flywheel etc. is not detailed
within this section, refer to the relevant information in the **OHV**

Engine section, **Job 7**, under **Checking for wear**. - information which
is common to all engine types.

● In view of the complexity of the diesel engine's camshaft drive
arrangement, the need for special tooling and the accuracy required in
adjusting camshaft timing and injection pump timing, we strongly
recommend that any work involving disturbance of the timing belt or
injection pump is entrusted to a FIAT dealer.

● The following information is provided only for those who have
technical experience of diesel engines, along with access to the
required tooling.

ℹ INSIDE INFORMATION: If you unbolt the whole of
the rear mounting bracket, be sure to replace the two

bolts into the gearbox casing (arrowed) to prevent oil
leakage. **ℹ**

Job 28. Diesel cylinder head - removal.

☐ **Step 1A:** Familiarise yourself with this drawing, showing
the cylinder head, block and other major components referred
to in the following text.

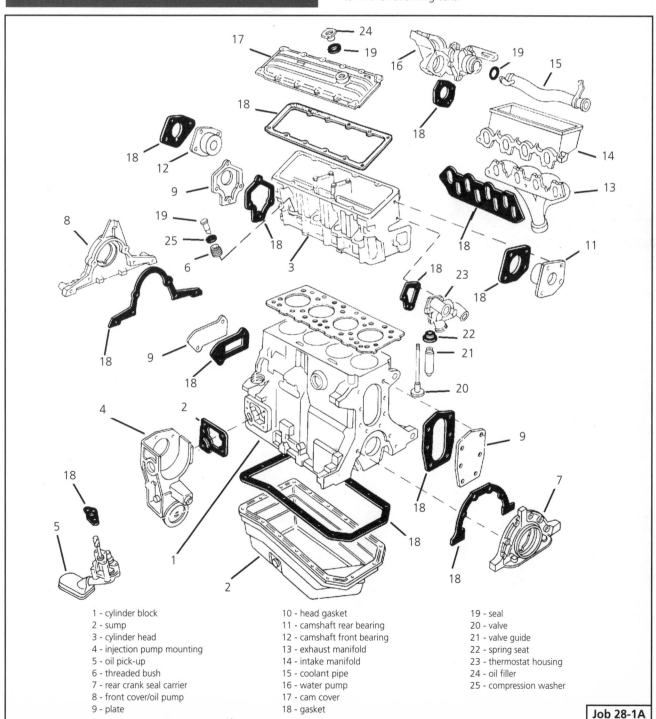

1 - cylinder block	10 - head gasket	19 - seal
2 - sump	11 - camshaft rear bearing	20 - valve
3 - cylinder head	12 - camshaft front bearing	21 - valve guide
4 - injection pump mounting	13 - exhaust manifold	22 - spring seat
5 - oil pick-up	14 - intake manifold	23 - thermostat housing
6 - threaded bush	15 - coolant pipe	24 - oil filler
7 - rear crank seal carrier	16 - water pump	25 - compression washer
8 - front cover/oil pump	17 - cam cover	
9 - plate	18 - gasket	

Job 28-1A

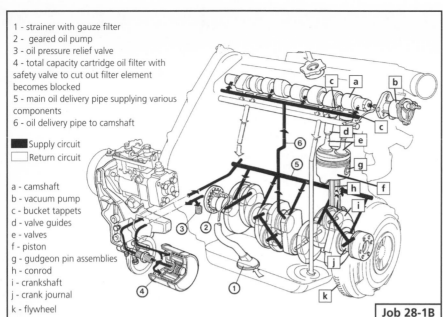

1 - strainer with gauze filter
2 - geared oil pump
3 - oil pressure relief valve
4 - total capacity cartridge oil filter with safety valve to cut out filter element becomes blocked
5 - main oil delivery pipe supplying various components
6 - oil delivery pipe to camshaft

■ Supply circuit
□ Return circuit

a - camshaft
b - vacuum pump
c - bucket tappets
d - valve guides
e - valves
f - piston
g - gudgeon pin assemblies
h - conrod
i - crankshaft
j - crank journal
k - flywheel

Job 28-1B

☐ **Step 1B:** This diagram of the diesel engine's lubrication system also illustrates the internal, 'moving' parts of the diesel engine.

☐ **Step 2:** Disconnect the battery earth lead and drain the cooling system. See *Part C, COOLING SYSTEM.*

☐ **Step 3:** Disconnect the air filter hose and remove the air filter housing.

Job 28-4

☐ **Step 4:** Disconnect the fuel feed and return pipes (arrowed) between engine and fuel filter.

☐ **Step 5:** Disconnect the accelerator cable and the manual timing advance cable (where fitted) from the injection pump.

☐ **Step 6:** Disconnect the heater plugs supply connector at the cylinder block

☐ **Step 7:** Disconnect the heater feed and return pipes and the brake servo vacuum pipe.

Job 28-8

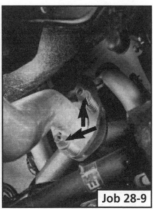
Job 28-9

☐ **Step 8:** Disconnect the radiator hoses and expansion tank pipe.

☐ **Step 9:** Disconnect the exhaust front pipe from the manifold by removing the nuts and springs.

☐ **Step 10:** Disconnect the breather pipe from the end of the air filter and remove the air filter.

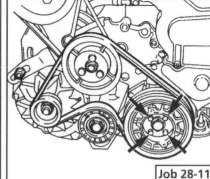
Job 28-11

☐ **Step 11:** Slacken the alternator mountings and remove the drive belt - later model illustrated. You will also have to remove the belt's drive pulley by undoing the four retaining bolts (arrowed).

☐ **Step 12:** Undo the bolt securing the dipstick guide tube (**a**) to the timing belt cover and remove the tube. Undo the remaining bolts (arrowed) and remove the top outer timing belt cover.

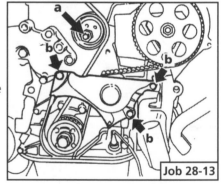
Job 28-12

☐ **Step 13:** Undo the three bolts (arrowed - **b**) and remove the bottom part of the timing belt cover.

Job 28-13

☐ **Step 14:** Undo the timing belt tensioner roller locking nut (see illustration *Job 28-13, part a*) and remove the timing belt.

☐ **Step 15:** Undo the camshaft sprocket securing bolt. To prevent the sprocket from turning, Fiat tool 1860473000 must be fitted through a sprocket hole into the backplate. Remove the sprocket.

1860473000
Job 28-15

Step 16: Unbolt and remove the inner timing belt cover.

Step 17: Undo the twelve bolts securing the camshaft cover and remove the cover.

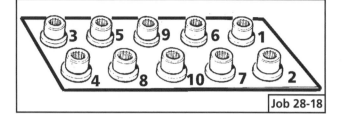

Job 28-18

Step 18: Slacken the cylinder head bolts half a turn at a time in the order shown until all are loose, then remove them. Don't forget the five smaller, outer bolts not shown here.

Step 19: Check that nothing remains attached to the cylinder head to prevent removal, grip the exhaust manifold and pull upwards to ease the cylinder head off its locating dowels. Lift it clear.

Job 29. Diesel cylinder head - refitting.

Step 1: Put the pistons at TDC - two at a time - and measure how much they protrude above the block surface. This is ideally done using a dial gauge and holder (FIAT tools 1895882000

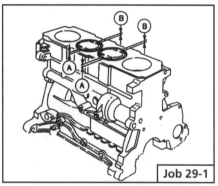

Job 29-1

and 1870404000, respectively) but if surfaces are very clean, and great care is taken, it is possible to take an average protrusion measurement based on measuring the protrusion at each side (**A**) and (**B**) of the piston crown, using a steel straight-edge and feeler gauges. Use the HIGHEST average measurement of the four pistons as your working figure.

Step 2: Now, referring to the illustration, select the appropriate one of the three available cylinder head gasket thicknesses as follows:

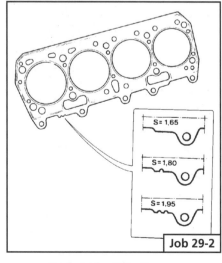

S= 1,65

S= 1,80

S= 1,95

Job 29-2

Measured protrusion
Up to 1.05 mm
1.05 - 1.20 mm
Over 1.20 mm

Gasket identification.
No notches (1.65 mm gasket)
One notch (1.80 mm gasket)
Two notches (1.95 mm gasket)

Step 3: Place the cylinder head gasket over the dowels in the block face with the word 'ALTO' facing upwards and carefully lower the head into position. Clean and lubricate the head bolts and allow to drain for 30 minutes before fitting.

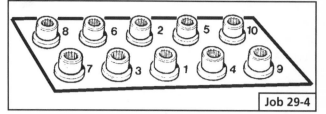

Job 29-4

Step 4: Continue refitting in the reverse order of removal, tightening the cylinder head bolts progressively to their correct torque and in the sequence shown here. Finally, tighten the five outer bolts to the correct torque. See **Chapter 3, Facts and Figures**. Refer to **Job 31.** for camshaft drive belt replacement and adjustment.

Job 30. Diesel cylinder head - overhaul.

Step 1: Undo the three nuts (arrowed) and remove the brake vacuum pump from the rear of the cylinder head.

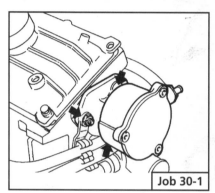

Job 30-1

Step 2: Unbolt and remove the inlet and exhaust manifolds (see illustration **Job 28-1A**).

Step 3: Unscrew and remove the injectors and the glowplugs (and the injector compression washers), taking care not to damage them. See **PART F, FUEL AND EXHAUST SYSTEMS**.

Step 4: Undo the retaining nuts and tap out the camshaft end-bearings with a suitable drift.

Step 5: Undo the centre bearing cap nuts evenly and progressively until there is no pressure. Remove both bearing caps, noting their positions so that you can refit them in the same order.

Job 30-4

Step 6: Remove the camshaft by moving it sideways, by enough to clear one end, then lift it out through the top.

Step 7: Remove the cam followers and keep them in order so that they are refitted in the same positions.

☐ **Step 8:** Using a suitable valve spring compressor, compress the spring of the first valve and remove the split collets. See the relevant petrol engine section.

☐ **Step 9:** Carefully release the spring compressor. Remove the valve spring cap, the spring and spring seat.

☐ **Step 10:** Withdraw the valve from its guide and remove the valve stem oil seal.

☐ **Step 11:** Remove the remaining valves and keep each set of components together and in the correct order, discarding the old stem seals.

☐ **Step 12:** Unscrew and remove the four threaded bushes which secure the pre-combustion chambers. FIAT use their tool No. 1850178000 for this purpose.

1850178000

Job 30-12

ℹ INSIDE INFORMATION: If you have no access to this tool, you will need to make a simple flat-bladed tool to locate in the slots provided in the bush. The tool blade should be 31.5 mm wide by 5 mm thick. ℹ

☐ **Step 13:** Remove the pre-combustion chambers by tapping them out with a small drift.

☐ **Step 14:** Thoroughly clean the cylinder head and components with paraffin or an engine cleaning solvent. Take great care not to gouge the face of the cylinder head. The valves are best cleaned with a rotary wire brush.

☐ **Step 15:** Check the cylinder head for distortion by using a straight edge along the machined surface, and a feeler gauge. Any distortion above 0.1 mm indicates the need for machining.

☐ **Step 16:** Valve guide wear can be checked by rocking the valve sideways in its guide. The guides should be replaced if a maximum movement of 0.35 mm is exceeded (in practice, scarcely detectable).

☐ **Step 17:** Lubricate the valve stems with clean engine oil then locate them in their respective guides after fitting new oil seals onto the tops of the guides. Take great care not to damage the seals!

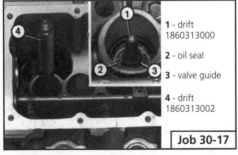

1 - drift 1860313000

2 - oil seal

3 - valve guide

4 - drift 1860313002

Job 30-17

making it easy ● *Two specialist tools are required for seal fitting if you are to avoid damaging the new seals. These are Nos. 1860313000 and 1860313002 respectively.*

● *They may be available from your FIAT agent on hire, but if not it is best to take the cylinder head to the agent for the seals to be fitted.*

☐ **Step 18:** Place the valve spring seat over the guide, then position the spring, followed by the cap. Compress the spring enough to allow you to engage the split cotters with the valve stem.

ℹ INSIDE INFORMATION: Use a little grease to keep them in place. Slowly release the compressor, checking that the collets are properly located. Tap the ends of the valve stems to bed them in. ℹ

☐ **Step 19:** Continue to assemble the head in the reverse order of dismantling and remember to lubricate all moving parts with engine oil during assembly. Refer to **Chapter 3, Facts and Figures** for specified tightening torques.

ℹ **Step 20:** *INSIDE INFORMATION: Valve clearance measurement and adjustment is now needed. Both measurement and shim replacement are carried out in the same manner as for the petrol OHC engine, **Job 16**, so refer to this and also to **Chapter 3, Facts and Figures** for specifications.* ℹ

Job 31. Diesel camshaft drive belt - replacement and adjustment.

GENERAL. Two different procedures are required, depending upon the age of your diesel engine, as modifications were made from engine No. 1723291-on to allow fine adjustment of camshaft timing. Both procedures require the use of FIAT special tooling, which it may be possible to hire from your local FIAT agent.

☐ **Step 1:** Follow **Job 28, Steps 11 to 13**.

ENGINES PRIOR TO ENGINE NO. 1723291

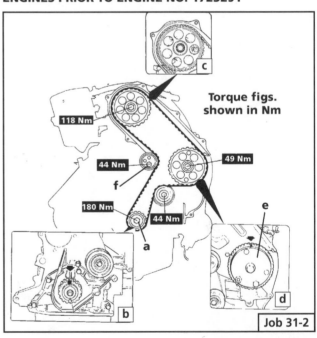

Torque figs. shown in Nm

Job 31-2

☐ **Step 2:** Use a spanner on the crankshaft bolt (**a**) to turn the engine until the timing marks on the crankshaft, camshaft and injection pump sprockets align with their respective reference marks. Align the crankshaft sprocket with the notch on the front cover (**b**). Align the camshaft sprocket with the hole in the timing belt cover (**c**). Align the injection pump sprocket with the reference on the timing belt rear guard (**d**).

Step 3: Using FIAT tool No. 1842128000 (see illustration *Job 31-2, part e*), lock the injection pump sprocket to prevent it turning.

Step 4: Slacken the belt tensioner nut (see illustration *Job 31-2, part f*), move the tensioner away from the belt and temporarily lock it in position.

Step 5: Ease the timing belt off the sprockets.

Step 6: Fit the new belt, first making sure that all of the timing marks still align.

Step 7: If you do not have access to the correct FIAT tensioning tool, see *Job 8, Step 9*, release the locknut, push the tensioner firmly into the belt and lock it up by tightening its bolt.

If you do have the FIAT special tool (a weighted bar), attach it to the tensioner, which will move to the position of correct tension. Lock the tensioner bolt. Remove the special tool locking the injection pump sprocket.

i INSIDE INFORMATION: If you can't put enough pressure on the tensioner with your fingers, carefully use a long screwdriver as a lever. Alternatively, push a pair of bolts into the two holes in the tensioner and lever between them to turn the tensioner. *i*

Step 8: Rotate the engine through two revolutions. If the belt is correctly tensioned you should just be able to twist it through a quarter-turn when gripping it between thumb and finger in the centre of its longest run between sprockets. Adjust as necessary.

Step 9: Refit the remaining parts in the reverse order, then check the injection timing (see *Chapter 5, Servicing Your Car, Job 39)*.

ENGINES FROM ENGINE NO. 1723291-ON

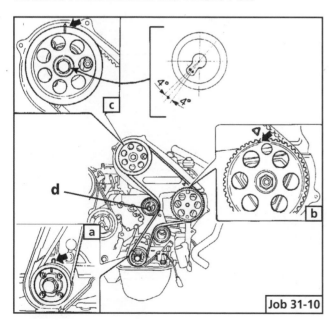

Job 31-10

Step 10: Turn the crankshaft in its normal direction of rotation until the marks on the crankshaft sprocket (**a**) and fuel injection pump sprocket (**b**) line up with the fixed marks on the engine. This will place cylinder No. 1 at Top Dead Centre TDC and set the camshaft for the power stroke of the same cylinder.

IMPORTANT NOTE: The hole for fixing the camshaft sprocket (**c**) has a fine-adjustment slot, so it is possible that the mark on the sprocket may not line up exactly with the mark on the cover.

Step 11: Undo the belt tensioner nut (see illustration *Job 31-10, part d*), then remove the timing belt.

Step 12: Undo the nut securing the brake vacuum pump to the cylinder head (see illustration *Job 30-1*), and remove it.

Step 13: Fit FIAT tool No. 1860932000 (for setting camshaft timing) to the vacuum pump end of the camshaft, matching the camshaft groove (**1**) with the lug (**2**) on the tool. Secure the tool to the cylinder head, positioning the centering dowel (**3**) as shown. The dowel must be perfectly centred on the tool, and if it isn't, you should adjust the hexagonal bolt (**4**) with a spanner, and centre it with tiny movements.

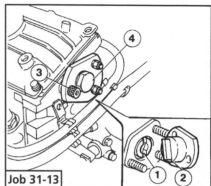

Job 31-13

Step 14: Remove the bolt (arrowed) which secures the front cover to the engine block, then fit the timing belt on the crankshaft sprocket.

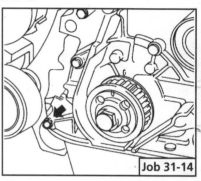

Job 31-14

Step 15: Fit FIAT tool No. 1860933000 for precise determination of TDC on cylinder No. 1. The tool must be secured firmly by two bolts to the crankshaft sprocket, and by another bolt to the crankshaft front cover (where the bolt was previously removed in *Step 14*).

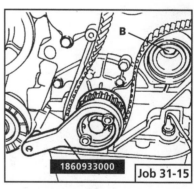

1860933000 Job 31-15

Step 16: Using FIAT tools 1860831000 and 1860848000, slacken the bolt securing the camshaft sprocket.

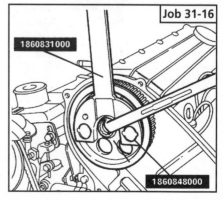

Job 31-16
1860831000
1860848000

Step 17: Continue fitting the timing belt in the following sequence: crankshaft sprocket, fixed tensioner, injection pump sprocket, timing sprocket, belt tensioner... and check that the mark on the injection pump lines up with the fixed mark on the rear cover.

Step 18: Fit tools 1860745100 and 1860745300 for tensioning the timing belt on the belt tensioner. Fit the knurled part on the graduated rod at the 60 mm mark.

ℹ INSIDE INFORMATION: If you do not have the correct tensioning tool, follow **Steps 7** and **8**. ℹ

Step 19: Tighten the camshaft sprocket bolt to the specified torque (see **Chapter 3, Facts and Figures**), then remove timing tools 1860933000 and 1860932000.

Step 20: Turn the crankshaft by two revolutions (clockwise), tighten the belt tensioner to the specified torque (see **Chapter 3, Facts and Figures**) and remove the tensioning tools. If the belt is correctly tensioned you should just be able to twist it through a quarter-turn when gripping it between thumb and finger in the centre of its longest run between sprockets. Adjust as necessary.

Step 21: Refit the remaining components in the reverse order of removal.

Job 32. Diesel engine - removal

This Job should be read in connection with **Job 23, Petrol engine and transmission, all types - removal**.

Step 1: Remove the cylinder head - see **Job 28**.

Step 2: While the car is still on the ground, slacken the front wheel bolts and slacken the hub centre nuts. You can then raise and support the car in such a way that it is possible to remove the power unit from below the engine bay. Tall axle-stands are best for the purpose. See **Chapter 1, Safety First.**

Step 3: Drain the engine oil.

Step 4: Disconnect the coolant temperature sender unit and the earth cable from the gearbox.

Step 5: Disconnect the starter motor and alternator wiring.

Step 6: Disconnect the speedometer cable. **See PART E: ELECTRICAL AND INSTRUMENTS, Job 5.**

Step 7: Disconnect the gear selector linkages (arrowed), after releasing the ball-coupling self-locking nuts.

Job 32-7

Step 8: Disconnect the clutch cable at the gearbox arm, and the reversing lights switch connector at the gearbox.

Step 9: Remove the front wheels and undo the hub centre nuts - see **PART G, STEERING AND SUSPENSION, Job 6, Step 2**.

Step 10: Remove the access panel from each wheel housing.

Step 11: Disconnect the track rod ends from the hub carriers, see **PART G, STEERING AND SUSPENSION, Job 3.**

Step 12: Undo the bolts securing the bottom of each front suspension strut to the hub carrier. See **PART G: STEERING AND SUSPENSION, Job 8.** Withdraw the drive-shafts from the hubs.

Step 13: Undo the nuts fixing the anti-roll bar (where fitted) to the track control arms. See **PART G: STEERING AND SUSPENSION, Job 7.**

Step 14: Remove the low-oil-pressure warning switch from the oil filter mounting.

Step 15: Support the weight of the power unit from above, using a suitable hoist or lifting crane. Alternatively, support the weight from below, using one or two trolley jacks and wood to spread the load.

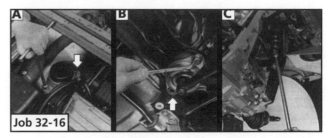

Job 32-16

Step 16: Undo the left-hand, right-hand and bottom power unit mounting bolts.

Step 17: Carefully lower the complete power unit, with drive-shafts, to the ground.

Job 32-17

Step 18: Unbolt and separate the transmission from the engine. See **Job 25**.

Job 33. Diesel engine - refitting

Refitting is the reverse of the removal operation. Make sure that all nuts and bolts are tightened to their specified torques - see **Chapter 3, Facts and Figures.** Check that all electrical connections are sound and that all fluid and vacuum hoses and unions are secure. Refer to **PART B: TRANSMISSION, Job 4.** for clutch refitting and alignment.

Job 34. Diesel engine - dismantling

This Job should be read in conjunction with **Job 14**. The engines are broadly similar although the information given in this Job takes priority for diesel engines.

Refer to the illustrations to **Job 28-1** when tackling the following work.

☐ **Step 1:** Remove the timing belt and cylinder head. See **Job 28.**

☐ **Step 2:** Remove the alternator, water pump and thermostat housing distribution pipe.

☐ **Step 3:** Remove the crankshaft timing belt sprocket.

ℹ️ INSIDE INFORMATION: Note that the bolt in the crankshaft nose which secures the crankshaft sprocket has a left-hand thread and must be undone clockwise. ℹ️

☐ **Step 4:** Unbolt the timing belt tensioner (see **Job 28, Step 17**) and idler pulleys.

☐ **Step 5:** Remove the injection pump sprocket.

ℹ️ INSIDE INFORMATION: You will need two FIAT tools for this operation. One (No. 1860473000) is to prevent the sprocket from turning when undoing the nut, and the other (extractor No. 1842128000) to pull the sprocket from the injection pump shaft. These may be available for hire from your FIAT agent. Alternatively it may be possible to improvise a means of preventing sprocket rotation, and a suitable three-leg puller may be carefully used to withdraw the sprocket. Take care not to lose the pump shaft Woodruff key. ℹ️

☐ **Step 6:** Unbolt and detach the support bracket from the rear of the injection pump. See **PART F: FUEL AND EXHAUST SYSTEMS**). Unbolt the pump flange and bracket nuts, and remove the pump and its front bracket (illustration **28-1, part 4**).

☐ **Step 7:** Remove and discard the old oil filter.

☐ **Step 8:** Remove the crankcase breather, the low-oil-pressure switch and the oil pressure gauge sensor from the front face of the engine.

☐ **Step 9:** Turn the engine upside down and remove the sump.

☐ **Step 10:** Remove the oil pick-up pipe and filter (see illustration **Job 28-1A, part 5**), and the oil return pipe.

☐ **Step 11:** Remove the front cover and oil pump assembly (**28-1A, part 8**).

☐ **Step 12:** Remove the rear crankshaft seal and carrier (**28-1A, part 7**).

☐ **Step 13:** Referring to the **OHC Engine** information in **Job 8**, and illustration **Job 28-1B**, check the big-end bearing caps and the connecting rods to make sure they have matching numbers starting from the timing cover end.

Otherwise, mark them with a centre punch. Make sure you know which way round each one goes!

☐ **Step 14:** Undo the big-end bolts and withdraw one piston/conrod assembly, keeping it with its bearing cap. Keep the shell bearing halves in their original locations if they are to be reused.

☐ **Step 15:** Remove the remaining piston/conrod assemblies.

☐ **Step 16:** Check the crankshaft main bearing caps and webs to see that they are correctly numbered from the timing cover end.

☐ **Step 17:** Remove the caps and half-shell bearings (illustration **28-1A**) and keep them in order.

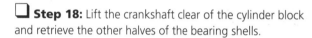

Job 34-17

☐ **Step 18:** Lift the crankshaft clear of the cylinder block and retrieve the other halves of the bearing shells.

All parts must be thoroughly cleaned for inspection - still keeping them in the right order for reassembly in case they are to be re-used.

Job 35. Diesel engine - reassembly.

CRANKSHAFT

☐ **Step 1:** Locate the main bearing shells so that their tabs engage with the slots. See relevant picture in OHC petrol engine.

☐ **Step 2:** Apply some grease to the smooth side of the thrust washers and 'stick' them in position on both sides of the rear main bearing web (at the flywheel end).

☐ **Step 3:** Oil the shells liberally with fresh engine oil and lower the crankshaft into position.

☐ **Step 4:** Fit the remaining halves of the shells into the bearing caps and position the remaining halves of the thrust washers, 'sticking' them in place on either side of the rear main bearing cap with grease.

☐ **Step 5:** Oil the journals and position the caps the right way round and in the correct order.

☐ **Step 6:** Screw the bolts in finger-tight and check that the crankshaft rotates freely and smoothly.

☐ **Step 7:** Tighten the bolts evenly and progressively until the specified torque setting is reached, see **Chapter 3, Facts and Figures.** Check again that the crankshaft rotates smoothly.

☐ **Step 8:** Check the crankshaft end float by using a feeler gauge between the thrust washer and the crankshaft. Thicker washers are available if required. See **Chapter 3, Facts and Figures**.

Step 9: Fit the rear oil seal carrier (with its new seal), using a new gasket. Lubricate the seal and lightly oil the gasket.

Job 35-9

Step 10: Position Nos. 1 and 4 crank pins at Top Dead Centre (TDC), then fit the flywheel with its TDC mark facing the cylinder head surface. Screw in the fixing bolts and tighten to their specified torque. See **Chapter 3, Facts and Figures**.

Step 11: Fit a new seal to the front cover/oil pump assembly, unless a new pump is being fitted, and install with a new gasket, lightly oiling both gasket and seal. Align the cover with the sump support plate.

Job 35-11

PISTON/CONNECTING ROD ASSEMBLIES

IMPORTANT NOTE: The pistons and connecting rods are to be fitted as assemblies. Their dismantling and reassembly is a job for your FIAT agent - not a DIY job.

Refer to **Job 7, OHV engine - reassembly, Part E.**, for information pertinent to the piston and connecting rod assemblies, particularly removal, installation and inspection of the piston rings.

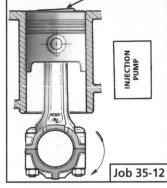

Job 35-12

Step 12: INSIDE INFORMATION: Each of the diesel's pistons must be fitted so that the higher part of the machined boss on the piston crown (arrowed) is on the injection pump side of the cylinder block.

Step 13: Refit the oil pump pick-up and return pipes.

Step 14: Refit the sump using a new gasket. Check that the drain plug is tight.

Step 15: Complete the reassembly by fitting all the external components in the reverse order. Refer to **Job 29** for cylinder head refitting.

PART B: TRANSMISSION AND CLUTCH

PART B: Contents

Job 1. Transmission removal (with engine in car).

It is possible to remove the gearbox without removing the engine, for clutch replacement or in order to fit an exchange gearbox, for example. The advantages of leaving the engine in the car are that there will be less dismantling to carry out and less weight to manhandle. Refer to **PART A: ENGINE, Jobs 23, 24, 32** and **33** for further information on removal of some of the components mentioned here.

IMPORTANT NOTE: If you intend fully removing the drive-shaft slacken the hub nut before raising the car. See **Job 9.**

Step 1: Ensure that you can support the car sufficiently high off the ground for the gearbox to be removed from beneath.

Job 1-2

Step 2: Make sure that the weight of the engine at the gearbox-end is supported from above the car or on a stand, from beneath. You may be able to make a home-made version of this FIAT workshop tool - arrowed.

FACT FILE: LATEST GEARBOXES

For the last couple of years of production, FIRE-engined Unos were fitted with the Punto-type gearbox. Removal procedure is similar, except...

● **A.** Disconnect the reverse gear inhibitor from its housing.

● **B.** Disconnect the gear selector rod, similar to other gearboxes.

A

● **C.** Disconnect the gear engagement cable (arrowed) from the control lever and mounting bracket.

C

Step 3: Remove the bonnet and disconnect the battery and the transmission earth cable.

Step 4: Disconnect the following items from the transmission (see *PART A: ENGINE, Job 23* for locations.):

- the speedometer cable
- the clutch cable
- the leads from the reversing light switch
- the starter motor from the bellhousing

Step 5: Undo these three bolts (arrowed) holding the gearbox to the engine and accessible in the engine compartment.

Job 1-5

Step 6: *With the car still on the ground, loosen the nuts fixing the constant velocity joints to the hubs. These require an enormous force to be tightened or released (see Chapter 3, Facts and Figures) and they will have been staked. There is a severe risk of pulling the car off supports if you attempt to undo these nuts while the car is raised off the ground. Slacken the front wheel nuts, raise the front of the car off the ground and support it securely, and remove the front wheels.*

Step 7: Support the gearbox from beneath the car and disconnect the exhaust pipe at the manifold. Remove the protective shields, when fitted.

Step 8: Remove the transmission end plate. See *PART A: ENGINE, Job 23*.

Step 9: Disconnect the gear change linkage by levering off the linkrod ball ends and spring clips (arrowed).

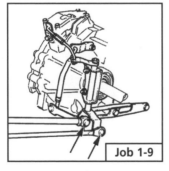

Job 1-9

Step 10: Remove the engine/transmission mounting from the centre-rear of the transmission. See *PART A: ENGINE, Job 27*.

ℹ INSIDE INFORMATION: With the mounting removed, refit the bolts into the gearbox to prevent oil leaks. Alternatively, if you intend stripping or transporting the transmission unit, drain the oil. ℹ

Step 11: Disconnect the hubs from the drive-shafts. See *Job 9*.

Step 12: Fix the drive-shafts where they protrude from the differential casing so that they cannot slide out - or remove them from the gearbox now, if you need to remove or dismantle them in any case. See *Job 9*.

Step 13: Remove the remaining bolts which secure the gearbox/differential unit to the engine, from beneath the car. You will also have to unbolt and remove the cover plate and the gearchange rod support bracket, where they share the engine-transmission bolts.

IMPORTANT NOTE: When working on non-FIRE OHC engines, it is necessary to remove the complete right-hand drive-shaft. See *PART G: STEERING AND SUSPENSION*.

Step 14: With the weight of the gearbox carefully supported (such as on a trolley jack) slide it free of the engine without putting any pressure on the clutch or the gearbox first motion shaft.

Job 1-15

Step 15: With the gearbox carefully balanced on its supports, it can be lowered to the ground and removed from beneath the car.

Job 2. Transmission - refitting (engine in car).

IMPORTANT NOTE: Refer to the illustrations in *PART A: ENGINE, Jobs 23, 24, 32 and 33* in connection with this Job.

Step 1: Refitting is the reverse of removal. Before starting, make sure that the clutch driven plate is still centralised. See *Job 3*.

Step 2: Fill the transmission with the correct grade of new FL oil. See *Chapter 3, Facts and Figures*.

Step 3: Check the clutch adjustment. See *Chapter 5, Servicing Your Car, Job 20*.

Step 4: When the brake calipers have been refitted, pump the brake pedal until its normal solid feel is restored.

Step 5: Use a self-grip wrench to reconnect the gear rod balls and sockets. Use new drive-shaft nuts, tightened to the correct torque and staked into the shaft grooves with a punch. See *Job 9*.

Job 3. Clutch - replacement.

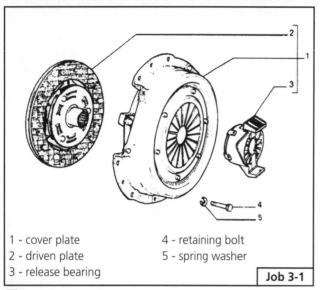

1 - cover plate
2 - driven plate
3 - release bearing
4 - retaining bolt
5 - spring washer

Job 3-1

Step 1: These first three numbered parts are the parts you will need to obtain, from your FIAT dealership.

FACT FILE:
● We strongly recommend that all three main components: clutch cover, driven plate and release bearing are replaced after a high mileage, ensuring longer life and smoother operation.

● If one is worn, they are all likely to be, so save yourself another big stripdown in the near future!

Step 2: Remove the transmission. See **Job 1.**

Step 3: Unscrew the clutch cover bolts (see **illustration Job 3-1, part 4**) progressively until the spring pressure is released, then remove the bolts.

Step 4: Ease the cover off its dowels and catch the driven plate as it falls.

Step 5:
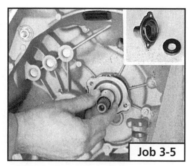

Job 3-5

INSIDE INFORMATION: Check the inside of the clutch bellhousing for contamination by oil. This indicates a leak from either the crankshaft rear seal or the gearbox input shaft seal (illustrated). A faulty seal should be replaced without delay. Oil can cause judder and slip. Here, the seal (inset) is being replaced. See **PART A: ENGINE, Job 21** for the position of the rear crankshaft seal. *i*

Step 6: Check the surface of the flywheel that mates with the clutch, for scoring, or significant micro cracking caused by excessive head generated by clutch slip. Replace the flywheel if in doubt.

Step 7: Check the release fork pivot, inside the bellhousing, for wear. Replace the bushes (see **inset**) if necessary, lubricating with a small quantity of molybdenum disulphide grease.

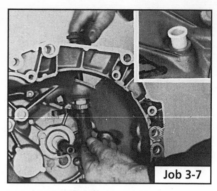

Job 3-7

Step 8: Clean oil or the protective film from the clutch cover and flywheel faces.

Step 9: Offer the driven plate to the flywheel with the side having the greatest hub projection facing outwards.

Step 10: Locate the clutch cover on the flywheel dowels and screw in the fixing bolts finger tight.

Step 11: Use an aligning tool to make sure that the clutch is centralised, otherwise the gearbox will not relocate on the engine and damage can be caused to the centre plate.

i INSIDE INFORMATION: There is no spigot bush or bearing in the crankshaft end, but there is an indentation which you can 'feel' with a normal clutch alignment tool allowing you to centralise the driven plate between the clutch cover release fingers. *i*

Step 12: Tighten the cover bolts evenly to the correct torque. See **Chapter 3, Facts and Figures**.

Step 13: Smear a little 'copper' grease on the release bearing guide and the gearbox input shaft.

Step 14: Refit the transmission. See **Job 2.**

Job 4. Clutch cable - refitting.

NB Late cars have hydraulic clutch - see **Job 13**.

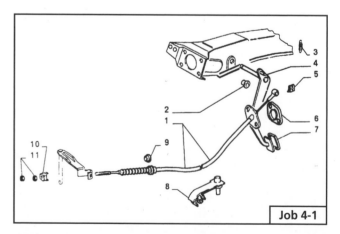

Job 4-1

Step 1: From under the bonnet, slacken the cable adjusting nut (11). Disconnect the cable from the release lever and outer cable bracket.

Step 2: From inside the car. Disconnect the cable from the foot pedal by removing the securing clip (see illustration *Job 4-1, part 5*) and pulling the cable end off its pivot.

Step 3: Unbolt the forked cable retaining plate from the bulkhead. Pull the cable out from inside the car.

Step 4: Fit the new cable in the reverse order and adjust. See *Chapter 5, Servicing Your Car, Job 20*.

Job 5. Gear lever and linkage - removal and refitting.

NOT SOME LATEST GEARBOXES - see *page 102*.

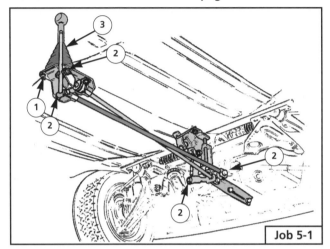

Job 5-1

Step 1: From under the car, undo the gaiter securing nuts (**1**).

Step 2: Dismantle the linkage by unscrewing the self locking nuts or removing the spring clips from the pivots (see illustration *Job 5-1, part 2*).

Step 3: From inside the car, pull up the gear lever boot (see *5-1, 3*) then withdraw the lever.

Step 4: Disconnect the relay lever from the control rod by prising the ball from its socket.

Step 5: The plastic bushes in the control rod ends can be removed for replacement by pressing them out in a vice using suitable spacers.

Step 6: The gear linkage relay mounted on the gearbox can sometimes seize and require replacement. The rods connected to the upper part are secured by 'C'- clips which should also be renewed.

Step 7: Refit in reverse order, using a self-grip wrench to reassemble the balljoints.

Job 6. Kickdown cable (automatic transmission) - replacement.

Step 1: Drain the automatic transmission oil and remove the sump. Discard the old gasket. See *Chapter 5, Servicing Your Car, Job 18*.

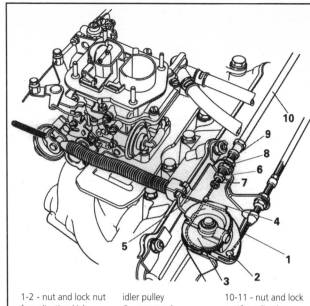

1-2 - nut and lock nut for adjusting kick-down cable	idler pulley	10-11 - nut and lock nut for adjusting accelerator control cable.
3 - kick-down control cable	6 - stop pawl	
4 - kick-down cable, end nipple	7 - accelerator control cable	12 - accelerator control cable.
5 - accelerator and kick-down control	8 - stop pawl adjustment and positioning screw	13 - kick-down control cable
	9 - adjustment screw lock nut	

Job 6-2

Step 2: Disconnect the cable from the throttle control idler pulley.

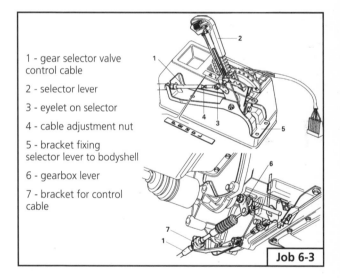

1 - gear selector valve control cable

2 - selector lever

3 - eyelet on selector

4 - cable adjustment nut

5 - bracket fixing selector lever to bodyshell

6 - gearbox lever

7 - bracket for control cable

Job 6-3

Step 3: Remove the securing clip and disconnect the kickdown cable (**1**) from the selector (**3**).

Step 4: Release the outer cable centring bush from its housing in the gearbox.

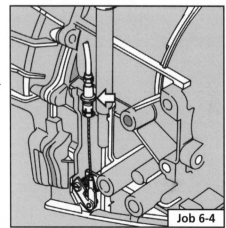

Job 6-4

105

ℹ Step 5: INSIDE INFORMATION! To do this, you will have to make a simple tool as shown here. There is no FIAT 'special tool' - each dealer has to make this one himself! Use the tool to push lightly upwards, so that the cable centring bush (*6-4* arrowed) comes out of its seat. **ℹ**

☐ **Step 6:** Fit the new cable in the reverse order. Use a new gasket when refitting the sump.

IMPORTANT NOTE: Readjust the cables if necessary. See *Jobs* **7** and **8**.

☐ **Step 7:** Refill the transmission with automatic transmission fluid. See *Chapter 3, Facts and Figures.*

Job 6-5

Φ 11 mm

300÷350 mm

Φ 13÷14 mm

Job 7. Kickdown cable (automatic transmission) - adjustment.

When carrying out *Steps 1* to *5*, refer to the illustrations in *Job 6*.

☐ **Step 1:** Make sure there is some slack in the cable.

☐ **Step 2:** With the accelerator fully depressed, check that the stop pawl (see illustration *Job 6-2, part 6*), part of the control cable (*6-2, part 7*), is at the end of its travel against the adjustment screw(*6-2, part 8*).

☐ **Step 3:** Make sure the kickdown cable can travel about 1 mm further by adjusting screw (see illustration *Job 6-2, part 8*) as necessary after releasing the locknut (*Job 6-2, part 9*).

☐ **Step 4:** With the accelerator pedal in the rest position, the stop pawl (see illustration *Job 6-2, part 6*), should be about 34 mm from the adjustment screw (*6-2, part 8*).

☐ **Step 5:** Check that the kickdown outer cable No. 13 has no sharp bends and that the inner cable No. slides freely inside it.

☐ **Step 6:** Retighten the locknut (see illustration *Job 6-2, part 9*)

Job 8. Automatic gear selector control cable - replacement.

☐ **Step 1:** Raise the car and support it securely on axle stands.

☐ **Step 2:** Manually select the 'P' (park) position, using the lever beneath the gearchange (see illustration *Job 6-3, part 6*).

☐ **Step 3:** Locate the lower end of the outer cable in the slot of the support bracket (see illustration *Job 6-3, 7*) and fit the end of the inner cable to the gear lever, (*Job 6-3, part 6*).

☐ **Step 4:** From inside the car, insert the other end of the outer cable in the slit in the bracket (see illustration *Job 6-3, 5*).

☐ **Step 5:** Put the gear lever inside the car (see illustration *Job 6-3, 2*) in the 'P' position, and holding the inner cable taut, check that the hole in the cable (*Job 6-3, part 3*) end aligns exactly with the selector pin. Adjust the selector cable (*Job 6-3, part 1*) until it does so, using the adjuster nut (*Job 6-3, part 4*).

> FACT FILE: CHECKING AUTO. TRANSMISSION SELECTION
>
> ● Now that you have completed the installation, and BEFORE USING THE VEHICLE ON THE ROAD, carry out the following checks:
>
> ● The engine should only start when you have selected either 'P' (park), or 'N' (neutral).
> ● The gear lever selector positions should agree with those indicated on the display panel.
> ● When 'R' (reverse) is selected, the reverse light should come on. With the ignition switched off, the buzzer should sound if any position other than 'P' (park) is selected.

Job 9. Drive shaft - removal and refitting.

IMPORTANT NOTE: For removal of the Turbo's drive-shaft, see also *PART A: ENGINE, Job 23, Step 25*.

☐ **Step 1:** Drain the transmission oil.

☐ **Step 2:** Ask a helper to apply the footbrake very firmly while you slacken the drive-shaft-to-hub nut, using a long bar for good leverage after opening out the staking on the nut, as far as possible. DON'T do so with the car off the ground because the very large force needed could pull it off its stands. Remove the nut after the car has been raised.

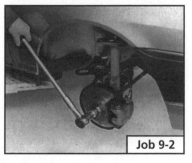

Job 9-2

☐ **Step 3:** Slacken the hub nuts on the side to be worked on. Jack up the front of the car and support on axle stands. Remove the roadwheel.

☐ **Step 4:** Unbolt the brake hose support clip from the suspension strut.

☐ **Step 5:** Disconnect the track rod end from the steering arm using a suitable splitter tool.

Job 9-5

Step 6: Remove the hub carrier securing bolts from the base of the front suspension strut and tap the carrier down and out of the clamp. Pull the top outwards.

Job 9-6

Step 7: Push or tap the drive-shaft splines (arrowed) out of the hub carrier, taking care not to damage the thread.

Job 9-7

Step 8: Support the drive-shaft while undoing the inboard flange bolts.

Job 9-8

Job 9-9

Step 9: Withdraw the shaft from the transmission.

Step 10: Refit in the reverse order, using a new drive-shaft nut tightened to the specified torque. See *Chapter 3, Facts and Figures*. Stake the nut into the drive shaft groove, as shown.

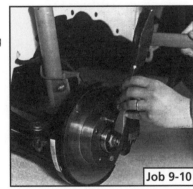
Job 9-10

Step 11: Refill the transmission with oil. See *Chapter 3, Facts and Figures.*

Job 10. Outer drive-shaft constant velocity joint - replacement

Step 1: You must first remove the drive-shaft. See *Job 9.*

Job 10-2

Job 10-3

Step 2: Remove the gaiter retaining clip...

Step 3: ...and pull the gaiter clear.

Step 4: Remove the circlip and pull the shaft from the CV joint.

Job 10-4

Step 5: Fit the new gaiter onto the shaft, followed by the new CV joint and circlip. Pack the joint with the grease supplied or with **FL Tutela MRM2** grease.

Step 6: Pull the gaiter over the joint and secure with the retaining band. The drive-shaft assembly is now ready for refitting.

Job 11. Inner 'c.v.' spider joint - replacement.

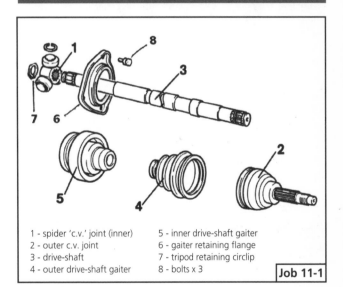

1 - spider 'c.v.' joint (inner) 5 - inner drive-shaft gaiter
2 - outer c.v. joint 6 - gaiter retaining flange
3 - drive-shaft 7 - tripod retaining circlip
4 - outer drive-shaft gaiter 8 - bolts x 3
Job 11-1

Step 1: Note the arrangement of the inner drive-shaft components.

Step 2: With the drive-shaft removed from the car (see **Job 9**), remove the circlip and pull the spider joint from the drive-shaft, or press the shaft out.

Job 11-2

Step 3: Remove the inner gaiter and retainer flange from the drive-shaft.

Step 4: After obtaining a new spider joint, if necessary, (available as a complete replacement item from your FIAT dealership), fit the new gaiter and its retainer to the shaft, followed by the spider joint and circlip. No lubrication is required prior to refitting the drive-shaft.

Job 12. Front hub/bearings - replacement

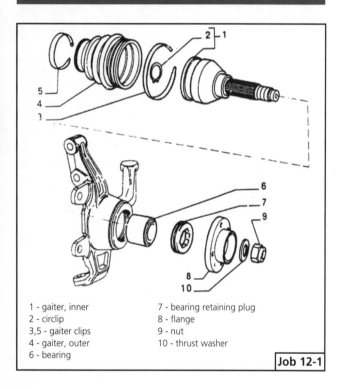

1 - gaiter, inner
2 - circlip
3,5 - gaiter clips
4 - gaiter, outer
6 - bearing
7 - bearing retaining plug
8 - flange
9 - nut
10 - thrust washer

Job 12-1

Step 1: Familiarise yourself with the front hub bearing components referred to here.

Step 2: Proceed as described in **Job 9, Steps 2 to 7**.

Step 3: Unbolt the brake caliper and tie it clear.

Step 4: Unbolt the brake disc and shield.

Step 5: Undo the track control arm balljoint nut and part the balljoint from the hub carrier using a suitable splitter tool. Remove the carrier.

Step 6: Grip the carrier in a vice and withdraw the hub, using a slide hammer. You may have to remove the bearing inner track from the hub if it comes out with it.

Step 7: Ease the staking on the bearing ring nut and unscrew from the hub carrier.

Step 8: Press out the old bearing.

Step 9: Clean the hub and press in the new bearing, putting pressure on the outer track only.

Step 10: Continue the assembly in the reverse order of dismantling and see **Chapter 3, Facts and Figures** for torque settings. Stake the nut - see **Job 9, Step 10**.

Job 13. Hydraulic clutch components

Very latest Unos used a hydraulic clutch in place of the cable arrangement used on the majority of cars. No adjustment is possible.

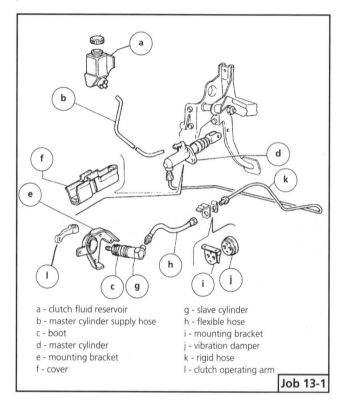

a - clutch fluid reservoir
b - master cylinder supply hose
c - boot
d - master cylinder
e - mounting bracket
f - cover
g - slave cylinder
h - flexible hose
i - mounting bracket
j - vibration damper
k - rigid hose
l - clutch operating arm

Job 13-1

Step 1: This is the layout of the hydraulic clutch components. Note that the master cylinder supply hose (**b**) is a low pressure hose. The method of disconnecting the rigid hose (**k**) and the flexible hose (**h**) is very similar to that for disconnecting the brake hoses in **PART H: BRAKES, Jobs 13** and **14**.

Removal of the master cylinder or slave cylinder, should replacement become necessary, can be easily discerned from the drawing shown here. Note that, if the clevis pin which holds the master cylinder to the pedal is worn, it should be replaced. The master cylinder bolts can be reached only after the cover (**f**) has been unclipped and removed. The slave cylinder is held to the gearbox casing by the bracket (**e**) and must first be disconnected from the clutch arm (**l**).

Step 2: These are the internal components of the clutch master and slave cylinders. Because the clutch components are not as safety critical as brake components, it is acceptable to extend their life by fitting new seals, when necessary. Note that you will need to use internal circlip pliers to remove the circlip from the pushrod on the master cylinder in order to dismantle it.

When you need to bleed the clutch hydraulic system, follow the procedure described for brake bleeding in **PART H: BRAKES, Job 15**. Because the circuit is far simpler, the procedure itself is likely to be both simpler and quicker to carry out. Note that the bleed screw (**f**) is normally covered by a cap (**e**) which must be removed before the bleed screw can be slackened.

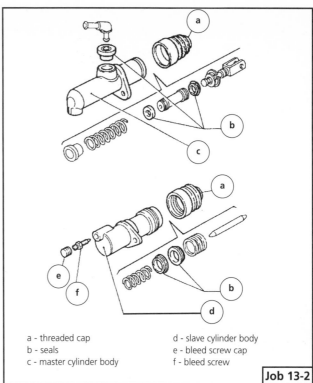

a - threaded cap
b - seals
c - master cylinder body
d - slave cylinder body
e - bleed screw cap
f - bleed screw

Job 13-2

PART C: COOLING SYSTEM

PART C: Contents

Job 1. Cooling fan and switch.
Job 2. Radiator - removal and refitting.

Job 3. Thermostat - replacement.
Job 4. Coolant pump - replacement.

Job 1. Cooling fan and switch

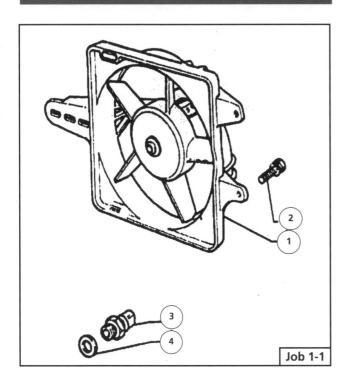

Job 1-1

Step 1: Undo the electrical connections from the thermostatic switch (**3**).

Step 2: Undo the mounting bolts (see illustration **Job 1-1, part 2**) and remove the complete assembly from the radiator.

Step 3: The thermostatic switch (see illustration **Job 1-1, part 3**) which controls the fan is located in the radiator header tank, except on non-FIRE OHC engines. See illustration **Job 4, Step 4B, part 11**.

Step 4: To remove, drain the cooling system, disconnect the switch and unscrew it from the radiator.

i **Step 5:** INSIDE INFORMATION: Test the switch using a test bulb and two leads. Connect one to a battery terminal and the other to one of the switch terminals. Now connect a wire between the remaining switch and battery terminal. *i*

Step 6: Lower the switch into water until the thread is just covered and the terminals remain dry.

Step 7: Heat the water slowly. The bulb should light just below boiling point (90 to 94 degrees Celsius) and go out when the temperature falls below 85 to 89 degrees Celsius.

Step 8: Refit with a new O-ring (see illustration **Job 1-1, part 4**) but do not over tighten.

Job 2. Radiator - removal and refitting

☐ **Step 1:** Drain the cooling system.

☐ **Step 2:** Disconnect the wires from the fan and the thermostatic switch. See *Job 1*.

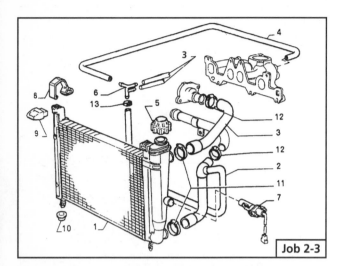

Job 2-3

☐ **Step 3:** Disconnect the top and bottom radiator hoses.

☐ **Step 4:** Undo the top securing clips. Remove the radiator and fan from the car.

☐ **Step 5:** Refit in the reverse order and fill the cooling system. See *Chapter 3, Facts and Figures* and *Chapter 5, Servicing Your Car*.

Job 3. Thermostat - replacement

IMPORTANT NOTE: For the location of the OHC 'FIRE' and non-FIRE thermostats, see illustration to *Job 4, Step 4A*. Both engine types' thermostats are in the same place on the block. The thermostat and housing are a complete unit and have to be replaced as one.

☐ **Step 1:** Drain the cooling system.

☐ **Step 2:** Disconnect the hoses from the thermostat housing, undo the

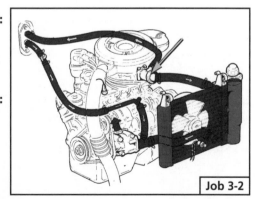

Job 3-2

nuts and remove the housing/thermostat assembly. This is the location of the OHV engine's thermostat (arrowed).

☐ **Step 3:** Clean the mating surfaces, fit the new unit and gasket.

☐ **Step 4:** Reconnect the hoses and refill the cooling system with the correct 50/50 **Paraflu** anti-freeze mixture, see *Chapter 5, Servicing Your Car*.

Job 4. Coolant pump - replacement

ℹ️ INSIDE INFORMATION! Pump types differ according to engine type, but the procedure for replacement is much the same. For the location of the OHV engine's water pump, see *Job 3, Step 2*. ℹ️

☐ **Step 1:** Raise the bonnet and remove the air cleaner.

☐ **Step 2:** Unplug the alternator leads, slacken the bolts and remove the drive belt. Remove the alternator.

☐ **Step 3:** Drain the cooling system.

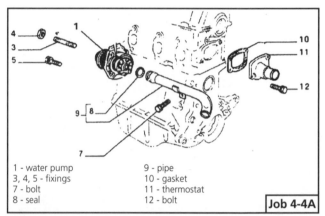

1 - water pump	9 - pipe
3, 4, 5 - fixings	10 - gasket
7 - bolt	11 - thermostat
8 - seal	12 - bolt

Job 4-4A

☐ **Step 4A:** Disconnect the hoses and the metal transfer pipe from the pump. This is the OHC FIRE engine's water pump.

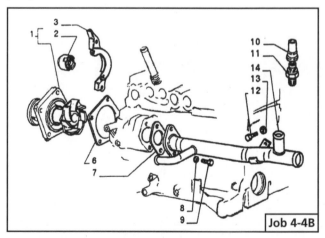

Job 4-4B

☐ **Step 4B:** Here is the location of the non-FIRE OHC engine's water pump (**1**). It bolts on to the end of the engine block. The coolant pipe bolts on to the rear of the water pump housing (**8** and **9**). It does not need to be removed when taking off the pump. Items **10** and **11** relate to the radiator fan thermostat. See *Job 3*.

☐ **Step 5:** Undo the four securing bolts and remove the coolant pump.

Step 6: Discard the old gasket and clean off the mating surfaces.

Step 7: Refit in reverse order using a new gasket.

Step 8: Adjust the drivebelt tension. See *Chapter 5, Servicing Your Car*.

Step 9: Fill the cooling system with the correct 50/50 **Paraflu** anti-freeze solution. See *Chapter 3, Facts and Figures.*

PART D: IGNITION SYSTEM

PART D: Contents

FACT FILE: FUEL INJECTION/ELECTRONIC IGNITION PRECAUTIONS

OBSERVE THE FOLLOWING PRECAUTIONS WHEN WORKING ON VEHICLES WITH FUEL INJECTION - ELECTRONIC IGNITION SYSTEMS:

● never start the engine when the electrical terminals are poorly connected or loose on the battery poles;

● never use a quick battery charger to start the engine;

● never disconnect the battery from the car circuit with the engine running;

● when charging the battery quickly, first disconnect the battery from the vehicle circuit;

● if the vehicle is placed in a drying oven after painting at a temperature of more than 80 degrees C, first remove the injection/ignition ECU;

● never connect or disconnect the ECU multiple connector with the ignition key in MARCIA position;

● always disconnect battery negative lead before carrying out electrical welding on vehicle.

Note that system contains one memory that is always active (stand-by memory) that stores learnt self-adaptive values. Because this data is lost when the battery is disconnected, this operation should be carried out as infrequently as possible.

Job 1. Ignition coil - replacement

See *Chapter 5, Servicing Your Car*, for more information about the ignition components.

Step 1A: NON-TURBO MODELS: Locate the coil, which is on the right-side inner wing on most early models, as shown, or near the battery on the opposite side

Job 1-1A

of the engine bay on most later models. This is an OHC engine with electronic ignition showing the Ignition Control

Unit (**a**); the distributor (**b**); and the coil (**c**). Disconnect the LT and HT leads from the coil, making a note of their exact terminal positions.

Step 1B: TURBO MODELS: On Turbo i.e. models detach the ignition amplifier multi-plug (the amplifier is attached to the coil bracket).

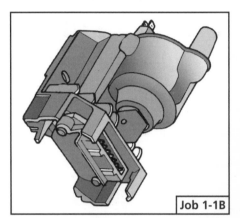

Job 1-1B

Step 2: Undo the coil mounting bolts/nuts and remove the coil.

Step 3: On models other than Turbo i.e., transfer the mounting bracket to the new coil and fit the assembly to the car in the reverse order.

Job 2. Distributor - removal and refitting

FACT FILE: DISTRIBUTOR TYPES

Step 1: Take note of the different types and locations of distributors.

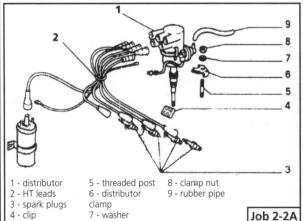

1 - distributor	5 - threaded post	8 - clamp nut
2 - HT leads	6 - distributor	9 - rubber pipe
3 - spark plugs	clamp	
4 - clip	7 - washer	

Job 2-2A

Step 2A: On the OHV engine the distributor is mounted vertically on the rear-side of the cylinder head (timing belt end).

FACT FILE:CONTINUED

☐ **Step 2B:**
On the majority of OHC non-FIRE engines and the 1.4 Turbo i.e., the distributor is at the front of the engine block at the timing belt end.

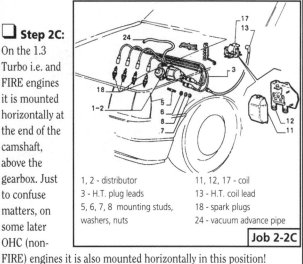

1 - distributor	6, 7, 8, 9 - clamp
2 - spark plugs	16 - clip
3 - H.T. plug leads	17 - H.T. coil lead
4 - clip	18 - coil - distributor
5 - vacuum advance pipe	

Job 2-2B

☐ **Step 2C:**
On the 1.3 Turbo i.e. and FIRE engines it is mounted horizontally at the end of the camshaft, above the gearbox. Just to confuse matters, on some later OHC (non-FIRE) engines it is also mounted horizontally in this position!

1, 2 - distributor	11, 12, 17 - coil
3 - H.T. plug leads	13 - H.T. coil lead
5, 6, 7, 8 mounting studs, washers, nuts	18 - spark plugs
	24 - vacuum advance pipe

Job 2-2C

☐ **Step 3:** Disconnect the battery earth lead, then turn the engine in a clockwise direction by use of the crankshaft pulley nut until the timing marks are in alignment. See *Chapter 5, Servicing Your Car, Job 27*.

☐ **Step 4:** Remove the distributor cap and check that the rotor arm contact is pointing at the number one segment inside the cap. If the rotor is pointing at number four, turn the engine another full turn and check that the rotor is now pointing at number one segment. On some horizontally mounted distributors there is a machined groove on the distributor body which is a cylinder No. 1 reference.

☐ **Step 5:** Mark the alignment of the rotor with the distributor body, and the alignment of the distributor base with the cylinder head or block, using typist's correction fluid or something similar.

☐ **Step 6:** Remove the distributor cap complete with leads, and disconnect the LT lead and vacuum pipe (where fitted).

☐ **Step 7A: OHV ENGINES AND SOME OHC ENGINES:** Undo the distributor clamp nut and remove the clamp (see illustration *Job 2-2A, part 6*).

☐ **Step 7B: FIRE AND SOME NON-FIRE OHC ENGINES (head-mounted, horizontal distributors):** Undo and remove the two or three distributor clamping nuts.

☐ **Step 8:** Remove the distributor from the cylinder head.

ℹ INSIDE INFORMATION: If the drive-shaft is displaced, just push it back - the timing won't be lost. ℹ

☐ **Step 9:** Refit by holding the distributor over its mounting hole with the mark on its base aligned with the one on the cylinder head or block, and the rotor aligned with the mark on the body.

☐ **Step 10:** Push the distributor home, turning the rotor very slightly if necessary, to engage the drive-shaft. Note that on cylinder head mounted distributors, the drive has an off-centre location and only fits one way.

ℹ INSIDE INFORMATION: On OHV models or OHC with the block-mounted distributor, you may have to start by slightly misaligning the rotor with its mark to compensate for the effect of its skew-gear drive turning it as it is pushed home. ℹ

☐ **Step 11:** Align the distributor with the mark on the cylinder head and refit the clamp plate and nut - or the two/three mounting nuts.

☐ **Step 12:** Reconnect the LT lead or multi-plug, distributor cap, HT leads, vacuum pipe (if fitted) and battery earth lead.

☐ **Step 13:** Start the engine and check the ignition timing. See *Chapter 5, Servicing Your Car, Job 27*.

Job 3. Electronic ignition

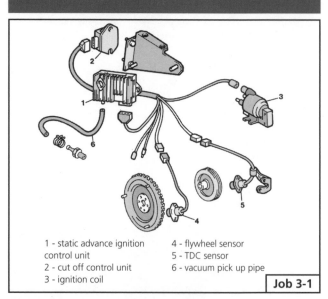

1 - static advance ignition control unit	4 - flywheel sensor
	5 - TDC sensor
2 - cut off control unit	6 - vacuum pick up pipe
3 - ignition coil	

Job 3-1

☐ **Point 1:** These are the electronic ignition components available as spares for the Uno ES 'Digiplex' electronic ignition system.

☐ **Point 2:** The electronic ignition can only be checked by using FIAT diagnostic equipment. Have the work carried out by your FIAT dealer.

PART E: ELECTRICAL AND INSTRUMENTS

PART E: Contents

See *FACT FILE: DISCONNECTING THE BATTERY* on *page 36*.

Job 1. System checks

Step 1: Decide whether you have enough knowledge or information to do this work yourself, or whether to consult it to your FIAT dealer or auto-electrician. You can waste money and cause further damage if you don't know what you're doing! PORTER MANUALS *Auto-Electrics Manual* explains everything in a simple-to-follow style.

Step 3: You should check the battery voltage only after it has been unused for at least two hours.

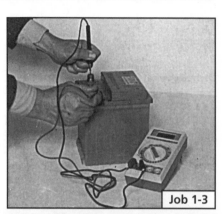

Job 1-3

Job 2. Alternator - removal and refitting

Refer to **Chapter 5, Servicing Your Car, Job 28** for information on alternator positions, access and belt tensioning.

Step 1: Disconnect the battery earth lead, then disconnect the plugs and/or individual leads (arrowed) from the back of the alternator (depending on type).

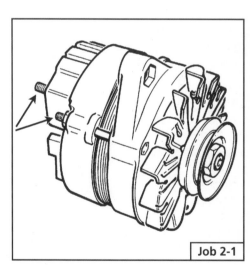

Job 2-1

Step 2: Slacken all alternator mounting nuts and bolts, including the adjuster bracket nut/bolt - if applicable - and push the alternator towards the engine to remove the drive belt.

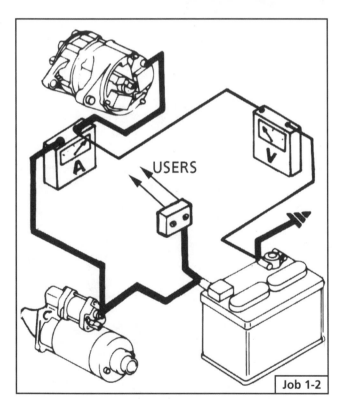

Job 1-2

Step 2: Before assuming that a flat battery is 'dead', have the charging system checked. This is the set-up for checking the maximum charge rate on Uno models with a built-in electronic regulator (the vast majority).

> *making it easy!* ● If any of the leads are capable of being removed the wrong way round, tag them as you remove them.

Step 3: Detach the air cooling hose from the rear of the alternator (fitted to later models only).

☐ Step 4:
Undo the mounting nuts/bolts and remove the alternator from its mountings. The mounting system for the Uno Diesel is shown here, and is a typical type of mounting.

Job 2-4

☐ Step 5: If the alternator has a cooling hose attachment, remove the cooling duct cover from the back of the alternator by releasing its fixing screws (arrowed). Note the position of the air outlet for refitting purposes.

Job 2-5

☐ Step 6: Refit in the reverse order and adjust the drive belt. See *Chapter 5, Servicing Your Car, Job 28*.

Job 3. Starter motor - removal and refitting

☐ Step 1: Disconnect the battery earth lead.

☐ Step 2A: MANUAL GEARBOX MODELS: Disconnect the cables from the rear of the starter motor solenoid (arrowed).

Job 3-2A

☐ Step 2B: AUTO. GEARBOX MODELS: This is the solenoid cable connection screw (arrowed) on the Hitachi starter motor fitted to Selecta models.

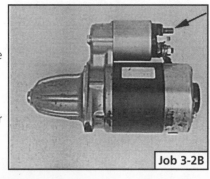

Job 3-2B

☐ Step 3:
Undo the mounting bolts and washers (**2, 3** and **4**) and remove the starter. On Turbo and 1.4 models the starter is withdrawn from below the car.

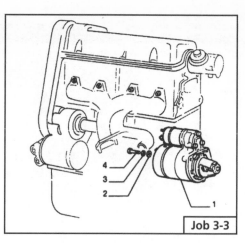

Job 3-3

☐ Step 4: Refit in the reverse order, ensuring that all electrical connections are clean and sound.

Job 4. Instrument panel - removal and refitting

☐ Step 1: Disconnect the battery earth lead.

☐ Step 2: It may help to first remove the steering wheel. Set the steering in the straight-ahead position. Lever out the centre insert (or unscrew the retaining screws from behind the steering wheel, if fitted). Remove the wheel retaining nut and pull the wheel from the column.

SAFETY FIRST!

● *As you bang it towards you with your hands to get it off the splines, take care not to bash yourself in the face! Leave the nut on the end of its thread and remove it once the wheel is loose on the splines.*

☐ Step 3: On early (pre-facelift) models, remove the instrument panel upper cover (**a**) by inserting your fingers at the sides and pulling the hood sharply upward off its retaining clips.

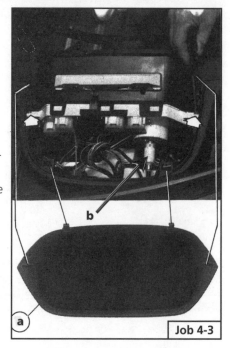

Job 4-3

Step 4: On early and later types, remove the two instrument panel fixing screws (arrowed). On later types pull the instrument panel forward. On early types pull the panel slightly towards you until you can

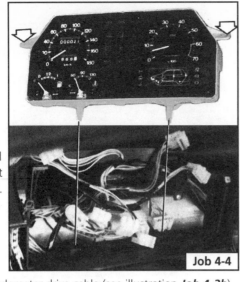

Job 4-4

undo the speedometer drive cable (see illustration **Job 4-3b**) by squeezing its plastic retaining ring.

i INSIDE INFORMATION: Turbo i.e. models with electronic digital instrumentation have no speedometer cable. On later Uno models it may be necessary to undo the facia lower trim panel (two screws and one nut) to gain access to the rear of the instrument panel from below. Some Turbo i.e. models have a rubber oil pressure pipe to the back of the panel, which also needs to be pulled free of the panel. *i*

Step 5: Take note of the electrical plug positions at the back of the panel, and disconnect the plugs. On later models this is done from below the dashboard. Also, on later models, the speedometer

Job 4-5

cable is disconnected by pulling its retaining ring sharply backwards.

Step 6: On early models remove the instrument panel upwards, so that its lower locating lugs (see **Step 4**) are freed.

Step 7: Refit in the reverse order, and reconnect the battery.

Job 5. Speedometer cable - replacement

i INSIDE INFORMATION: The following does not apply to Turbo i.e. models fitted with digital instrumentation. *i*

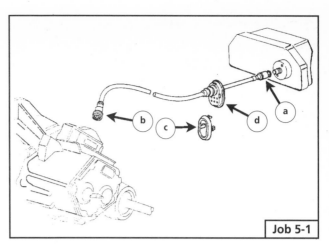

Job 5-1

Step 1: Disconnect the cable (**a**) from the instruments - see **Job 4.**

Step 2: At the gearbox end of the speedometer cable, undo the knurled nut (see illustration **Job 5-1, part b**) securing the cable to the gearbox.

Step 3: Remove the bulkhead grommet clip (see illustration **Job 5-1, part c**) and the grommet (**part d**) and withdraw with the cable.

Step 4: Refit in the reverse order.

Job 6. Windscreen wiper motor (early models) - replacement

Step 1: Disconnect the battery earth lead.

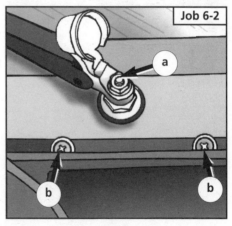

Job 6-2

Step 2: Remove the single wiper arm by lifting the cover, undoing its retaining nut (**a**) and carefully pulling it from the splined shaft.

Step 3: Undo the bezel nut holding the wiper arm drive shaft in place - visible with the wiper arm out of the way...

Step 4: ...then pull back the weather strip from above the motor and, with the bonnet open, undo the two mounting screws (see illustration **Job 6-2, part b**).

Step 5: Pull the motor and its cover out from under the scuttle and unplug the wires.

Step 6: Refit in the reverse order, making sure the wiper arm position is correct.

Job 7. Windscreen wiper motor (later models) - replacement

☐ **Step 1:** Disconnect the battery earth lead.

☐ **Step 2:** Remove the bonnet, see *PART I: BODY AND INTERIOR.*

☐ **Step 3:** Remove the wiper arm by undoing its retaining nut and pulling it from the splined drive shaft. See illustration *Job 6-2.*

☐ **Step 4:** Undo the air intake grille fixing screws and remove the washer reservoir filler cap (where applicable).

☐ **Step 5:** Withdraw the grille and disconnect the windscreen washer hose.

☐ **Step 6:** If necessary, remove the washer reservoir for access to the motor.

☐ **Step 7:** Undo the two motor mounting screws, withdraw the motor and detach its plastic cover.

☐ **Step 8:** Unplug the electrical connector and remove the motor.

☐ **Step 9:** Refit in the reverse order, making sure that the wiper arm position is correct.

Job 8. Tailgate wiper motor - replacement

☐ **Step 1:** Disconnect the battery earth lead.

☐ **Step 2:** Undo the nut securing the wiper arm to its shaft and remove the arm and blade.

☐ **Step 3:** From under the tailgate, unclip the wiper motor cover.

☐ **Step 4:** Undo the mounting screws (arrowed), unplug the wires (arrowed, inset) and remove the motor.

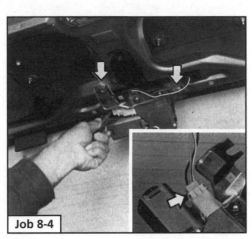

Job 8-4

☐ **Step 5:** Refit in the reverse order.

Job 9. Windscreen washer pump - replacement

FACT FILE: WINDSCREEN WASHER TYPES

☐ **Step 1:** Note that on early models the pumps for front and rear washers are moulded into the washer reservoir/'plastic bag' in the engine compartment (**a**). It is not possible to repair the pumps or detach them from the bag. If a pump fails, the complete reservoir/pump assembly requires replacement.

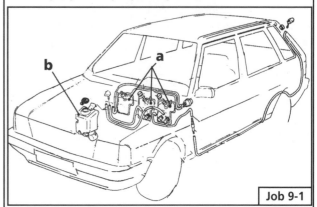

Job 9-1

● Similarly, on some later models with the bulkhead-mounted rigid square reservoir (**b**), only the reservoir/pump assembly can be renewed.

● Turbo and other later models have a rigid plastic reservoir mounted on the scuttle. On this arrangement the washer pump is a push-fit into the back of the reservoir.

● The following procedure relates to pump replacement on models with a replaceable pump.

☐ **Step 2:** Disconnect the battery earth lead, then follow steps *1 to 6 in Job 7.*

Job 9-3

Job 9-4

☐ **Step 3:** Drain the fluid from the washer reservoir.

☐ **Step 4:** Pull out the defective pump from the reservoir, check the condition of the pump seal, and push the replacement pump into the hole in the reservoir and clip into the reservoir body..

☐ **Step 5:** Refit in the reverse order.

Job 10. Radio aerial (pillar-mounted) - replacement

☐ **Note 1:** Aerials can be either roof-, windscreen pillar- or wing-mounted. If your Uno has an original pillar-mounted aerial, this is retained by two screws at the top and one at the bottom of the pillar.

ℹ️ **Note 2:** INSIDE INFORMATION: When replacing the aerial, to make cable-routing as easy as possible, unplug the old aerial cable from the radio and leave it in place. Cut the old cable where it joins the aerial. Use insulation tape to attach the new aerial cable's radio-end and use the old cable to pull it through the correct route. Plug the new cable into the radio. ℹ️

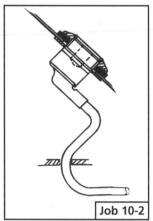

Job 10-2

Job 11. Headlight - replacement

☐ **Step 1:** Open the bonnet.

☐ **Step 2:** On early (pre-facelift) models undo the two securing screws (**a**) from the top of the bonnet closing panel. Pull the headlight forward and off its ball-stud (**b**).

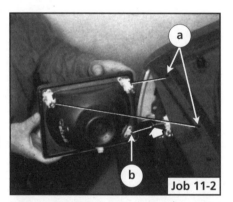

Job 11-2

☐ **Step 3:** On later models, working inside the engine bay, behind the headlight, undo the three nuts (arrowed) which secure the light unit to the body front panel.

Job 11-3

☐ **Step 4:** Disconnect the wiring multi-plug and pull the headlight forwards from its recess.

☐ **Step 5:** If you wish to remove the front indicator unit, unclip its multi-plug or the bulb holder from inside the engine bay.

☐ **Step 6A: EARLY MODEL:** Undo the two retaining screws from the front of the light

Job 11-6A

☐ **Step 6B(i): LATER MODELS:** Prise the unit's plastic retaining tag from inside the engine bay using a screwdriver...

Job 11-6B(i)

☐ **Step 6B(ii):** ...and remove the sidelight/indicator unit.

☐ **Step 7:** Refit components in the reverse order.

Job 11-6B(ii)

Job 12. Rear light cluster - replacement

See *Chapter 5, Servicing Your Car, Job 7* for further information.

☐ **Step 1:** Remove the two studs which secure the boot trim, and pull back the carpet for access.

☐ **Step 2:** Lift the retaining tab and detach the wiring plug.

☐ **Step 3:** From inside the load compartment, undo the three nuts securing the light unit to the body and remove the light unit.

☐ **Step 4:** Refit in the reverse order.

Job 13. Front fog lights - replacement

Step 1: Raise the front of the car and support it securely. See *Chapter 1, Safety First!*

Step 2: Reach under the bumper to unplug the wiring connector from each fog light and to undo the two retaining nuts.

Step 3: Withdraw each light from the front of the car, tilted downwards.

Step 4: Refit in the reverse order and check light alignment.

Job 14. Fuel gauge sender unit - replacement

IMPORTANT NOTE: Read *Chapter 1, Safety First!* before carrying out any work on the fuel system.

The fuel tank should be less than 3/4 full before carrying out this job.

IMPORTANT NOTE: Disconnect the battery before starting work.

Step 1: From within the boot, tilt the rear seat forward, lift the floor covering and raise the plastic panel in the floor to expose the unit.

Step 2: Disconnect the one or two (depending on type) fuel hoses and the electric wires from the sender unit (arrowed).

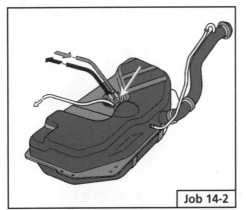

Job 14-2

Step 3: Undo the knurled securing ring and remove the unit.

Job 14-3

Step 4: Refit in the reverse order using a new sealing ring.

Job 15. Diesel glow plugs - check and replacement

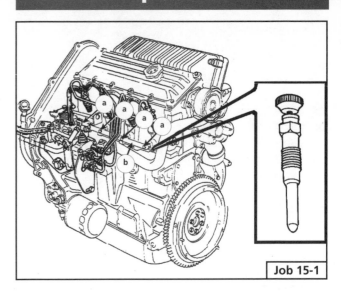

Job 15-1

Step 1: Disconnect the battery earth lead. Undo the retaining nut at each plug top (**a**), and remove the bridging strip (**b**) from between the glow plugs (complete glow plug - inset).

Step 2: With the wire or connecting strap removed, unscrew each plug from the cylinder head by just a couple of turns using a ring spanner or socket.

Step 3: Clean away dirt from around the plugs, then fully unscrew and remove them. It's a good idea to blank off the plug hole with cloth to prevent dirt from entering.

Step 4: Examine the condition of each plug by wiping soot away and examining for erosion of the element sheath.

Step 5: Check the internal resistance of each glow plug by connecting across a resistance meter. You are looking for a resistance of 5 ohms or less. If the reading is much higher than this, or is infinity, the plug must be renewed.

IMPORTANT NOTE: It is false economy to renew only one glow plug at a time - we recommend a complete set of new plugs if any one plug is in poor condition.

Step 6: Refit the glowplugs and tighten to their specified torque, see *Chapter 3, Facts and Figures.* Overtightening a glow plug can damage it!

Step 7: Refit the bridging strip and connect the supply lead.

Job 16. Electric window motors - replacement

IMPORTANT NOTE: See *PART I, BODY AND INTERIOR, Job 8* for door trim information, and *Job 9* for illustrations for this Job.

Step 1: With the relevant window fully closed, remove the door trim panel.

☐ **Step 2:** Disconnect the window motor electric plug.

☐ **Step 3A:** Have a helper support the window glass while you unbolt the complete window motor and regulator assembly from the door.

☐ **Step 3B: LATER (FACELIFTED) MODELS:**
The window glass is separated from the regulator mechanism by inserting circlip pliers into the holes in the plastic retainer (see *PART I, BODY AND INTERIOR. Job 9-4B*).

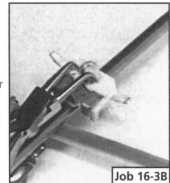
Job 16-3B

☐ **Step 4: ALL MODELS:** If necessary, disconnect the electrical connector (**1**), detach the drive cable (**3**) from the window motor (**2**) by removing the securing clip (**7**) from the cable outer sleeve and pulling it from the motor drive housing. Note the window mounting (**4**); the drive cable guide (**6**); the protective sleeve (**5**). For later type of regulator, see *page 151*.

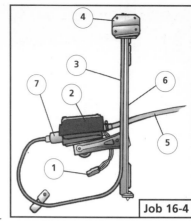
Job 16-4

☐ **Step 5:** Refit in the reverse order, ensuring that the top and bottom mounting bolts are adjusted to allow free sliding movement of the window glass.

PART F: FUEL AND EXHAUST SYSTEMS

PART F: Contents

FACT FILE: FUEL INJECTION/ELECTRONIC IGNITION PRECAUTIONS

OBSERVE THE FOLLOWING PRECAUTIONS WHEN WORKING ON PETROL-ENGINED VEHICLES WITH FUEL INJECTION - ELECTRONIC IGNITION SYSTEMS:

• never start the engine when the electrical terminals are poorly connected or loose on the battery poles;

• never use a quick battery charger to start the engine;

• never disconnect the battery from the car circuit with the engine running;

• when charging the battery quickly, first disconnect the battery from the vehicle circuit;

• if the vehicle is placed in a drying oven after painting at a temperature of more than 80 degrees Celsius, first remove the injection/ignition ECU;

• never connect or disconnect the ECU multiple connector with the ignition key in MARCIA position;

• always disconnect battery negative lead before carrying out electrical welding on vehicle.

Note that some systems contain one memory that is always active (stand-by memory) and that stores learnt self-adaptive values. Because this data is lost when the battery is disconnected, this operation should be carried out as infrequently as possible.

SAFETY FIRST!

• *The high pressure pipework on a fuel injection system can retain its pressure for days even after the engine has been switched off.*

• *When you disconnect the pipework, a jet of fuel can be emitted under very high pressure - strong enough to penetrate the skin or damage the eyes.*

• *NEVER work on the fuel pipework when the engine is running (except when bleeding Diesel injectors - see Job 18.*

• *ALWAYS place a rag over a union while it is being undone until all the pressure has been let out of the system.*

• *You are recommended to wear strong rubber gloves and goggles when disconnecting the fuel injection system's high pressure pipework. Always disconnect VERY slowly, letting pressure out progressively. See Job 8 for details of how to depressurise the system.*

• *Disconnect the battery negative earth before working on the fuel system.*

• *Work outdoors and away from sources of flame or ignition.*

• *ALWAYS wear rubber gloves - don't let your skin come into contact with fuel.*

Job 1. Fuel system types

It's a good idea to familiarise yourself with the type of fuel system fitted to your car. These are the main types.

1 - carburettor
2 - fuel supply pipe from the pump to the carburettor
3 - fuel supply pump
4 - fuel supply pipe from the tank to the pump
5 - fuel return pipe from the carburettor to the tank
6 - tank ventilation pipe
7 - fuel tank
8 - fuel filler
9 - fuel tank breather pipe

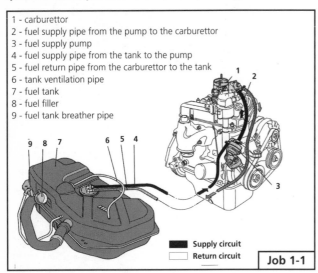

Supply circuit
Return circuit

Job 1-1

Type 1: This is the 903cc OHV engine's fuel system.

1 - fuel supply pipe from the pump to the carburettor
2 - carburettor
3 - fuel return pipe from the carburettor to the tank
4 - fuel supply pipe from the tank to the pump
5 - fuel filler
6 - fuel tank breather pipe
7 - fuel tank
8 - tank ventilation pipe
9 - fuel supply pipe

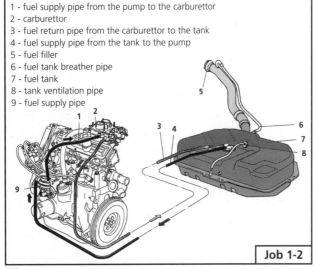

Job 1-2

Type 2: This is a typical non-FIRE OHC engine fuel systems - the 1116cc engine's, to be specific.

1 - fuel tank breather pipe
2 - fuel filler
3 - fuel tank
4 - immersed electric fuel pump
5 - fuel return pipe from injection unit to tank
6 - fuel supply pipe from tank to fuel filter
7 - fuel supply pipe from filter to injection unit
8 - fuel pressure regulator
9 - injector holder turret
10 - butterfly position sensor
11 - fuel filter

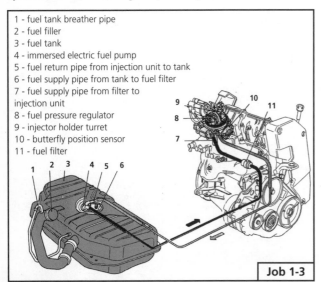

Job 1-3

Type 3: The larger non-FIRE OHC engine's fuel system, with its fuel pump in the tank.

1 - fuel tank breather pipe
2 - fuel filler
3 - tank ventilation pipe
4 - fuel tank
5 - secondary fuel filter
6 - electric fuel pump
7 - pipe supplying fuel to injectors
8 - injectors
9 - fuel recovery pipe between the injectors and the pressure regulator
10 - fuel supply pipe from the filter to the distribution pipe
11 - fuel pressure regulator
12 - main fuel filter
13 - fuel supply pipe
14 - fuel return pipe from the pressure regulator to the tank

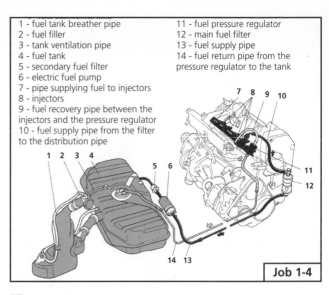

Job 1-4

Type 4: There was more complexity to the 1300 and 1372cc Turbo i.e. fuel system.

1 - fuel supply pipe
2 - fuel supply pipe from the pump to the carburettor
3 - carburettor
4 - fuel return pipe from the pump to the tank
5 - fuel supply pipe from the tank to the pump
6 - fuel tank
7 - fuel tank breather pipe
8 - fuel filler
9 - fuel tank ventilation pipe

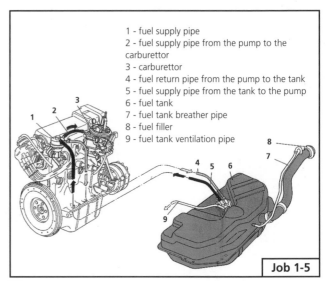

Job 1-5

Type 5: The FIRE 999cc and 1108cc engines used this fuel system.

1 - rotary injection pump
2 - fuel recover pipe from the injectors
3 - fuel supply pipe from the filter to the injection pump
4 - injectors
5 - external fuel filter with manual priming pump
6 - fuel supply pipe from the tank to the filter
7 - excess fuel return pipe from the fuel pump to the tank
8 - fuel tank
9 - fuel filler
10 - tank breather pipe
11 - tank ventilation pipe

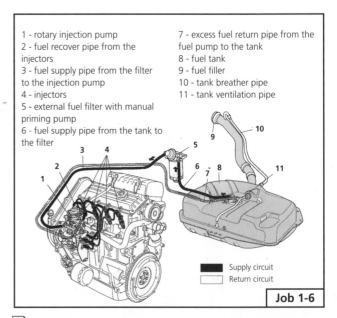

Supply circuit
Return circuit

Job 1-6

Type 6: The Diesel and Turbo Diesel fuel systems are very similar, although the Turbo Diesel was not sold in the UK.

Job 2. Carburettor
- removal and refitting

Step 1: Disconnect the battery earth lead, then remove the air cleaner. See *Chapter 5, Servicing Your Car.* Don't forget to check for hoses fitted to the underside of the air filter housing and for supplementary mounting brackets. Illustrated is an earlier type of air filter.

Job 2-1

Step 2: Disconnect coolant hoses from the carburettor body, and plug them.

Step 3: Disconnect the throttle and choke controls. See *Jobs 3* and *4*.

Step 4: Disconnect the fuel lines from the carburettor and plug the ends.

making it easy! ● *Ensure that fuel delivery and return fuel lines are identified for refitting in their correct positions.*

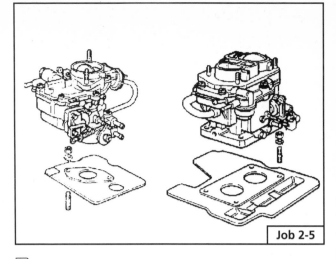

Job 2-5

Step 5: Unscrew the carburettor mounting nuts and remove the unit from the intake manifold (or on the cylinder head, on OHV engines).

Step 6: Clean the mating flanges, fit a new carburettor base gasket and refit/reconnect in the reverse order.

Step 7: Reconnect the battery earth lead.

Refer to illustrations in *Job 1* for typical layouts.

Job 3. Petrol injection unit
- removal and refitting

1 - current limiter resistor for injector
2 - coolant temperature sensor
3 - throttle valve angular position sensor
4 - injector
5 - intake air temperature sensor
6 - fuel filter
7 - fuel pressure regulator
8 - electric motor for regulating engine idle speed.
9 - Bosch SPI system diagnostic socket
10 - SPI system electronic control unit
11 - safety ventilation valve
12 - fuel filler fitting
13 - electric fuel pump
14 - fuel tank
15 - ignition switch
16 - SPI system relay
17 - electric fuel pump relay

18 - electronic rev counter*
19 - ignition coil
20 - ignition diagnostic socket
21 - Digiplex 2 electronic ignition ECU*
22 - battery
23 - catalytic converter
24 - point for checking CO upstream of catalytic converter
25 - Lambda probe
26 - HT distributor
27 - TDC and RPM sensor*
28 - spark plugs
29 - active carbon trap filter
30 - Bosch solenoid (normally open) for fuel vapour cut-off
31 - Elbi solenoid (normally closed)
32 - two-way vent valve

* 1372CC AND 1498CC ENGINES ONLY

Job 3-1A

FACT FILE: INJECTION SYSTEMS

Step 1A: First, identify your system! The single-point injection unit of non-Turbo models looks rather like a carburettor and is fitted on the inlet manifold. The following procedure relates to removal and refitting of this unit alone.

FACT FILE: INJECTION SYSTEMS (continued)

❑ **Step 1B:** The Bosch Jetronic multi-point injection system of Turbo i.e. engines is electronically controlled and comprises numerous components around the engine bay. Due to its complexity, we do not cover any system repair work in this manual, other than replacement of the electric fuel pump (see *Job 8*) and the fuel filter (see *Chapter 5, Servicing Your Car*). Removal of the inlet manifold of Turbo i.e. models is detailed in *Job 14*.

1 - electronic injection control unit
2 - diagnostic socket
3 - control relays
4 - battery
5 - injector cooling fan
6 - air flow meter (debimeter)
7 - water temperature sensor
8 - supplementary air valve
9 - injectors (n degree 4)
10 - fuel delivery manifold to injectors
11 - fuel pressure regulator
12 - fuel filter
13 - throttle case
14 - butterfly valve switch
15 - thermal switch for injector cooling fan activation.

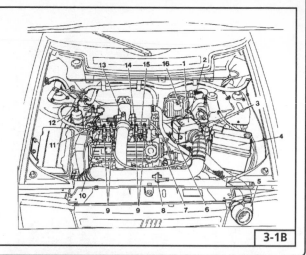

3-1B

❑ **Step 2:** Disconnect the battery earth lead. Depressurise the fuel system - see *Job 8*.

❑ **Step 3:** Remove the air cleaner assembly and the rubber sealing ring from around the top of the injection unit.

❑ **Step 4:** Disconnect all electrical connections from the injector unit, making a written note of their positions.

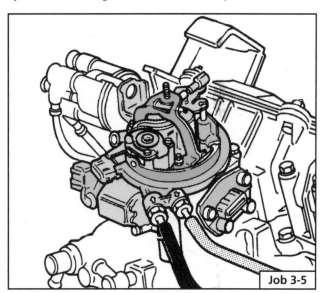

Job 3-5

❑ **Step 5:** Release the clips and disconnect the fuel supply and return hoses from the unit.

❑ **Step 6:** Disconnect the breather hose from the unit.

❑ **Step 7:** Release the clip securing the throttle link rod to the injection unit throttle lever, then detach the link rod from the lever.

❑ **Step 8:** Release the four Allen-type through-bolts in the top of the injection which retain it to the manifold, then lift the unit and its base gasket from the manifold.

❑ **Step 9:** Refit in the reverse order, making sure mating faces are clean and the base gasket is new.

❑ **Step 10:** Reconnect the battery earth lead.

Job 4. Accelerator cable, carburettor engines - replacement and adjustment.

FACT FILE: CARBURETTOR CONTROLS

There are several different systems in use:

❑ **Step 1A:** These are two of the most common throttle cable set-ups. One is adjusted by turning the plastic ball-

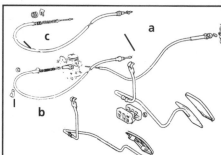

a - choke cable
b - throttle cable - ball and socket
c - throttle cable - clip and quadrant

Job 4-1A

joint at the end. The other (with a clip-in cable) is adjusted by removing the locating clip and adjusting the shroud - see *Job 5, Step 1B* for a similar system.

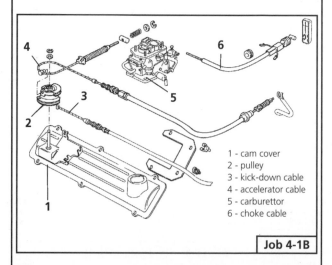

1 - cam cover
2 - pulley
3 - kick-down cable
4 - accelerator cable
5 - carburettor
6 - choke cable

Job 4-1B

❑ **Step 1B:** These are the threaded adjusters on the throttle cable set-up used on Selecta automatic models, with a second, kick-down cable. See *PART B: TRANSMISSION, Jobs 6 and 7* for adjustment of the kick-down cable and mechanism.

Step 2: Remove the air cleaner assembly.

Step 3A: BALL AND SOCKET TYPE: Pull the plastic socket (**a**) off the ball joint (**b**) on the carburettor.

Step 3B: CLIP-ON OR SCREW-ON TYPES: Slacken the adjuster and unscrew or unclip from the carburettor.

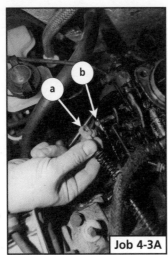

Job 4-3A

Step 4: BALL AND SOCKET TYPE: Unclip the sleeve (see illustration **Job 4-3A, part b**) from the steel bracket.

Step 5: From inside the car, unhook the cable nipple from the fork at the top of the pedal arm.

Step 6: Pull out the bulkhead grommet and release the cable.

> *making it easy!* ● *There are so many different types of cable that you are strongly advised to take the old one with you to check that the new one is exactly the same, when buying a replacement.*

Step 7: Refit in the reverse order - not forgetting the grommet!

Step 8: Check that, when the new cable is fitted:
● there is just the slightest amount of free-play in the cable with the throttle closed.
● the carburettor lever is back against its stop with the throttle fully open.

Job 5. Accelerator cable, petrol injection and diesel engines - replacement and adjustment.

FACT FILE: FUEL INJECTION CONTROLS

Fuel-injected petrol engines may have a combination of rigid link and throttle cable, or two throttle cables. Some have a ball jointed end and threaded adjuster. Others have adjuster nuts at the end of the cable outer.

Step 1A:
If the cable end does not have a ball-joint, cable adjustment is carried out at the cable outer sleeve abutment bracket after any locknuts have been slackened (arrowed) This specific system is the one fitted to the Turbo i.e. but is typical of the cable-and-quadrant type.

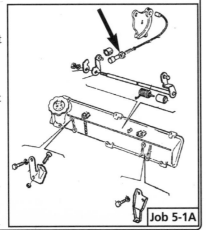

Job 5-1A

FACT FILE: FUEL INJECTION CONTROL (continued)

Step 1B:
This is a later Single Point Injection system but the principles of all are similar. The cable (**1**) should be neither too taut nor too loose with the throttle released.

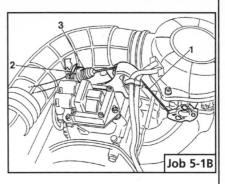

Job 5-1B

When the throttle pedal is fully pressed down, the throttle valve in the SPI body should be fully open. On this system, you release the locking tab (**2**) and slide the sheath (**3**) until the cable adjustment is right. Finally, refit the tab on the grooves on the end of the sheath.

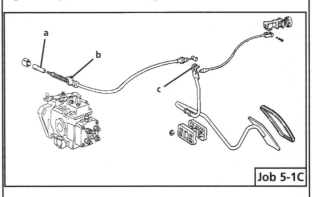

Job 5-1C

Step 1C: The following procedure refers to this, the ball-stud-ended cable fitted to most models, including the diesel.

IMPORTANT NOTE: It is not possible to adjust the engine idle speed on non-Turbo petrol engines - they are self-setting. If the idle speed needs adjustment, there is a fault - see your FIAT dealer.

Step 2: Prise the cable end socket from the carburettor/diesel injection pump or throttle relay lever ball stud. (See **illustration Job 1C, part a.**)

Step 3: Remove the cable outer sleeve from its abutment bracket. It is secured either by a clip or a locknut. (See illustration **Job 1C, part b.**)

Step 4: Working from inside the car, free the cable from the fork at the top of the accelerator pedal arm. (See illustration **Job 1C, part c.**)

Step 5: Draw the cable through the bulkhead.

Step 6: Refitting is the reverse of removal, but you should adjust the cable by slackening the end-socket locknut, turning the socket to achieve correct adjustment, and locking the nut again. Adjustment is correct when, with the pedal fully depressed, the throttle is fully open, yet there is free play in the cable when the throttle is shut. In the case of the non-Turbo single-point injection system, check the throttle linkage adjustment as detailed in **Step 7.**

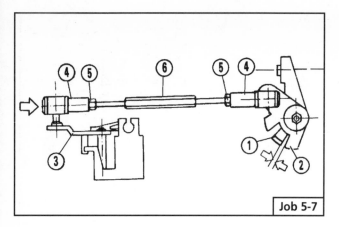

Job 5-7

☐ **Step 7: NON-TURBO, BOSCH SINGLE-POINT INJECTION ONLY:** Check that the throttle linkage adjustment:

• With the engine at normal operating temperature (cooling fan having cut in) check that the lever (**3**) is at rest against its stop.
• Now check that the throttle cable is neither taut nor very slack, so that there is no free play in the accelerator pedal.
• If adjustment is required in either case, slacken the locknut at the end of the throttle cable outer sleeve and turn the cable adjuster nut to correct.
• Under accelerator pedal depression the throttle valve lever (**2**) must complete a stroke of between 0.2 and 0.5 mm before starting to open the throttle valve (fixed to lever **1**). Check this with a feeler gauge. If outside these limits, adjust by slackening link-rod locknuts (**5**) and turning the centre section (**6**) of the rod to lengthen or shorten the rod as required.
• Finally, recheck the clearance between (**2**) and (**1**).

Job 6. Carburettor choke cable - replacement and adjustment

Refer to the illustrations in **Jobs 4** or **5**.

☐ **Step 1:** Remove the air cleaner and release the inner and outer cables from the carburettor screw-nipple and abutment clamp respectively.

☐ **Step 2:** From inside the car, pull the choke control lever fully out and undo its top hinge screw.

☐ **Step 3:** Pull the choke cable assembly back far enough to unplug the warning light lead and release the inner cable from the lever.

☐ **Step 4:** Pull the cable through the bulkhead.

☐ **Step 5:** Fit the new cable in reverse order and adjust the inner cable so that the lever is pulled out 2 to 3 mm before securing at the carburettor end.

Job 7. Mechanical fuel pump - replacement.

PRE-'92, NON-TURBO PETROL MODELS ONLY

FACT FILE: FUEL PUMP LOCATION

• If a mechanical fuel pump is fitted to your vehicle, it will be located on the side of the timing cover (OHV), on the front of the cylinder block adjacent to the distributor (non-FIRE OHC) or on the cylinder head adjacent to the distributor (FIRE OHC engine).
• The method of replacement is the same in all cases.
For the location and replacement of electric fuel pumps, see **Job 8**.

☐ **Step 1:** Disconnect the battery earth lead.

☐ **Step 2:** Disconnect both fuel hoses from the pump and plug the end of the inlet hose.

☐ **Step 3:** Undo the two securing nuts and remove pump, pushrod (arrowed), spacer and gaskets.

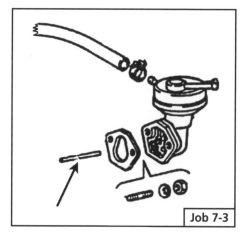

Job 7-3

☐ **Step 4:** Refit in the reverse order, using new gaskets. The inner gasket should always be 0.3 mm thick. The outer one is available in 0.3, 0.7 and 1.2 mm thicknesses from your FIAT dealer, allowing for fuel pressure adjustment. Pressure is higher with a thin gasket and lower with a thick one, and the correct pressure is 0.176 bar.

making it easy • If you have a micrometer or a good vernier caliper, clean the old gaskets, measure their thickness, and fit new gaskets of the same thickness. Alternatively, on OHV engines, check that when the pushrod is fully retracted, it projects between 1.0 mm and 1.5 mm beyond the spacer block outer gasket.

☐ **Step 5:** Reconnect the battery earth lead.

IMPORTANT NOTE: Some cars may have a pump with a lever, not a pushrod. In this case, **Step 4** becomes irrelevant.

Job 8. Electric fuel pump - replacement.

IMPORTANT NOTE: Read **Chapter 1, Safety First!** before carrying out any work on the fuel system.

FACT FILE: FUEL PUMP LOCATION

● First, locate your fuel pump!

● Turbo i.e. models have the pump (**1**) mounted under the car in front of the fuel tank. Behind it is the pre-pump fuel filter (**2**). Renew when replacing it.

● On all other models the pump (**1**) is integrated with the fuel sender unit (**2**) inside the fuel tank. Parts **3** and **4** are fuel return and supply pipes respectively.

● For vehicles fitted with a mechanical fuel pump, see **Job 7**.

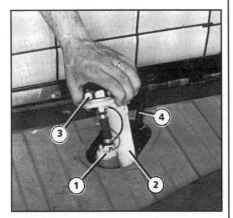

SAFETY FIRST!

● **FUEL INJECTED PETROL MODELS ONLY:**
Depressurise the fuel system before starting work - this is important because fuel remains under pressure in the system long after the engine has been switched off. Depressurisation is achieved by removing the fuel pump relay then running the engine until it dies. The relay is mounted on the near-side suspension turret and may be under a removable cover.

☐ **Step 1: ALL VEHICLES:** Switch off the ignition and disconnect the battery leads, starting with the earth lead.

PART A: NON-TURBO MODELS ONLY

☐ **Step A1:** Tilt the rear seat cushions forward, lift the luggage area cover and raise the fuel tank access cover to expose the pump/sender unit top.

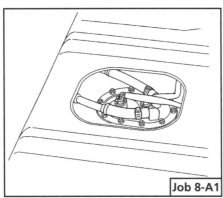
Job 8-A1

☐ **Step A2:** Disconnect the wires from the pump and sender unit.

☐ **Step A3:** Detach the fuel supply and return hoses from the pump, noting their position for correct refitting later.

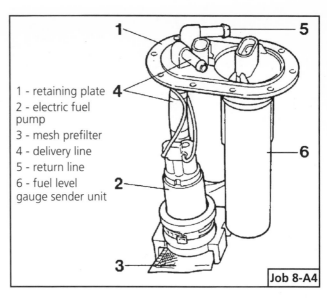

1 - retaining plate
2 - electric fuel pump
3 - mesh prefilter
4 - delivery line
5 - return line
6 - fuel level gauge sender unit

Job 8-A4

☐ **Step A4:** Undo the fixing nuts and remove the sender/pump assembly.

☐ **Step A5:** Refit in the reverse order using a new unit gasket and making sure that all connections are good and secure.

☐ **Step A6:** Reconnect the battery leads and refit the fuel pump relay.

PART B: TURBO I.E. MODELS ONLY

☐ **Step B1:** Raise the rear of the car and support on axle stands. See **Chapter 1, Safety First**.

☐ **Step B2:** If a protective shield is fitted over the fuel pump (**1**) under the car, detach it. (Item **2** is the pre-pump fuel filter.)

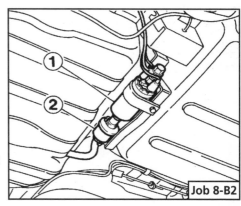
Job 8-B2

☐ **Step B3:** Disconnect the electrical wires from the fuel pump terminals, noting their positions.

☐ **Step B4:** Disconnect the inlet and outlet fuel hoses from the pump, undo the pump retaining clamp, and remove the pump.

☐ **Step B5:** Fit the new pump and any other components in the reverse order of removal, and make sure that all connections are secure.

☐ **Step B6:** Reconnect the battery earth lead and refit the fuel pump relay.

Job 9. Fuel tank - removal and refitting.

SAFETY FIRST!

● *We recommend that you carry out all of this work out of doors.*

IMPORTANT NOTE: Read **Chapter 1, Safety First!** before carrying out this work!

making it easy !   ● Plan ahead! Before starting this work, run the car's fuel level as low as possible.

☐ **Step 1:** Disconnect the battery leads starting with the earth lead.

☐ **Step 2:** Syphon any remaining fuel from the tank and into a suitable closed container.

☐ **Step 3:** Disconnect the fuel sender wiring and any fuel hoses from within the boot (model-dependent - see **PART E: ELECTRICAL AND INSTRUMENTS, Job 14**).

☐ **Step 4:** Disconnect the filler and breather hoses from the tank, working from underneath the car.

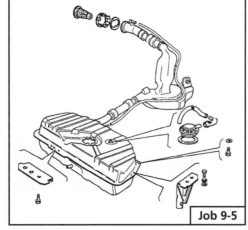

☐ **Step 5:** On Turbo i.e. models disconnect the fuel hose from the front of the tank.

Job 9-5

☐ **Step 6:** Free the handbrake cable from its bracket at the side of the tank.

☐ **Step 7A: STEEL FUEL TANKS:** Using a trolley jack to support the tank (fitted with a wooden plank across its lifting pad to prevent damage) undo the peripheral mounting brackets on vehicles with a steel fuel tank.

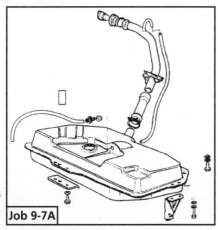

Job 9-7A

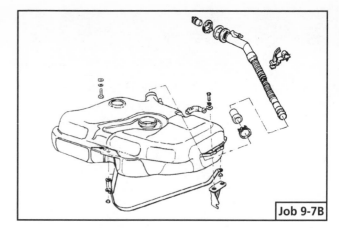

Job 9-7B

☐ **Step 7B: PLASTIC FUEL TANKS:** Undo the strap securing bolts on vehicles fitted with a plastic tank.

☐ **Step 8:** Lower the tank enough to check whether any hoses remain attached, then lower it fully to the ground.

☐ **Step 9:** Refit in the reverse order, making sure all connections are sound. Reconnect the battery leads.

Job 10. Hot air hoses/ thermo-valves - general.

ℹ INSIDE INFORMATION: The good operation of the thermostatic valve in the air cleaner of carburettor petrol models (usually where the heated air pipe from the manifold enters) relies on air hoses that are in good condition. Replace any that are doubtful before suspecting the valve to be faulty. These valves usually give little trouble and usually only suffer from sticking, caused by dirt. ℹ

Job 11. Lambda sensor (i.e. engines) - replacement.

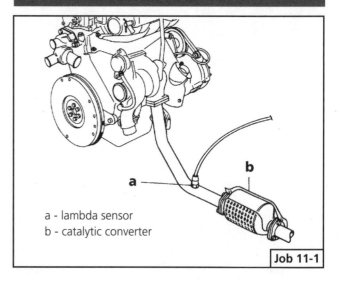

a - lambda sensor
b - catalytic converter

Job 11-1

☐ **Step 1:** Raise the front of the car and support on axle stands. See **Chapter 1, Safety First!** You will find the Lambda sensor screwed either into the exhaust manifold or into the exhaust front downpipe - depending on exact Uno model.

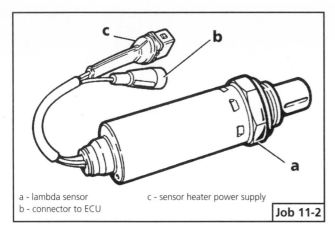

a - lambda sensor   c - sensor heater power supply
b - connector to ECU

Job 11-2

☐ **Step 2:** Trace the wiring back from the sensor and release it from any securing clips until you reach the main loom and then disconnect it.

FACT FILE:

● The Lambda sensor is very fragile and should not be knocked or dropped.

● We recommend that a new one is fitted only by your FIAT dealer, who can test the old one to see whether it is working properly.

● No cleaners should be used on the sensor.

☐ **Step 3:** Before refitting, check that the sensor sealing ring is in good condition, and lubricate the thread of the sensor with a high-temperature anti-seize compound.

Job 12. Fuel evaporation system.

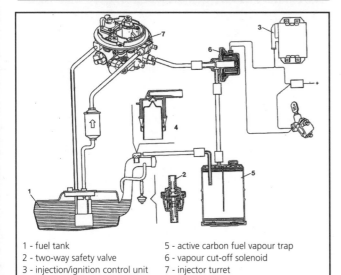

1 - fuel tank
2 - two-way safety valve
3 - injection/ignition control unit
4 - float valve
5 - active carbon fuel vapour trap
6 - vapour cut-off solenoid
7 - injector turret

Job 12-1

☐ **Point 1:** A complex control system exists on later models to prevent evaporative losses of fuel vapour to the atmosphere, and to control fuel tank pressure under different temperature conditions.

☐ **Point 2:** The system comprises a charcoal canister which absorbs fuel vapour from the fuel tank, mostly while the vehicle is standing, then re-injects them when the engine is running. The valves which regulate the system are controlled by the engine's electronic control unit.

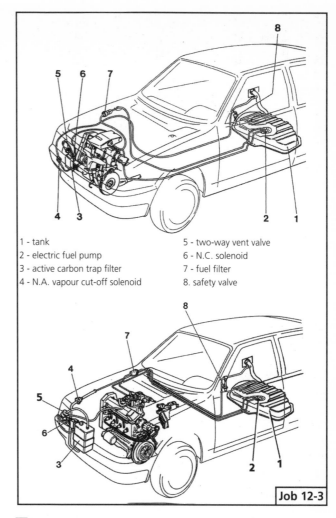

1 - tank
2 - electric fuel pump
3 - active carbon trap filter
4 - N.A. vapour cut-off solenoid
5 - two-way vent valve
6 - N.C. solenoid
7 - fuel filter
8. safety valve

Job 12-3

☐ **Point 3:** Other than occasional replacement of the charcoal canister, no system maintenance is needed. However, a fault with the system can lead to running problems, and diagnosis and rectification must be left to a FIAT dealer. For reference, the top illustration shows component and fuel-line positions on FIRE-engine cars; the lower illustration covers non-FIRE OHC engine cars fitted with this system.

Job 13. Exhaust system - replacement.

ℹ INSIDE INFORMATION: ● The exhaust manifold is mounted on the side of the cylinder head and may have ducting attached to it which supplies hot air to the carburettor at low temperatures.

● It is secured by studs, nuts and washers. When refitting it, always use a new gasket and tighten all retaining nuts evenly.

● The catalytic converter of later petrol models is replaced just as any other section of the exhaust system, if it is damaged or becomes ineffective. **ℹ**

☐ **Step 1:** Raise the front of the car and support on axle stands. See **Chapter 1, Safety First!**

☐ **Step 2:** Disconnect the exhaust downpipe from the manifold (or turbocharger). Some models have a spring link between the manifold and exhaust pipe, which should first be detached.

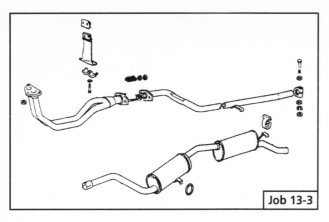

Job 13-3

☐ **Step 3:** Release the flexible exhaust mountings from the entire length of the system. Some models, such as this one, have a ball-type coupling between the front pipe and the following section, secured by spring-loaded bolts. This coupling makes it easier to remove the exhaust system leaving the downpipe in position.

Illustration *Job 11-1* shows a later system with a catalytic converter in the front pipe, and a Lambda sensor. See *Job 11* for Lambda sensor precautions.

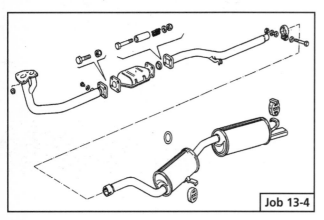

Job 13-4

☐ **Step 4:** If you are not replacing the whole system, unclamp the section to be replaced. Other systems, such as the Turbo i.e. shown here, use flanges and clamp bolts.

making it easy / • *Use penetrating oil and tap with a hammer to help part the sections.*
• *Apply several doses of penetrating oil over a couple of days for best results.*

☐ **Step 5:** Refit by loosely assembly the complete system and attaching it to its rubber hangers and the manifold/turbo/downpipe. Align the system, ensuring sufficient clearance along its length, then tighten all the clamps and manifold/turbo/downpipe nuts.

making it easy / • *When reconnecting the system, use a heatproof exhaust joint sealer.*
• *This both seals joints and makes it easier to part them again later.*

☐ **Step 6:** Lower the car to the ground, run the engine and check for exhaust leaks.

Job 14. Turbocharger - replacement.

PART A: 1.3 TURBO I.E. ONLY

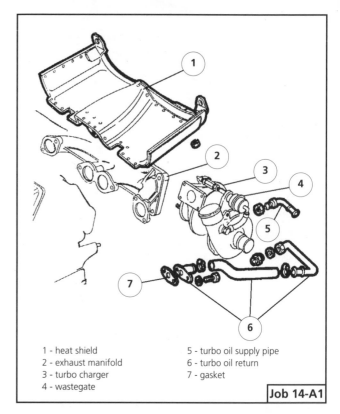

1 - heat shield
2 - exhaust manifold
3 - turbo charger
4 - wastegate
5 - turbo oil supply pipe
6 - turbo oil return
7 - gasket

Job 14-A1

☐ **Step A1:** Disconnect and remove the fuel injection system airflow meter.

☐ **Step A2:** Detach the wound hose from the duct which cools the fuel injectors.

☐ **Step A3:** Detach the turbocharger air hoses from the turbocharger.

☐ **Step A4:** Unbolt and remove the inlet manifold assembly.

• Next you must detach the intake ducting from the throttle body, disconnect the throttle cable and all electrical wiring and air/vacuum pipes to the manifold/throttle housing/air chamber assembly.
• Detach the two wiring harness brackets from the manifold/air chamber assembly, the throttle housing support bracket.
• Disconnect the fuel supply pipe to the injectors, remove the cooling duct for the injectors, the fuel pressure regulator and the injector cable shield.
• Remove the fuel rail and injectors, and the alternator heat shield.
• Remove the exhaust heat shield, noting that two inlet manifold securing nuts are only accessible once the heat shield has been removed.

☐ **Step A5:** Remove the heat shield from the alternator.

☐ **Step A6:** Detach the exhaust pipe heat shield.

Step A7: Unscrew the nuts connecting the exhaust downpipe to the turbocharger unit.

Step A8: Disconnect the oil supply pipe union at the turbocharger, and the oil return hose.

Step A9: Drain the cooling system - see *Chapter 5, Servicing Your Car* - then detach the coolant supply union at the turbocharger, using an open-ended spanner.

Step A10: Detach the bracket which supports the exhaust manifold (from beneath the car).

Step A11: Undo the exhaust manifold bolts, then withdraw the manifold from the engine, complete with the turbocharger unit.

Step A12: Refit all components in the reverse order of removal, using new gaskets.

PART B: 1.4 TURBO I.E. ONLY

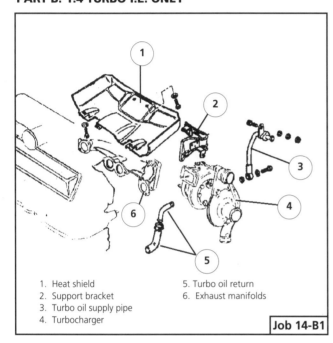

1. Heat shield
2. Support bracket
3. Turbo oil supply pipe
4. Turbocharger
5. Turbo oil return
6. Exhaust manifolds

Job 14-B1

Step B1: Raise the front of the car and support on axle stands. See *Chapter 1, Safety First!* Disconnect the battery earth lead.

Step B2: Unbolt and remove the inlet manifold.

● Next you must detach the intake ducting from the throttle body, disconnect the throttle cable and all electrical wiring and air/vacuum pipes to the manifold/throttle housing/air chamber assembly.
● Disconnect the fuel supply pipe to the injectors, remove the cooling duct for the injectors, the fuel pressure regulator and the injector cable shield.
● Finally, remove the exhaust heat shield and disconnect the inlet manifold support bracket (at the front of the manifold, securing it to the cylinder head).

Step B3: Working underneath the car, disconnect the exhaust downpipe.

Step B4: Undo the turbocharger mounting bracket securing bolts from the engine block.

Step B5: Drain the cooling system - see *Chapter 5, Servicing Your Car* - then detach the coolant supply and return pipes from the turbocharger.

Step B6: Disconnect the oil supply pipe banjo union from the turbocharger.

Step B7: Disconnect the air intake hose from the turbocharger.

Step B8: From underneath the car, detach the large pipe which connects the turbocharger to the intercooler.

Step B9: Disconnect the oil return pipe running from the turbocharger to the sump pan.

Step B10: Undo the upper bolts securing the turbocharger support bracket.

Step B11: Now undo the bolts securing the coolant pipe to the water pump, and remove the pipe.

Step B12: Lift the turbocharger and inlet manifold upward off the engine.

Step B13: Refit all components in the reverse order of removal, using new gaskets.

Job 15. Turbo i.e. intercooler - removal and refitting.

Step 1: Raise the front of the car and support on axle stands - see *Chapter 1, Safety First!*

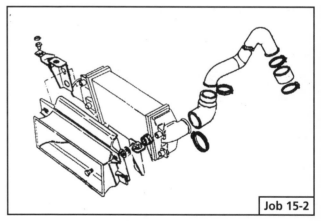

Job 15-2

Step 2: Working under the near-side of the front valance, undo the large worm-drive clips securing the air intake and outlet ducts to the intercooler.

Step 3: Remove the intercooler mounting bolts and withdraw the intercooler from the car.

Step 4: If necessary, separate the intercooler from its air intake mouth by undoing the four mouth securing bolts.

Step 5: Install in the reverse order.

Job 16. Diesel injection pump - removal and refitting.

IMPORTANT NOTE: This job involves removal and refitting of the timing belt, and requires specialised FIAT tooling. For these reasons it is best left to a FIAT dealer or diesel specialist.

☐ **Step 1:** Disconnect the battery earth lead.

☐ **Step 2:** Remove the timing belt. See *PART A: ENGINE, Job 31.*

☐ **Step 3:** Undo and remove the injection pump drive sprocket securing nut (**a**).

Job 16-3

☐ **Step 4:** Withdraw the sprocket from the pump drive-shaft using FIAT extractor tool No. 1842128000 (*Step 3*).

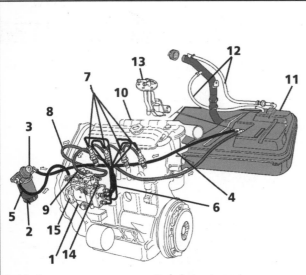

1 - injection pump
2 - fuel filter
3 - primer
4 - fuel supply to filter
5 - fuel supply to pump
6 - injector pipes
7 - injectors
8 - fuel return to tank
9 - fuel return to pump
10 - air chamber/intake manifold
11 - fuel tank
12 - tank breather
13 - tank sender
14 - shut-off solenoid
15 - pump timing marks

Job 16-5

☐ **Step 5:** Use a split-ring spanner to undo the injector pipes (**6**) from the back of the pump, slackening them progressively to release any residual fuel pressure.

☐ **Step 6:** Disconnect the pump shut-off solenoid (see illustration *Job 16-5, part 14*), wire, fuel delivery and return pipes, throttle cable (and fast idle cable, if fitted).

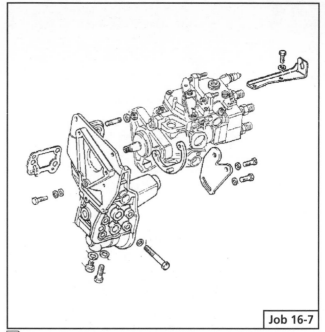

Job 16-7

☐ **Step 7:** Mark the relationship of the pump drive flange to its mounting on the engine (see illustration *Job 16-5, part 15*). Remove the nuts securing the pump flange, then undo the pump rear mounting bracket nuts and lift off the pump.

☐ **Step 8:** Refit the pump, but only loosely nip up its flange nuts.

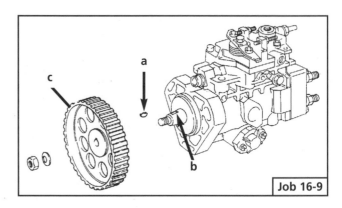

Job 16-9

☐ **Step 9:** Ensure that the pump drive-shaft Woodruff key (**a**) is in place (**b**) then refit the pump drive sprocket (**c**). Align the sprocket edge reference mark with the one on the mounting backplate (at approx. '12 o'clock').

☐ **Step 10:** Tighten the sprocket centre nut to 49 Nm, then fit FIAT tool No. 1842128000 to the sprocket, tightening its bolt to lock the sprocket (see *Step 3*).

☐ **Step 11:** Refit the timing belt, ensuring correct alignment of the crankshaft and camshaft sprockets (see *PART A: ENGINE, Job 31*).

☐ **Step 12:** Refit/reconnect the remaining components in reverse order, then adjust the injection timing, bleed the fuel system, and, if a new pump is fitted, adjust the idle speed (see *Chapter 5, Servicing Your Car, Job 38*). Tighten the pump mounting nuts after adjusting the timing.

☐ **Step 13:** Reconnect the battery earth lead.

Job 17. Diesel injectors - remove and refit.

Step 1: Clean thoroughly around each injector to prevent dirt from entering the cylinders when removing the injectors.

Step 2: Unscrew the fuel pipe union at the injector, using a flare nut wrench (split ring spanner).

Step 3: Loosen the union at the injection-pump-end of each injector pipe. Disconnect the fuel-return unions at the injector and move the return pipes away.

Step 4: Unscrew the injector using a deep 27 mm A/F socket, or, preferably, a proper injector socket (arrowed). Collect the injector and its base washer. All seals should be renewed every time the injector is removed.

Job 17-4

Step 5: Thoroughly clean the injector bore before refitting, as dirt here can cause cylinder leakage. So can the re-use of a sealing washer, so always renew them.

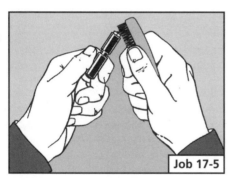
Job 17-5

Job 17-6

Step 6: Injector efficiency and spray pattern can only be checked by your FIAT dealer, or a Diesel or injection specialist with test equipment. An inexpensive check, while the injectors are out.

Step 7: Refit the injector, tightening it to the specified tightening torque. See **Chapter 3, Facts and Figures**.

Step 8: Reconnect all parts in the reverse order. Run the engine at a fast idle initially to clear air from the high pressure side of the fuel system.

Job 18. Bleeding diesel fuel system.

PART A: BLEEDING AIR FROM THE SYSTEM

If the engine stalls because of lack of fuel or if fuel low pressure lines have been disconnected or fuel filter has been changed, bleed the system as follows:

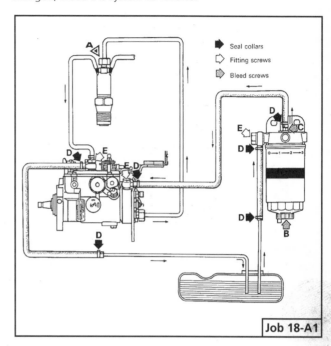

Seal collars
Fitting screws
Bleed screws

Job 18-A1

Step A1: Unscrew the unions fastening the delivery lines to the four injectors (**A**).

Step A2: Start the engine and run until fluid emerges from the loose injector fitting.

Step A3: Keep the engine running and tighten the four injector fittings.

ℹ️ INSIDE INFORMATION: If the engine will not start, check all fuel inlet pipe union points (see illustration **Job 18-A1, part D**) and also the pipe fittings (**Job 18-A1, part E**). Replace seal washers to eliminate the possibility of air leaks. ℹ️

PART B: BLEEDING WATER FROM DIESEL

Bleed off water from the fuel filter as follows:

Step B1: Unscrew the water bleed screw (**Job 18-A1, part B**) under the filter.

Step B2: Unscrew air bleed screw (**Job 18-A1, part C**) above the filter.

Step B3: Let water and fuel emerge until no more water is present, then tighten, firstly the water bleed screw (**B**) under filter, and then bleed the air bleed screw (**C**) above the filter.

PART G: STEERING AND SUSPENSION

PART G: Contents

Job 1. The systems explained.

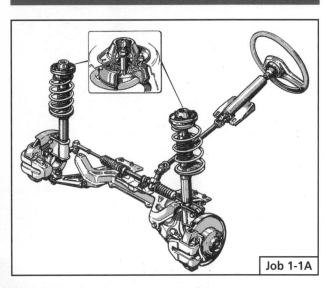

Job 1-1A

Point 1A: All Uno front suspension and steering layouts are virtually identical. This is the general layout, shown here for left-hand drive.

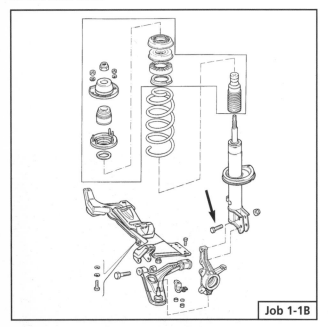

Job 1-1B

Point 1B: This is the front shock absorber strut and its attachments to the hub carrier (two bolts - one arrowed) and to the bodywork, at the top. The shock absorber is surrounded with a coil spring.

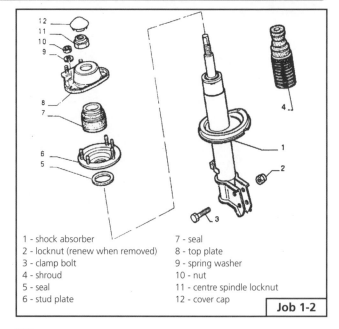

1 - shock absorber
2 - locknut (renew when removed)
3 - clamp bolt
4 - shroud
5 - seal
6 - stud plate
7 - seal
8 - top plate
9 - spring washer
10 - nut
11 - centre spindle locknut
12 - cover cap

Job 1-2

Point 2: This is the shock absorber assembly without the spring. We recommend that dismantling is carried out by your FIAT dealer. See *Job 8, Step 7*. You must NEVER remove the central nut (*part 11*) holding the coil spring onto the strut without using a purpose-made coil spring compressor, as described in *Job 8*.

Job 1-3

Point 3: All Uno rear suspension layouts are virtually identical. This is the rear axle beam assembly with its coil springs and shock absorbers.

Job 2. Steering wheel - removal and refitting.

❏ **Point 1:** Refer to *PART E: ELECTRICAL AND INSTRUMENTS, Job 4*, for details of steering wheel removal and refitting.

Job 3. Track rod end balljoint - replacement.

❏ **Step 1:** Slacken the bolts of the front wheel on the relevant side of the car, raise the front of the car and support on axle stands. See *Chapter 1, Safety First!*

❏ **Step 2:** Undo the nut on the track rod end until it is near the end of the TRE stud, but do not remove it.

Job 3-2

❏ **Step 3:** Release the TRE stud from its taper in the steering arm using a splitter tool.

Job 3-3

❏ *i* **Step 4:** INSIDE INFORMATION: A sharp blow to the side of the eye often momentarily distorts the eye and releases the ballpin from its taper. *i*

❏ **Step 5:** Remove the nut. Disconnect the TRE balljoint from the steering arm and undo the locknut which secures it to the steering tie rod.

Job 3-4

❏ **Step 6:** Unscrew the TRE from the tie rod, counting the exact number of turns needed to remove it.

Job 3-6

❏ **Step 7:** Clean and grease the tie bar threads before fitting the new balljoint to prevent future seizure. Fit the new balljoint in reverse order and, before using the car further, take it to your FIAT dealership or tyre specialist to have the front wheel

alignment set. This is NOT a job you can do at home but is DOES need doing as soon as possible to avoid severe tyre wear and dangerous braking and steering!

❏ **Step 8:** Refit and tighten the wheel, and lower the car to the ground.

Job 4. Steering rack gaiter - replacement.

❏ **Step 1:** Remove the Track Rod End (TRE) balljoint. See *Job 3*.

❏ **Step 2:** Undo the securing clip from each end of the gaiter and pull the gaiter off the tie rod.

Job 4-2

❏ **Step 3:** Wipe away contaminated grease and replace with new (lithium-based molybdenum disulphide grease). Secure the new gaiter in position at both ends with new bands or screw-type clips.

❏ **Step 4:** Complete the reassembly in the reverse order.

❏ **Step 5:** Refit the TRE balljoint. See *Job 3*.

Job 5. Steering rack - replacement.

❏ **Step 1:** Slacken the front wheel bolts, raise the front of the car and support on axle stands. See *Chapter 1, Safety First!* Remove the front wheels.

❏ **Step 2:** Undo the Track Rod End (TRE) balljoint nuts then separate the balljoints from the steering arms with a splitter tool. See *Job 3*.

❏ **Step 3:** Locate the steering column lower coupling, adjacent to the pedals inside the car, then undo and remove the pinch bolt and nut (arrowed).

Job 5-3

Note that this steering column has been disconnected at the upper end - not necessary here.

Step 4: Undo the four rack mounting bolts from under the front suspension crossmember, and remove the rack mounting clamps.

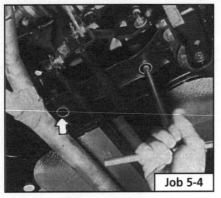

Job 5-4

Step 5: With an assistant inside the car, helping to separate the steering column pinch-joint from the rack pinion, pull the rack assembly away from the bulkhead and withdraw it from beneath a wheel arch.

making it easy / **Step 6:** *The replacement rack should be centred* before installation.

• *Measure the total travel of a TRE when the steering is moved moved from lock to lock. Go back half this distance and your rack is centred.*

Step 7: Place the steering wheel in the dead ahead position and engage the rack pinion splines with the column coupling.

Step 8: Continue refitting in the reverse order of removal.

Step 9: Take your car to your nearest FIAT dealership or tyre specialist to have the front wheel alignment set before using the car further. This is NOT a job you can do at home but is DOES need doing as soon as possible to avoid severe tyre wear and dangerous braking and steering!

Job 6. Track control arm - replacement.

IMPORTANT NOTE: If the arm bushes or the arm balljoint (strut bottom balljoint) are worn, the entire arm assembly must be replaced.

i INSIDE INFORMATION: It may be possible to disconnect the track control arm outer balljoint from the hub carrier without removing the hub from the car. (See **PART A: ENGINE.**) However, you will probably damage the balljoint gaiter - which will mean having to buy a complete, new track control arm! Avoid this very real risk by following PART B. *i*

Step 1: Slacken the relevant front wheel bolts, raise the front of the car and support on axle stands. See **Chapter 1, Safety First.** Unless you are following PART B, slacken the hub centre nut. See **Job 9.** Remove the front wheel.

PART A: HUB REMAINING IN PLACE

Step A2: Remove the nut from the track control arm balljoint.

i INSIDE INFORMATION: Some mechanics refer to the Track Control Arm as the lower wishbone. *i*

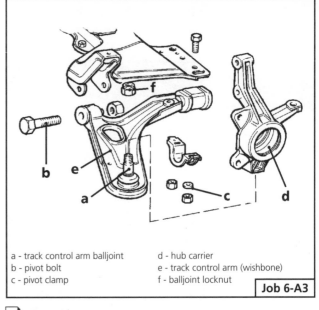

a - track control arm balljoint
b - pivot bolt
c - pivot clamp
d - hub carrier
e - track control arm (wishbone)
f - balljoint locknut

Job 6-A3

Step A3: Using a splitter tool, part the balljoint from the hub carrier.

Step A4: Undo the inboard pivot bolt and nut and remove the pivot clamp.

Step A5: Remove the track control arm from the car. Now go to **Step 6.**

PART B: HUB REMOVED FROM CAR

Step B2: Lift the securing staking on the hub centre nut (drive-shaft nut - arrowed), undo the nut and remove it, together with its washer. (See **Job 9.**) Refit the nut by a couple of turns and tap on it with a mallet to free the outboard drive-shaft joint from the hub.

Step B3: Undo the track control arm inboard clamp and pivot bolts. On Turbo models remove the anti-roll bar (see **Job 7**).

Step B4: Pull the strut/hub outwards while pulling the drive-shaft out of the hub carrier from the rear.

Step B5: Undo the track control arm ball joint retaining nut (behind the hub carrier), and use a ball joint splitter to separate the ball joint from the bottom of the hub carrier. If inner bushes are worn, or if the balljoint rubber shroud is damaged, you must replace the entire arm with a new FIAT part. Remove the arm from the car.

Step 6: Refitting is the reverse of the removal procedure.

Step 7: Lower the car to the ground and tighten the wheel bolts.

Job 7. Front anti-roll bar (Turbo i.e.) - removal and refitting.

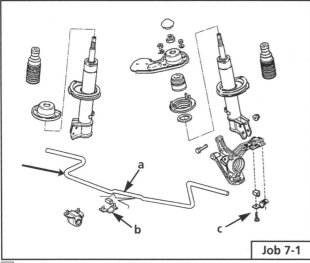

Job 7-1

☐ **Step 1:** Note the differences in the Turbo i.e.'s front suspension, in particular, the addition of an anti-roll bar (**a**).

☐ **Step 2:** Raise the front of the car and support on axle stands. See **Chapter 1, Safety First!**

☐ **Step 3:** Disconnect the gearchange linkages. See **PART B: TRANSMISSION AND CLUTCH.**

☐ **Step 4:** Working under the front of the car, undo the four bolts which retain the two anti-roll bar clamps to the underside of the car (one of them shown here - see illustration **7-1, part b**).

☐ **Step 5:** Working underneath each suspension track control arm, remove the two nuts or bolts which retain the anti-roll bar end clamps (see illustration **7-1, part c**) to the arms, and collect the clamps.

☐ **Step 6:** Withdraw the anti-roll bar from under one wheelarch.

☐ **Step 7:** Refit in the reverse order of removal. Before retightening the anti-roll bar mounting bolts and nuts, the car must be laden with the equivalent of four passengers and 40 kg of luggage, or the anti-roll bar will not control body roll properly. Also observe the tightening torques specified in **Chapter 3, Facts and Figures**.

Job 8. Front suspension strut - replacement.

☐ **Step 1:** Slacken the bolts of the relevant front wheel, then raise the front of the car and support on axle stands, so that the front wheels hang free. See **Chapter 1, Safety First!**

☐ **Step 2:** Remove the relevant wheel then detach the bracket which holds the brake hose to the suspension strut.

☐ **Step 3:** Remove the two bolts which secure the hub carrier to the base of the strut. Separate the hub carrier and strut. Also, see **Job 1, Point 1B**.)

Job 8-3

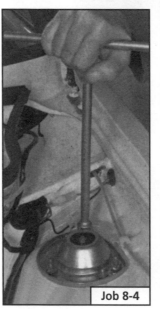

Job 8-4

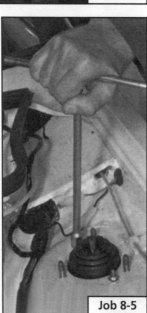

Job 8-5

☐ **Step 4:** Working under-bonnet, undo the nuts securing the strut-top reinforcement plate to the bodywork turret.

☐ **Step 5:** Remove the plate and then remove the two strut top mounting nuts. Note that on some models ancillary components may be attached to the plate or other strut-top fixings.

☐ **Step 6:** Lower the suspension strut to the ground.

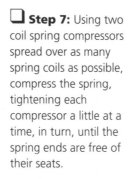

Job 8-6

☐ **Step 7:** Using two coil spring compressors spread over as many spring coils as possible, compress the spring, tightening each compressor a little at a time, in turn, until the spring ends are free of their seats.

Job 8-7

☐ **Step 8:** Hold the strut centre rod from turning, with the aid of an open-ended spanner, and undo the large nut securing the rod to the top mounting assembly.

☐ **Step 9:** Pull off the mounting together with its bearing, the spring seat, seat cushion, coil spring and rubber bellows. See **Job 1, Point 1B**.

FACT FILE: COIL SPRINGS

● If a coil spring is cracked, sagged or heavily rusted, replace the front springs AS A PAIR. FIAT springs are colour-coded with a stripe of either yellow or green paint. Use only a matching pair.

☐ **Step 10:** Refit all components in reverse order, making sure the coil spring is properly seated with the large coil at the bottom and the end of the coil, tight against the stop in the spring seat. Tighten to the specified tightening torques (see **Chapter 3, Facts and Figures**) only when the car is back on its wheels.

ℹ️ INSIDE INFORMATION: On cars built before 1985 it is necessary to seal the top mounting to the turret with silicone sealant to prevent water from getting into the strut bearing. ℹ️

Job 9. Front wheel bearing - replacement.

IMPORTANT NOTE: When disconnecting the outer end of the track control arm (or bottom wishbone) from the balljoint mounting on the hub carrier, you may have the greatest difficulty in removing the balljoint without destroying the gaiter. If you do so, you will have to fit a complete, new track control arm! You will probably be better off removing the hub carrier and track control arm, still connected together, then splitting the ball joint when off the car. See **Job 6**.

ℹ️ **Step 1:** INSIDE INFORMATION: ● The hub nut requires a great deal of torque to undo!
● Lever off the dust cap and slacken the centre hub nut (shown here being staked) while the car is still on the ground.

● Try to lift the staking from the groove in the drive-shaft. If it won't all come clear, don't worry! It will unroll as the nut is undone.
● You will need an extra-long lever (about half-a-metre long) to undo the hub nut.
● Slacken the wheel bolts while the car is on the ground. ℹ️

making it easy! ● The hub and bearing can be drifted out from the hub carrier. But if you have difficulty doing so, you could remove the hub carrier and take it to your FIAT dealer for bearing replacement.

☐ **Step 2:** Raise and support the car on axle stands. Remove the road wheel. Remove the hub/drive-shaft nut.

☐ **Step 3:** Remove the brake caliper, the disc and the disc shield. See **PART H: BRAKES.**

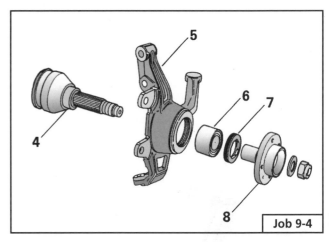

Job 9-4

☐ **Step 4:** Remove the hub carrier (**5**). Disconnect the balljoint from the bottom of the carrier to the track control arm (although you may be better off removing the hub carrier and track control while still attached - see **Job 6**). Disconnect the track rod end balljoint. See **Job 3**. Disconnect the hub carrier from the bottom of the strut. See **Job 8**.

☐ **Step 5:** Support the hub carrier horizontally across the open jaws of a large vice, or a pair of supports on the bench. Carefully drift the drive-shaft (see illustration, **Job 9-4, part 8**) out of the bearing (**part 6**).

☐ **Step 6:** If the bearing inner race comes off with the drive-shaft, carefully separate them, working all the way round with a cold chisel, as shown.

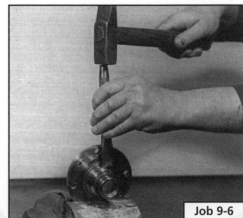

Job 9-6

Step 7: Remove the inner bearing race ring nut (see illustration *Job 9-4, part 7*). Note that, when refitted the nut is tightened to 50 Nm and staked - see

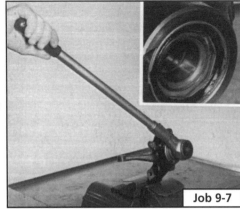

Job 9-7

inset. You may wish to have this special nut fitted by your FIAT dealer, if you don't have the correct adaptor for your torque wrench.

Step 8: Place the hub carrier back onto the vice, or supports, and carefully drift out the outer race, taking GREAT CARE not to mark the bearing housing.

Step 9: Fit the new bearing as a complete assembly (inner and outer races together) to the hub carrier. Press or drift on the OUTER RACE ONLY, inserting the bearing EVENLY until it is fully seated.

IMPORTANT NOTE: The bearing is 'sealed for life' and needs no additional grease.

making it easy! ● If you have a large enough vice, start the bearing off - until it is flush with the carrier - by pressing it in with the jaws of the vice. Then finish off with a drift, tapping at evenly spaced positions around the bearing.

Step 10: Refit a NEW bearing ring nut (see illustration *Job 9-4, part 7*), tightening and staking as described in *Step 7*.

Step 11: Reassemble the front suspension and brakes in the reverse order of removal. See relevant Jobs for detailed information. Use a NEW hub nut.

FACT FILE: STAKING THE HUB NUT

Step 12A: Use a cold chisel with an edge ground to an angle of about 60 degrees to stake the collar of the nut. USE A NEW NUT EACH TIME IT IS REPLACED.

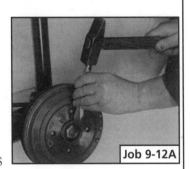

Job 9-12A

Step 12B: Make sure the staked-down section of the collar fits in the stub axle slot in the opposite direction to the direction of the nut rotation, as shown.

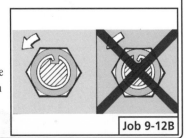

Job 9-12B

Job 10. Rear shock absorbers and coil springs - replacement.

Step 1: Slacken the rear wheel bolts, raise the rear of the car and support on axle stands placed beneath the body. See *Chapter 1, Safety First*.

Job 10-2   Job 10-3

Step 2: Support the outer end of the axle with a trolley jack (but don't compress the suspension!) then remove the relevant road wheel.

Step 3: From inside the luggage area hold the shock absorber shaft top with an open-ended spanner and undo the spindle nut.

Job 10-4   Job 10-5

Step 4: Carefully lower the trolley jack to decompress the spring and free the top of the shock absorber.

Step 5: From under the car, undo the shock absorber lower mounting bolt and withdraw the shock absorber downwards.

Step 6: Refit in the reverse order, observing the tightening torques specified in *Chapter 3, Facts and Figures*.

Step 7: If you need to remove the rear suspension coil springs, follow the above procedure. In addition, undo the two nuts and washers (arrowed) which secure the spring top mounting assembly to the bodywork, and lift off the mounting assembly. The spring can now be removed.

Job 11. Rear axle bushes - removal and installation.

Refer also to illustration *Job 1, Point 3*.

Step 1: Slacken the rear wheel bolts, raise the rear of the car and support on axle stands under the body. See *Chapter 1, Safety First!* Remove the rear wheels.

Step 2: Remove the centre bolt from each axle bush then lever down the forward end of the axle so that it clears its underfloor brackets.

Job 11-2

Step 3: Press the axle bushes out with a two-legged puller bearing on a socket which in turn bears on the bush. Push the new bushes in by the same method.

Job 11-3

making it easy! ● Smear the new bushes with brake fluid when pressing them into their locations in each forward arm of the axle. This will ease insertion.

● Ordinary oil or grease destroys rubber!

Step 4: Refit in the reverse order. Tighten the axle bush bolts to the specified torque (see **Chapter 3, Facts and Figures**) only when the car is back on its wheels with the equivalent of four occupants and 40 kg of luggage on board.

Job 12. Rear wheel bearings - replacement.

IMPORTANT NOTE: FIAT hub bearings have a much longer service life because they are factory built into the hub. The bearing races cannot be replaced separately.

Step 1: Slacken the bolts of the relevant rear wheel. Lever off the hub centre grease cap, lift the staking on the hub centre nut (see **Job 9**) and slacken the hub nut with a 30 mm socket and long bar.

Step 2: Raise the rear of the car and support on axle stands. See **Chapter 1, Safety First!** Remove the wheel and the brake drum (or the brake caliper and disc - Turbo i.e.) - see **PART H: BRAKES**.

Step 3: Remove the hub nut and the thrust washer from beneath it.

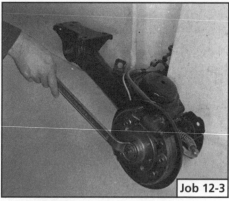

Job 12-3

Step 4: Pull the hub from the stub axle, using a two- or three-leg puller if necessary. If the bearing pulls apart, leaving the inner race on the stub axle, it should be removed using a suitable puller.

Job 12-4

ℹ INSIDE INFORMATION: In rare, extreme cases, the inner race just won't budge! Try pouring boiling water over it, then try again. DON'T heat with a flame. In the worst possible case, the inner race can be cut off with a cutting wheel on an angle grinder. **ℹ**

Step 5: Lightly grease the stub axle, then tap on the new hub assembly (complete with ready-assembled bearing) using a tubular drift in contact with the wheel bearing inner track.

Job 12-5

IMPORTANT NOTE: The bearing is 'sealed for life' and needs no additional grease.

Step 6: Refit the hub nut washer, fit a NEW hub nut and tighten it to the specified torque (see **Chapter 3, Facts and Figures**) while rotating the hub flange. Stake the nut locking collar into the slot in the stub axle, using a drift. See **Job 9**.

making it easy! ● You will find it easier - and safer - to tighten the hub nut up to its correct torque with the wheel in place and the car on the ground.

Step 7: Refit the remaining components in the reverse order (referring also to **PART H: BRAKES**), lower the car and tighten the wheel bolts.

PART H: BRAKES

PART H: Contents

Job 1. Understanding Uno brakes.

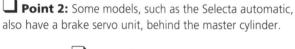

Job1-1A

☐ **Point 1A:** This is the layout of the standard model braking system. Obviously, the brake pedal is on the other side on right-hand drive cars. The master cylinder (and servo, if fitted) can be on either side, according to model.

Job1-1B

1 - vacuum switch
2 - pressure modulators
3 - electronic control unit relay feed
4 - anti-lock braking system warning light remote control switch
5 - anti-lock braking system warning light
6 - electronic control unit
7 - brake lights switch
8 - rpm sensor

☐ **Point 1B:** Turbo i.e. models have disc brakes all round, instead of the Uno's usual front disc/rear drum arrangement and later models have optional anti-lock brakes.
Apart from checking that the hydraulic and electrical connections are sound, anti-lock brakes are not repairable. Individual components and friction materials can be replaced but otherwise, consult your FIAT dealer.

☐ **Point 2:** Some models, such as the Selecta automatic, also have a brake servo unit, behind the master cylinder.

☐ **Point 3:** Selecta front brakes are of a different type.

Job 2. Front brake pads . replacement

IMPORTANT NOTE: Copper-impregnated grease should be lightly smeared on the edge of the caliper piston where it touches the pad and on all sliding surfaces to prevent seizure.

PART A - CALIPER WITH NO INSPECTION OPENING

This is the type of brakes fitted to the majority of Unos.

The amount of dismantling needed in order to replace the brake pads of this caliper type is the same as for checking them. See *Chapter 5, Servicing Your Car, Job 49*.

PART B - CALIPER WITH INSPECTION OPENING ONLY

These are the brakes fitted to Selecta automatics, for instance.

ℹ INSIDE INFORMATION: The brake pads should be replaced when the friction material thickness falls to the minimum of 1.5 mm. This can - theoretically - be checked through the opening in the caliper body. However, you can see far more clearly, and check the piston rubbers at the same time, if you swivel the caliper out of the way. **ℹ**

☐ **Step B1:** Slacken the front wheel bolts, raise the front of the car and support on axle stands. See *Chapter 1, Safety First!* Remove the front wheels.

☐ **Step B2:** Undo the lower guide bolt of the caliper cylinder housing. Slacken the top bolt but don't remove it.

☐ **Step B3:** Unplug the sensor wiring if fitted. Swing the cylinder housing upwards and tie it clear.

Step B4: Remove the pads complete with anti-rattle springs.

Step B5: Using a spray-on brake cleaner clean away all dirt and dust, taking care not to inhale it. See *Chapter 1, Safety First!*

Step B6: Loosen the cap on the master cylinder, push in the caliper pistons to allow for the extra thickness of the new pads, syphoning off excess fluid from the reservoir to prevent spillage.

Step B7: Reassemble in the reverse order, tightening new cylinder housing bolts to the specified torque, see *Chapter 3, Facts and Figures.*

IMPORTANT NOTE: Always use new FIAT caliper mounting bolts - they are of a special self-locking type - when refitting the caliper.

Step B8: Pump the brake pedal to bring the pads into contact with the discs, and top up the brake fluid.

Step B9: Refit the road wheels and lower the car to the ground.

See *Chapter 5, Servicing Your Car,* for illustrations relating to this.

Job 3. Front brake caliper - replacement.

Step 1: Slacken the front wheel bolts, raise the front of the car and support on axle stands. See *Chapter 1, Safety First!* Remove the front wheels.

Step 2: Clean dirt from the union at the caliper end of the flexible hose and slacken the union.

Step 3: Disconnect the pad wear warning sensor wire, where fitted. (See illustration *Job 3-A4, inset*.)

Follow *Step 4-on* in *PART A* or *PART B*, according to the type of bracket fitted to your vehicle.

PART A - CALIPER WITH NO INSPECTION OPENING

Step A4:
Pull out the small locking block spring clips then slide out the locking blocks.

Job 3-A4

Step A5: Lift off the brake pads and caliper body.

Step A6: Unscrew the caliper body from the brake hose, then cap the hose end or clamp the hose using only a purpose-built brake hose clamp.

Job 3-A5

Step A7: Check the condition of the brake hose, replace it if it is showing signs of cracking or perishing or if it has rubbed or chaffed against any other component, then fit the new caliper in reverse order and bleed the front brake circuit. See *Job 15*.

a, b - spanner positions - see text
1. brake caliper
2. seals and bleed screw
3. bleed screw
4. cap
5. guide pins
6. guide pin bushes
A. piston fluid seal and dust seal
B. guide pin gaiters
C. brake pads

Job 3-B4

PART B - CALIPER WITH INSPECTION OPENING

Step B4: Gently pull the caliper outwards to ease the piston a little way back into its bore, or use a flat blade to lever the pad and piston back into the bore. Prevent each guide pin from turning, using a slim, open-ended spanner (point *a*) while unbolting the upper and lower guide pin bolts (point *b*). Lift off the caliper.

Step B5: Check the condition of the brake hose, replace it if necessary, then fit the new caliper in reverse order. Use NEW guide pin bolts tightened to the torque specified in *Chapter 3, Facts and Figures*, then bleed the front brake circuit, see *Job 15*.

Step B6: Refit the wheels, lower the car to the ground, and tighten the wheel bolts.

Job 4. Front brake disc - replacement.

Step 1: Remove the caliper and pads, see *Jobs 2* and *3*.

Job 4-2

Step 2: Knock back the locktabs (where fitted) of the caliper support bracket securing bolts, then unbolt and remove the caliper support bracket.

Step 3: Undo the disc fixing bolt (arrowed) and wheel locating spigot (here with a spanner) and remove the disc.

Step 4: Thoroughly clean the disc mating face on the hub drive flange, and its counterpart on the disc, then reassemble in reverse order. Degrease the disc surfaces with alcohol before fitting the brake pads.

Job 4-2

Job 5. Rear brake shoes - replacement.

i INSIDE INFORMATION! When the lining thickness is down to a minimum of 1.5 mm, replace the shoes as a complete axle set. *i*

making it easy!
- *Before removing the shoes, mark them F(front) and R(rear) respectively, so that you can compare old and new shoes and ensure refitting in the correct positions.*
- *Complete work on one side at a time so that you have always got the other side as a visual guide.*

Step 1: Jack up the rear of the car and support on stands.

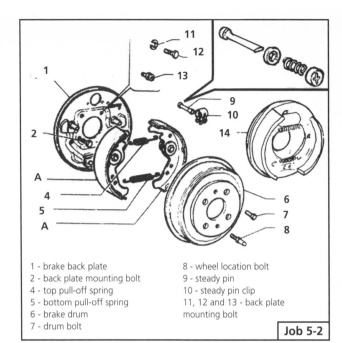

1 - brake back plate
2 - back plate mounting bolt
4 - top pull-off spring
5 - bottom pull-off spring
6 - brake drum
7 - drum bolt

8 - wheel location bolt
9 - steady pin
10 - steady pin clip
11, 12 and 13 - back plate
mounting bolt

Job 5-2

Step 2: Unscrew the drum securing bolts (**7** and **8**) and remove the drum (**6**). See *Chapter 5, Servicing Your Car.*

Step 3: Wash the brake dust away with FIAT brake cleaner, taking care not to inhale any brake dust.

Job 5-3

Step 4: Undo the shoe steady pin by levering off the spring. (see illustration *Job 5-2, part 10*)...

Job 5-4

Step 5: ...and removing the pin through the rear of the backplate. The earlier type is shown in illustration *Job 5-2, inset*.

Job 5-5

❑ **Step 6:** Use self-locking grips to hold the top spring while you disengage it.

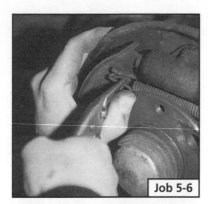

Job 5-6

❑ **Step 7:** Use larger grips to unhook the bottom of the shoe - to take the pressure off the spring - and remove the spring.

Job 5-7

❑ **Step 8:** You now have to turn the cut-outs on the hub flange (arrowed) so that the auto-adjusters clear the flange.

Job 5-8

ℹ️ **Step 9:** INSIDE INFORMATION: While the shoes are off, check the wheel cylinder for leaks - peel back each rubber shroud - and push the pistons to-and-fro to make sure that they move freely. Replace if any problems are found. Then wrap stiff wire around the wheel cylinder - it stops the piston from popping out! ℹ️

Job 5-9

❑ **Step 10:** When reassembling, put a smear of lithium-based brake grease (not ordinary grease!) on all the working contact surfaces including those shown on

Job 5-10

the backplate, except the wheel cylinder piston ends.

❑ **Step 11:** Ensure that the springs are in the correct positions.

❑ **Step 12:** Do not forget to fit the shoe retaining pins and securing clips.

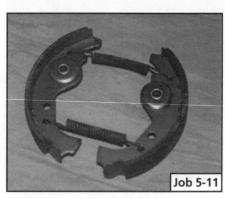

Job 5-11

making it easy ❑ **Step 13:** Compare with the other side for correct assembly.

● Repeat the whole operation on the second side using your first one as a guide if necessary.

❑ **Step 14:** Centralise and align the shoes by tapping them towards the centre of the hub with a soft mallet. This moves them against the pressure of the self adjuster springs.

❑ **Step 15:** Clean the dust from the drums and check their condition. Use a piece of fine emery cloth to de-grease them. Refit the brake drums and securing bolts.

❑ **Step 16:** Pump the brake pedal a few times to bring the linings into contact with the drums. Refit the road wheels and lower the car to the ground. Check the wheel nuts for tightness.

Job 6. Rear wheel cylinder - replacement.

❑ **Step 1:** Remove the brake shoes. See *Job 5*.

❑ **Step 2:** Disconnect the brake pipe from the back of the wheel cylinder (see *point a*) and seal the pipe end.

Job 6-2

❑ **Step 3:** Undo the fixing bolts (see illustration *Job 6-2*, arrowed) and remove the wheel cylinder from the backplate.

❑ **Step 4:** Fit the new cylinder to the backplate and connect the brake pipe. We strongly recommend that you do not attempt to overhaul a seized, leaking or damaged wheel cylinder. Replace it with a new unit from your FIAT dealership.

❑ **Step 5:** Refit the brake shoes, drum and road wheel.

Step 6: Bleed the rear brake hydraulics. See *Job 15.*

Job 7. Rear brake disc pads (Turbo i.e.) - replacement.

Step 1: Slacken the rear wheel bolts, and raise and safely support the rear of the car - see *Chapter 1, Safety First!* - and remove the wheels.

Step 2: Detach the clip which secures the inboard end of the brake hose to the suspension strut.

Step 3: To prevent each caliper guide pin from turning, use a slim, open-ended spanner while unbolting the upper and lower guide pin bolts, then withdraw the caliper body up and rearwards.

Job 7-3

Step 4: Remove the brake pads. Clean away all dirt and brake dust, taking care not to inhale any. See *Chapter 1, Safety First!*

Job 7-4

Step 5: Locate the new pads in the caliper mounting frame. Their anti-rattle springs should already be attached to them.

Step 6: Retract the caliper piston to make room for the new, thicker pads, by rotating the piston clockwise using fine-nosed pliers engaged in the slots in the piston face. If necessary, syphon excess brake fluid from the reservoir to prevent spillage.

Job 7-6

Step 7: Refit the caliper using new bolts obtained from a FIAT dealer, tightened to their specified torque (see *Chapter 3, Facts and Figures*).

Step 8: Pump the brake pedal repeatedly to bring the pads into contact with the disc, then top up the brake fluid as necessary. Note that it may be necessary to pump the pedal up to fifty times to effect adjustment.

Step 9: Check the handbrake adjustment.

Step 10: Refit the wheels and lower the car to the ground.

Job 8. Rear brake caliper (Turbo i.e.) - replacement.

This job is carried out in the same way as pad replacement (*Job 7*) with the addition of the following:

Step 1: Disconnect the handbrake cable from the caliper by pulling on the cable end until it can be slipped out of its groove in the caliper lever. If necessary, back off the handbrake cable adjustment. See *Job 16.*

Step 2: Slacken the brake flexible hose at the caliper before lifting off the caliper. Once the caliper is removed, unscrew it from the flexible hose.

Job 8-2

Step 3: Refit all components in the reverse order, referring to *Job 7.*

Step 4: Bleed the relevant rear brake. See *Job 15.*

Job 9. Rear brake disc (Turbo i.e.) - replacement.

Step 1: Remove the caliper and pads as in *Job 8*, but do not disconnect the brake hose from the caliper. Support the weight of the caliper, so as not to strain the hose.

Step 2: Unbolt the caliper support bracket (inset) from the hub, using a hex-type socket drive or Allen key.

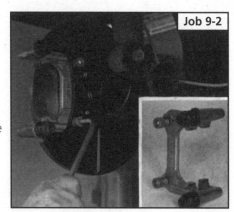
Job 9-2

Step 3: Remove the disc fixing screws (see *Job 4, Step 3*) and lift off the disc.

Step 4: Refit in the reverse order of removal, but thoroughly clean the disc and hub flange mating faces. Apply locking fluid to the caliper mounting frame bolts before tightening them to the specified torque - see *Chapter 3, Facts and Figures.*

Job 10. Master cylinder - replacement.

☐ **Step 1:** Raise the bonnet and protect the wings from brake fluid spillage.

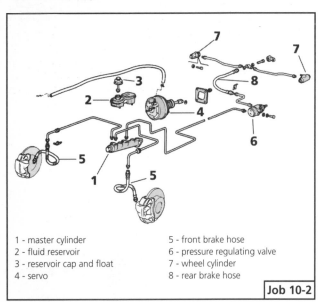

1 - master cylinder
2 - fluid reservoir
3 - reservoir cap and float
4 - servo
5 - front brake hose
6 - pressure regulating valve
7 - wheel cylinder
8 - rear brake hose

Job 10-2

☐ **Step 2:** Locate the master cylinder on the engine compartment bulkhead.

● On most models it is mounted on the brake servo, but it bolts directly to the bulkhead on non-servoed models.

● Disconnect the electrical leads from the reservoir cap, then remove the cap and level float.

☐ **Step 3:** Unscrew the pipe unions and move them clear of the master cylinder. Use a container to catch lost fluid.

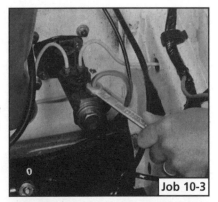

Job 10-3

☐ **Step 4:** Undo the two master cylinder mounting nuts and remove the master cylinder.

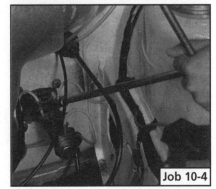

Job 10-4

☐ **Step 5:** Fit the new cylinder in reverse order ensuring sound connection of the fluid pipe unions.

☐ **Step 6:** Bleed the complete brake system as in *Job 15*.

Job 11. Servo - check remove and refit.

WHERE APPLICABLE

ℹ️ INSIDE INFORMATION:

● Before condemning the servo for lack of efficiency, check the condition of the one-way valve and vacuum pipe connecting it to the inlet manifold.

● Ease the valve out of the front of the servo and disconnect the pipe from the inlet manifold.

● Check that you can only blow one way through the valve - from the servo end towards the inlet manifold (or brake vacuum pump - Diesel models).

● The vacuum pipe can suffer failure in many ways. Age can harden it until it cracks, causing an air leak which sometimes results in a whistling noise and rough slow-running.

● Loose connections could also produce the same result. The other type of vacuum hose failure is an implosion - where the hose is sucked flat by the vacuum - often because oil has softened the hose.

● This is not so easily detected, as it rarely upsets the engine performance and resumes its normal shape shortly after the engine is stopped.

● The inner lining can also deteriorate, causing a blockage. ℹ️

Refer to the illustration with *Job 10-2*.

☐ **Step 1:** Remove the master cylinder. See *Job 10*.

☐ **Step 2:** On Turbo i.e. models, undo the coolant expansion tank fixing and move the tank away from the servo.

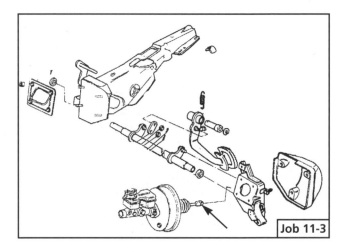

Job 11-3

☐ **Step 3:** From inside the car, disconnect the servo pushrod (arrowed) from the pedal by removing the split pin or circlip securing it to the pedal peg. Undo the four servo mounting nuts and washers. On Turbo i.e. models, working under the left-hand side of the dashboard, remove the three nuts securing the plastic cover to the brake transverse linkage, remove the split pin or circlip securing the servo pushrod to the actuating lever on the cross-shaft, and detach the pushrod from the lever.

Step 4:
Working under the bonnet, disconnect the servo vacuum hose (arrowed) from the servo, remove the servo and be careful not to spill fluid onto the paintwork.

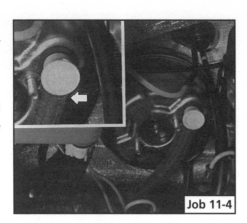

Job 11-4

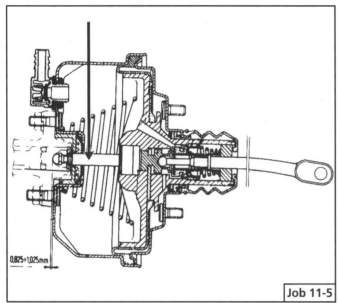

0.825÷1.025mm

Job 11-5

Step 5: Measure the projection of the servo piston pushrod (arrowed). With the master cylinder fitted there should be a clearance of between 0.825 and 1.025 mm between the primary piston face and the end of the pushrod. Use the mating surfaces of the master cylinder and servo as the reference point.

Step 6: Turn the adjusting screw on the servo as necessary and apply locking fluid to the thread when finished.

Step 7: Complete reassembly in the reverse order and bleed the brakes. See *Job 15*.

Job 12. Pressure regulating valve - replacement and adjustment.

FACT FILE: PRESSURE REGULATING VALVE

● The regulating valve is located under the car and connects to the rear axle via a lever and spring. It is also known as the Load Proportioning Valve. It alters the balance of the brakes, front to rear, according to the amount of load on the rear of the car.

Step 1: Raise the rear of the car and support on axle stands. See *Chapter 1, Safety First!*

Step 2:
Unscrew the valve pipe unions, pull the pipes clear of the valve and cap their ends. See *Job 14*.

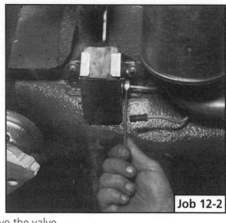

Job 12-2

Step 3:
Undo the valve mounting bolts, release the link spring and remove the valve.

Step 4: Refit in reverse order and adjust as follows.

Step 5: Park the car, unladen, on level ground. Add the following ballast to the luggage compartment immediately behind the rear seat: 3-door models - 65 kg; 5-door models - 55 kg. On Turbo i.e. models this ballast weight should be 45 kg.

Step 6:
Working under the car, slacken the valve bracket securing bolt (**1**), then attach a weight of 6 kg* to the bracket eye (**2**) and

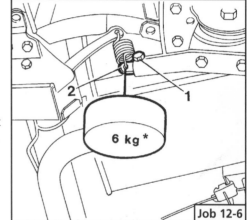

6 kg *

Job 12-6

retighten the securing bolt. **IMPORTANT NOTE: On Turbo i.e. models this weight * should be 10 kg.**

Step 7: Now fully tighten the bracket bolt (see illustration *Job 12-6, part 1*).

Step 8: Remove the weights, lower the car to the ground, then bleed the rear brakes. See *Job 15.*

Job 13. Flexible hoses - replacement.

i INSIDE INFORMATION: When disconnecting brake pipes or hoses, it is essential to minimise brake fluid loss. This can be done by unscrewing the master cylinder reservoir cap, laying a sheet of plastic across the opening, and refitting the cap. This will prevent atmospheric pressure from pushing the fluid out of opened lines. **i**

☐ Step 1: Undo the rigid pipe union (*a*) connecting to the hose where hose and pipe join at the support bracket. Take care not to damage the bracket or tear it off the body.

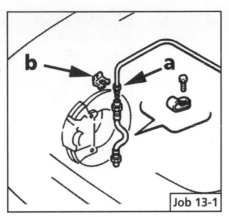

Job 13-1

☐ Step 2: Pull out the clip (see illustration **Job 13-2, part b**) which secures the hose to the bracket, then unscrew the hose union at its other end.

making it easy!
• *If the pipe starts to twist with the union, grip the pipe as lightly as possible, and see if you can stop it from turning.*
• *If not, cut through the pipe with a junior hacksaw and replace the length of rigid pipe.*

☐ Step 3: Fit the new hose in reverse order, making sure that the hose is not twisted when refitting the rigid hose.

☐ Step 4: Check that the hose cannot chafe anywhere over the whole range of steering and suspension movement.

☐ Step 5: Bleed the hydraulic system, see **Job 15.**

Job 14. Metal pipes - replacement.

i INSIDE INFORMATION: When disconnecting brake pipes or hoses, it is essential to minimise brake fluid loss. This can be done by unscrewing the master cylinder reservoir cap, laying a sheet of plastic across the opening, and refitting the cap. This will prevent atmospheric pressure from pushing the fluid out of opened lines. A pipe spanner makes the job *much* easier! *i*

☐ Step 1: Undo the unions at each end of a pipe length. Patience is often required because of the union seizing both in its threads and on the pipe. See **MAKING IT EASY!** after **Job 13, Step 2**. Use penetrating oil to help free seized unions, and use a split-ring spanner rather than an open-ended one, to reduce the risk of rounding off the union nuts.

☐ Step 2: Detach the pipe length from its securing clips and remove it.

making it easy! **☐ Step 3:** *Where possible, use the old pipe as a pattern to shape the new one prior to fitting.*

☐ Step 4: Follow the original route and secure the pipe in the body clips.

☐ Step 5: Connect the unions and bleed the system. See **Job 15.**

Job 15. Brake bleeding.

i INSIDE INFORMATION: Unless the master cylinder or pressure regulating valve has been disturbed, it will only be necessary to bleed the end of the braking system which has been opened. Start bleeding at the left-hand rear brake. *i*

☐ Step 1: Push a tight fitting length of plastic or rubber tubing onto the first bleed screw and immerse the other end in a small quantity of brake fluid

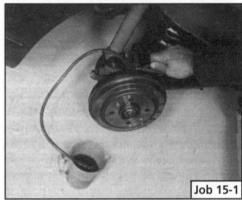

Job 15-1

contained in a glass jar so that no air can accidentally be pulled up the tube.

☐ Step 2: Undo the brake bleed screw (at the drum brake backplate or on the disc caliper body) by half a turn. Have your helper push the brake pedal to the floor and hold it there while you lock up the bleed valve. Then release the pedal slowly. Repeat several times, with the following suggested dialogue:

YOU. (*Open bleed screw*) "Open!" (*called out loud*)
HELPER. (*Pushes pedal down*) "Down!"
YOU. (*Close bleed screw*) "Closed!"
HELPER. (*Lets pedal up*) "Up!" - repeated, as necessary.

IMPORTANT NOTE: Take great care not to let the master cylinder run out of brake fluid. Otherwise you will introduce fresh air into the system and have to start again. Use ONLY fresh brake fluid from a previously unopened container.

☐ Step 3: Top up the fluid reservoir frequently while repeating the bleeding operation until all air is expelled from the brake line (no bubbles appear in the tube or jar).

☐ Step 4: Bleed each remaining brake in the same way, going to the right-hand front next, followed by the right-hand rear, and finishing with the left-hand front brake.

SAFETY FIRST!
• *After completing the bleeding operation, and with your helper's foot firmly on the brake pedal, check all connections for leaks.*
• *Remember to top up the fluid, replace the master cylinder cap and reconnect the wires to it.*

Job 16. Handbrake cable - replacement.

FACT FILE: HANDBRAKE CABLE

● The handbrake cable mechanism comprises a primary cable from the handbrake lever to the off-side rear brake, and a secondary cable which runs from the centre of the rear axle to the near-side rear brake.

● If the handbrake won't hold even though it is properly adjusted, check the rear brake mechanism for seizure or for oil or fluid contamination or severe wear of the brake shoes.

❏ **Step 1:** Chock the front wheels at front and rear, and raise the rear of the car and support on axle stands. See *Chapter 1, Safety First!*

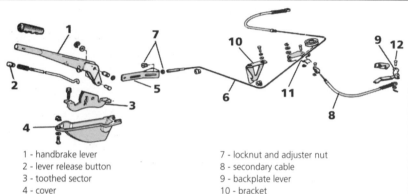

1 - handbrake lever
2 - lever release button
3 - toothed sector
4 - cover
5 - lever arm
6 - primary cable

7 - locknut and adjuster nut
8 - secondary cable
9 - backplate lever
10 - bracket
11 - compensating pulley and bracket
12 - clevis pin

Job 16-2

❏ **Step 2:** From under the floorpan, slacken the cable at its handbrake lever (**5**) by undoing the locknut and adjuster nut (**7**).

❏ **Step 3:** Working at the off-side rear brake backplate, remove the split pin and the clevis pin (see illustration *Job 16-2, part 12*) from the handbrake mechanism lever at the backplate, then pull back the spring around the cable end to free the cable from its bracket on the suspension strut.

TURBO I.E. ONLY

On models with rear disc brakes, push back the caliper lever to free the handbrake inner cable from it, then detach the outer cable from its abutment.

❏ **Step 4:** Fully disconnect the primary cable end from the handbrake lever, then detach the cable from its guides and from the compensating pulley (see illustration *Job 16-2, part 11*) on the axle.

❏ **Step 5:** Disconnect the secondary cable (see illustration *Job 16-2, part 8*) from the compensating pulley bracket by removing the clevis pin split pin and withdrawing the clevis.

❏ **Step 6:** Disconnect the other end of the cable from the backplate as detailed in *Step 3* and detach the cable from its guides.

❏ **Step 7:** Refit in the reverse order, using new split pins, and adjust the cable. See *Chapter 5, Servicing Your Car.*

PART I: BODY AND INTERIOR

PART I: Contents

Job 1. Bonnet - removal and refitting.
Job 2. Bonnet release system - removal and refitting.
Job 3. Radiator grille - removal and refitting.
Job 4. Tailgate - removal and refitting.
Job 5. Tailgate release system - removal and refitting.
Job 6. Front bumper - removal and refitting.
Job 7. Rear bumper - removal and refitting.

Job 8. Door trim panel - removal and refitting.
Job 9. Window regulator - removal and refitting.
Job 10. Door lock/handle (3-door) - removal and refitting.
Job 11. Door lock/handle (5-door) - removal and refitting.
Job 12. Door removal - replacement and adjustment.
Job 13. Door mirror replacement.

Job 1. Bonnet - removal and refitting.

❏ **Step 1:** Using the prop, support the bonnet in the open position.

❏ **Step 2:** Use a felt pen or masking tape to mark out the hinge positions, then get a helper to support the bonnet while you undo the four hinge bolts (two at each side). Lift the bonnet clear.

Job 1-2

☐ **Step 3:** Refit in the reverse order but tighten the bolts just enough to position the bonnet, then lower it carefully and check for an equal gap between wings and bonnet, and for proper alignment of its leading edge. Make any minor adjustments and when you are satisfied, fully tighten the hinge bolts.

making it easy! ☐ **Step 4:** When you and your assistant replace the bonnet, place a piece of cloth under each back corner so that it doesn't damage your car's bodywork.

Job 2. Bonnet release system - removal and refitting.

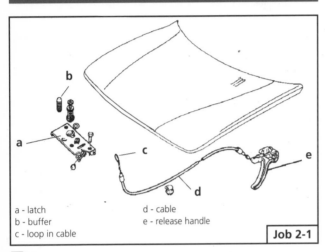

a - latch
b - buffer
c - loop in cable
d - cable
e - release handle

Job 2-1

☐ **Step 1:** Take note of the bonnet lock/release components.

☐ **Step 2:** Remove the clip that retains the bonnet release handle (under the left-hand side of the dashboard, early models; right-hand side for later model).

☐ **Step 3:** Open the bonnet and remove the radiator grille. See *Job 3.*

☐ **Step 4:** At the bonnet latch (on the car's front panel) unhook the looped end of the release cable from the latch lever.

☐ **Step 5:** Release the cable outer sleeve from any retaining clips, then withdraw the cable assembly from inside the car.

☐ **Step 6:** Refit in the reverse order of removal.

☐ **Step 7:** The operation of the release mechanism can be adjusted by varying the position of the bonnet striker post. Slacken the

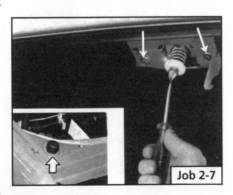

Job 2-7

post adjustment lock bolts (arrowed), and align the post assembly centrally with the opening in the latch.

☐ **Step 8:** You can also vary the release effort by screwing the striker post in or out (see illustration *Job 2-7,* screwdriver position). Bonnet levelling (relative to the wings) is achieved by screwing in or out the rubber buffers (inset, illustration *Job 2-7*) at the corners of the bonnet closing panel.

☐ **Step 9:** EARLY MODELS ONLY: The striker post can only be moved from side-to-side if the large locknut is slackened off. Height adjustment (screwdriver position) is the same as on later cars.

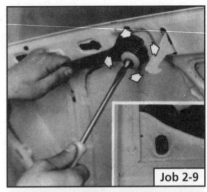

Job 2-9

☐ **Step 10:** The closing plate catch can also be adjusted by slackening the bolts and moving the striker assembly.

Job 2-10

SAFETY FIRST!

● *Do not drive unless both the bonnet catch and safety catch are fitted and work properly.*

Job 3. Radiator grille - removal and refitting.

☐ **Step 1A:** On pre-facelift non-Turbo models, open the bonnet and remove the securing screw from the upper centre of the grille louvres. Using a screwdriver, release the two plastic upper retainers (near each headlight) then pull the grille upwards and away from the car.

☐ **Step 1B:** On later models open the bonnet and remove the retaining screws visible along the top edge of the grille, and lift off the grille.

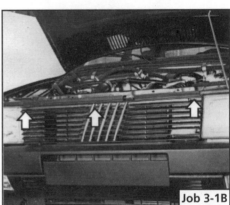

Job 3-1B

☐ **Step 2:** Refit in the reverse order.

Job 4. Tailgate
- removal and refitting.

Step 1A: If you have to remove the hinges, use a felt pen to draw around the hinge plates where they fit against the inside of the tailgate (see illustration *Job 1B, point a*) so that they can be refitted later in exactly the same position.

Step 1B: If you don't *have* to remove the hinges, tap out each hinge pin, after removing the circlip. This avoids having to re-site the hinges.

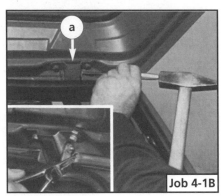

Job 4-1B

Step 2: Disconnect the following:
● The leads from the rear screen heater.
● The leads from the wiper motor.
● The plastic tube from the windscreen washer jet.

Step 3: Raise the tailgate and have a helper support its weight. Disconnect the tailgate strut by prising out the plastic lug from each end of the strut and withdrawing it from the car.

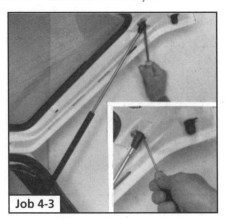

Job 4-3

Step 4: The hinge bolts can now be removed (if necessary) and the tailgate carefully lifted away.

making it easy. **Step 5:** *When you and your assistant replace the tailgate, place a piece of cloth under each top corner so that it doesn't damage your car's bodywork.*

Step 6: Refit all components in the reverse order, making sure that the tailgate sits correctly and that its release latch works correctly.

Step 7: The tailgate lock is adjusted, if necessary, by slackening the two bolts. Also, see *Job 5*.

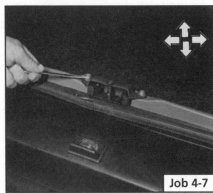

Job 4-7

Step 8: The position of the buffers - they screw in and out - affects the fit of the tailgate and therefore the operation of the closing mechanism.

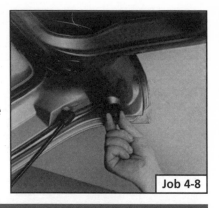

Job 4-8

Job 5. Tailgate release system
- removal and refitting.

Note that not all Uno models have a remote release system.

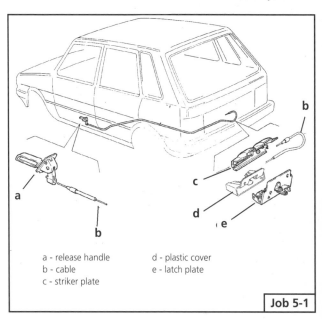

a - release handle   d - plastic cover
b - cable   e - latch plate
c - striker plate

Job 5-1

Step 1: Peel back the carpeting and undo the two screws which secure the remote release handle to the floor between driver's door and seat.

Step 2: Follow the instructions given in *Job 4* for the bonnet release cable, noting that you may have to remove sundry trim items to gain full access to the cable assembly.

Step 3: Working underneath the tailgate, remove the two bolts which secure the latch plate to the tailgate.

Step 4: Detach the rod which links the latch plate to the lock barrel assembly, and remove the latch plate.

Step 5: Remove the plastic cover from the tailgate latch's striker plate on the car body. Mark the position of the striker plate and remove its two securing bolts and the plate.

Step 6: Refit all components in the reverse order. If the striker plate needs re-alignment to make the tailgate close more smoothly, loosen its two securing bolts and move it by very small amounts at a time before testing it again, tightening when good closing is achieved.

Job 6. Front bumper
- removal and refitting.

PART A - NON-TURBO CARS

☐ **Step A1:**
Remove both
wheel arch liners
(screws, arrowed).

Job 6-A1

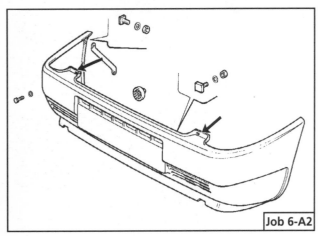

Job 6-A2

☐ **Step A2:** Remove the radiator grille (see *Job 3*) and the two bumper upper fixing screws (arrowed).

☐ **Step A3:** Remove the three fixing bolts from inside the lower edge of the bumper.

☐ **Step A4:** Undo the bumper side-stay nuts at the bumper wrap-around, and lift the bumper clear.

☐ **Step A5:** Refit in reverse order.

PART B - TURBO I.E. CARS

Follow the procedure set out in *Job 6* but in addition, disconnect the following:

☐ **Step B1:**
From 'inside' the
liner cavity,
remove the
bumper lower
fixing bolt.

Job 6-B1

☐ **Step B2:** Unbolt
the bumper from the
support rods.

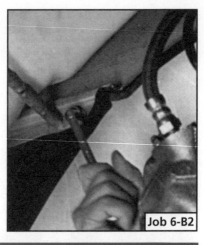

Job 6-B2

Job 7. Rear bumper
- removal and refitting.

Step 1: Reach under the bumper, squeeze together the retaining tabs securing the number plate light, pull the lamp clear and unplug its wires.

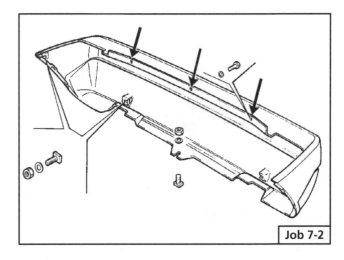

Job 7-2

☐ **Step 2:** From under the car, remove the three bumper lower edge and two side fixing bolts.

☐ **Step 3:** Open the tailgate and unscrew the three upper fixing bolts (see illustration *Job 7-2, arrowed*). Lower the bumper from the car.

☐ **Step 4:** Refit in reverse order.

Job 8. Door trim panel
- removal and refitting.

☐ **Step 1:** Undo
the fixing screws
from the door
armrest/grab
handle. If it is of
the removable type
(i.e. not a one-
piece moulding
with the door trim
panel) remove it
downwards.

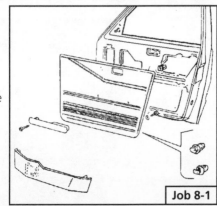

Job 8-1

Note that on later models, both armrest and tidy-bin are integral with the door trim panel - see **Step 5**.

❑ **Step 2:** Undo the tidy-bin screws.

❑ **Step 3:** Ease the interior door release handle escutcheon forward and remove it. The handle can now be withdrawn and its control rod disconnected.

Job 8-3

❑ **Step 4:** Remove the window winder handle by releasing its circlip, hidden between handle and door trim panel.

Job 8-4

❑ **Step 5:** Lever the trim panel off the door by sliding a flat blade between it and the door, adjacent to each press-stud, and prising outwards. Take great care not to over-force the press-studs and rip them out of the trim panel.

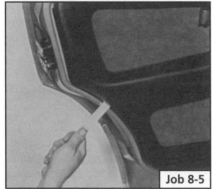

Job 8-5

Peel back the polythene sheet which is stuck over the door opening, trying not to rip it. The polythene will stick back in place.

Job 9. Window regulator - removal and refitting.

❑ **Step 6:** Refit in reverse order.

See **PART E: ELECTRICAL AND INSTRUMENTS Job 16** for Electric Window Motor Replacement.

❑ **Step 1:** With the window fully wound up, remove the door trim panel and polythene sheet. See **Job 8**.

❑ **Step 2:** Have a helper support the weight of the window, then remove the two bolts which secure the window frame to the regulator mechanism.

❑ **Step 3:** Undo all the bolts securing the regulator to the door.

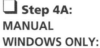

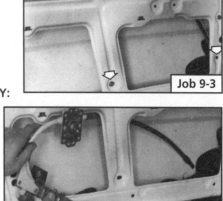

Job 9-3

❑ **Step 4A: MANUAL WINDOWS ONLY:** Detach the regulator cable from its clips and remove the regulator assembly from the door.

Job 9-4A

❑ **Step 4B: ELECTRIC WINDOWS ONLY:** You will have to temporarily reconnect the window switch and lower the windows. Use bent long-nosed pliers on the window glass retaining pin (inset, position arrowed) and

Job 9-4B

separate the window glass from the electric window device.

❑ **Step 5:** Lift the window glass, move it forwards and remove it.

❑ **Step 6: ELECTRIC WINDOWS ONLY:** Remove the bolts (arrowed)...

Job 9-6

❑ **Step 7:** ...and lift out the electric window device. For the earlier type of regulator and more detailed information, see **PART E: Job 16, Step 4**.

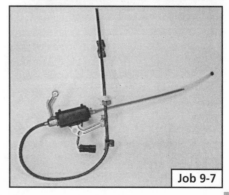

Job 9-7

Job 10. Door lock/handle (3-door) - removal and refitting.

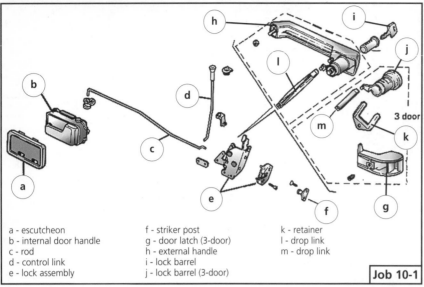

a - escutcheon
b - internal door handle
c - rod
d - control link
e - lock assembly
f - striker post
g - door latch (3-door)
h - external handle
i - lock barrel
j - lock barrel (3-door)
k - retainer
l - drop link
m - drop link

Job 10-1

☐ **Step 1:** Take note of the arrangement of the door lock components.

☐ **Step 2:** Remove the door trim panel, see **Job 8**. Remove the securing screw from the trailing edge of the door, then detach the exterior door handle.

☐ **Step 3:** Undo the screws which secure the window glass guide, then remove the guide.

☐ **Step 4:** Undo the door lock fixing screws and remove the lock.

☐ **Step 5:** Refit in the reverse order.

Job 11. Door lock/handle (5-door) - removal and refitting.

Refer to the illustration for **Job 10, Step 1.**

☐ **Step 1:** Remove the door trim panel, see **Job 8**.

☐ **Step 2:** Undo the lock securing bolts and withdraw the lock sufficiently to disconnect the plunger link rod. Remove the lock.

☐ **Step 3:** The exterior handle and lock barrel can be removed by undoing the two screws from inside the door.

☐ **Step 4:** Refit in the reverse order.

Job 12. Door removal - replacement and adjustment.

☐ **Step 1: FRONT AND REAR (5-door) DOORS:** Each door has two hinges. Mark around the edge of the hinge onto the door frame with a felt pen so that the door can be refitted in the same place.

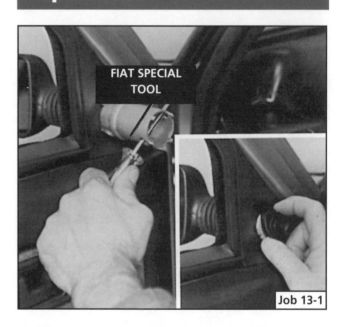

Job 12-2

☐ **Step 2:** Unbolt each hinge by undoing the door bolts (**a**) while a helper supports the door.

☐ **Step 3:** Adjust the front-to-back and up-and-down position by slackening the B-post bolts (see illustration **Job 12-1, parts b**) and moving the hinge. To move the door in-and-out at its front edge, pack the hinges with shims.

Job 13. Door mirror - replacement.

FIAT SPECIAL TOOL

Job 13-1

☐ **Step 1:** Remove the rubber bellows (inset) and unscrew the ring screw. If you don't have access to the special tool illustrated, use a self-grip wrench, or a blunt drift, taking care not to cause damage.

☐ **Step 2:** Have an assistant hold the mirror as it is disconnected. It can now be lifted away, with its plastic trim.

CHAMPION 'READING' YOUR SPARK PLUGS

Champion explain how the condition of spark plug firing ends can act as a guide to the state of tune and general condition of the engine. The examples shown are assumed to be the correct grade for the engine.

NORMAL

Core nose lightly coated with grey-brown deposits. Electrodes not burning unduly - gap increasing by about 0.01 mm every 1,250 miles (with the use of unleaded fuel). Spark plugs correct for engine.

HEAVY DEPOSITS

Possible causes: Fuel or oil additives. Excessive upper cylinder lubricant. Worn valve guides. Unvarying speed (stationary engine). Replace spark plugs.

OIL FOULING

Deposits can short-circuit firing end, weakening or eliminating spark. Causes: worn valve guides, bores or piston rings, or while new engine is running-in. Temporary use of next hotter grade of spark plug may stop the misfire. Replace spark plugs. Cure oiling problem.

CARBON FOULING

Look for dull black sooty deposits. (Unleaded fuel carbon fouling can appear similar to oil fouling). Deposits can short circuit the firing end, weakening or eliminating the spark. Check for: Over-rich mixture, faulty choke or clogged air filter. Replace spark plugs.

SPLIT CORE NOSE

(May first appear as hair-line crack). Probably caused by: Over-advanced ignition timing. Faulty distributor advance mechanism. Use of low octane fuel. Weak mixture. Manifold air-leaks. Cooling system problems. Incorrect gap-setting technique.

INITIAL PRE IGNITION

Caused by serious overheating. Causes are those listed for overheating, but may be more severe. Corrective measures are urgently needed before engine damage occurs. Discard plugs in this condition.

OVERHEATING

Likely causes are: Over-advanced ignition timing, or faulty distributor advance mechanism. Use of low octane fuel. Weak mixture. Discard spark plugs showing signs of overheating, and cure the cause.

FACT FILE: CORRECT INSTALLATION

- Make sure seating areas are perfectly clean.
- Insert plug finger tight to seat. Ensure plug 'spins' freely.
- Have dealer 'chase' out threads in engine, if necessary.
- PLUGS WITH SEATING GASKET: Tighten a further 1/4 turn with plug spanner.
- PLUGS WITH TAPER SEATS: Tighten a further 1/16th turn ONLY - no further!
- Overtightening can damage cylinder head or make taper seat plugs impossible to remove.

RECOMMENDED FL LUBRICANTS - FOR YOUR FIAT UNO

COMPONENT/ CAPACITY	UNO 45 903, 999cc 1983-1990	UNO 45 903, 999cc 1990-1992	UNO 1.0 i.e. 999cc 1992-1994	UNO 55, 60 1116cc 1983-1990	UNO 60 1108cc 1990-1992	UNO 1.1 i.e. 1108cc 1992-1994	UNO SELECTA 1116, 1372cc 1987-1994	UNO 70 1299, 1301cc 1983-1990	UNO 70 1372cc 1990-1992	UNO 1.4 i.e. 1372cc 1992-1994	UNO TURBO (c) 1299, 1301cc 1985-1990	UNO TURBO (c) 1372cc 1990-1994	UNO 6... 16... 1987
ENGINE	VS Europa	VS Europa	VS Europa	VS Europa	VS Europa	VS Europa	VS Europa	VS Europa	VS Europa	VS Europa	Selenia 20K	Selenia 20K	VS Ma...
CAPACITY	3.5/3.8 L	3.8 L	3.8 L	4.1 L	3.8 L	3.8 L	4.1 L	4.1 L	4.1 L	4.1 L	4.1 L	4.1 L	4
MANUAL G-BOX	Tutela ZC90	Tutela ZC80/S	Tutela ZC80/S	Tutela ZC90	Tutela ZC80/S	Tutela ZC80/S		Tutela ZC90	Tutela ZC80/S	Tutela ZC80/S	Tutela ZC90	Tutela ZC80/S	Tutela 2.0...
CAPACITY	2.4 L	2.4 L	2.4 L	2.4 L	2.4 L	2.4 L		2.4 L	2.4 L	2.4 L	2.9 L	2.0 L	2.0
AUTO G-BOX							Tutela CVT						
CAPACITY							3.5 L (a)						
DIFFERENTIAL (S)	From Gearbox	From Gearbox	From Gearbox	From Gearbox	From Gearbox	From Gearbox	From Gearbox	From Gearbox	From Gearbox	From Gearbox	From Gearbox	From Gearbox	From G...
CAPACITY	-	-	-	-	-	-	-	-	-	-	-	-	
STEERING BOX	Tutela K854	Tutela K854	Tutela K854	Tutela K854	Tutela K854	Tutela K854	Tutela K854	Tutela K854	Tutela K854	Tutela K854	Tutela K854	Tutela K854	Tutela
CAPACITY	127 g	127 g	127 g	127 g	127 g	127 g	127 g	127 g	127 g	127 g	127 g	127 g	12
C.V. JOINTS	Tutela MRM2	Tutela MRM2	Tutela MRM2	Tutela MRM2	Tutela MRM2	Tutela MRM2	Tutela MRM2	Tutela MRM2	Tutela MRM2	Tutela MRM2	Tutela MRM2	Tutela MRM2	Tutela
CAPACITY	80 g (each)	80 g (each)	80 g (each)	80 g (each)	80 g (each)	80 g (each)	80 g (each)	80 g (each)	80 g (each)	80 g (each)	80 g (each)	80 g (each)	80 g
BRAKE FLUID	Tutela Plus 3	Tutela Plus 3	Tutela Plus 3	Tutela Plus 3	Tutela Plus 3	Tutela Plus 3	Tutela Plus 3	Tutela Plus 3	Tutela Plus 3	Tutela Plus 3	Tutela Plus 3	Tutela Plus 3	Tutela
CAPACITY	0.33 L	0.33 L	0.33 L	0.33 L	0.33 L	0.33 L	0.37 L	0.33 L	0.33 L	0.33 L	0.37 L (c)	0.37 L (c)	0....
COOLANT	Paraflu 11	Paraflu 11	Paraflu 11	Paraflu 11	Paraflu 11	Paraflu 11	Paraflu 11	Paraflu 11	Paraflu 11	Paraflu 11	Paraflu 11	Paraflu 11	Para...
CAPACITY	4.6 L (b)	4.6 L (b)	4.6 L (b)	6.2 L (b)	4.7 L (b)	4.7 L (b)	6.2 L (b)	6.2 L (b)	6.2 L (b)	6.2 L (b)	6.9 L (b)	7.7 L (b)	8.9
SCREENWASH	Arexons DP1	Arexons DP1	Arexons DP1	Arexons DP1	Arexons DP1	Arexons DP1	Arexons DP1	Arexons DP1	Arexons DP1	Arexons DP1	Arexons DP1	Arexons DP1	Arexo...

NOTES: a) Drain/Refill Capacity   b) Cooling System at a Concentration of 50% coolant to 50% water   c) If ABS Breaking System Fitted: Use 0.45 L Tutela Top 4   CHANGE PERIODS: see *Chapter 5, Service Intervals*

IMPORTANT NOTE: Not all of the components listed here are fitted to all models.

CHAPTER 7
WIRING DIAGRAMS

KEY: COMPONENT NUMBERS 1981-1986

00200	Alternator
00203	Alternator
00208	Alternator with built-in regulator
00500	Battery
01001	Starter motor
01002	Starter motor
01202	Rear front electric window motor
01203	Left front electric window motor
01206	Windscreen wiper motor
01207	Rearscreen wiper motor
01252	Right front door locking motor
01253	Left front door locking motor
01254	Right rear door locking motor
01255	Left rear door locking motor
01400	Electric windscreen washer pump
01401	Electric rearscreen washer pump
01402	Headlight washer pump
01405	Ignition coil
01420	Electric fuel pump
01500	Radiator cooling fan
01502	Injector cooling fan
01504	Heater fan
02001	Engine cut-out solenoid on injection pump
02010	Fuel injector
02011	Fuel injector
02012	Fuel injector
02013	Fuel injector
02015	Supplementary air valve
02210	Accelerator pump outlet cut-out solenoid on carburettor
02215	Supplementary air valve
02400	Ignition coil
02405	Ignition coil with ECU
02490	Static advance ignition control unit
02492	Microplex ignition system control unit
03000	Engine oil pressure switch
03002	Right front door open switch
03003	Left front door open switch
03004	Right rear door open switch
03005	Left rear door open switch
03006	Handbrake 'on' warning light switch
03007	Brake lights switch
03008	Reversing lights switch
03015	Handbrake applied warning light switch
03028	Radiator thermal switch
03029	Coolant overheating thermal switch
03034	Injector cooling fan thermostatic switch
03035	Accelerator pump outlet cut-out solenoid thermostatic switch
03036	Radiator thermostatic switch with two operating ranges
03053	Map reading light switch
03054	Main external lights switch
03059	Fog lights switch
03060	Rear fog lights switch
03085	Micro-switch on pedal for accelerator pedal travel of 16-24 mm
03086	Micro-switch on pedal for accelerator pedal travel of 3-7 mm
03110	Heated rear windscreen switch
03112	Rear window washer switch
03114	Heater fan switch
03123	Air pressure switch
03142	Choke warning light switch
03144	Reset switch
03145	Display switch
03150	Rear drive engaged warning light switch
03305	Right door pillar courtesy light switch
03306	Left door pillar courtesy light switch
03315	Push button for electric windscreen washer pump
03319	Push button for horn
03336	Push button for headlight flashers
03500	Ignition switch
03505	Butterfly valve cut-off switch
03506	Throttle position switch

03511	Multiple switch on selector lever
03530	Right front electric window switch
03531	Left front electric window switch
03546	Rearscreen wash/wipe switch
03550	Hazard warning lights switch
04010	Direction indicators switch
04020	Headlights, main bean and dipped
04022	Headlights, main beam and dipped, side lights switch
04032	Windscreen wash/wipe control
04214	Fuel injection system control relay
04215	Antiskid system failure relay
04225	Radiator fan 2nd speed engagement relay feed
04241	Foglights relay feed
04248	Headlight washer remote control switch with timer
04260	Electric windows motor relay feed
04279	Starter inhibitor relay
04283	Antiskid system relay
04291	Horn relay feed
04292	Heater rear windscreen relay
04305	Automatic transmission electronic control unit relay feed
04441	Dim-dip cut-out
04450	Remote control shunt to cut out lights in daytime
04500	Windscreen wiper intermittent device
04580	Flashers unit for direction indicators and hazard warning lights
04581	Direction indicator flashers unit
04600	Distributor
04601	Distributor
04700	Coolant temperature sender unit
04701	Electronic injection coolant temperature sender unit
04720	Oil pressure sender unit
04730	Speedometer impulse generator
05004	Right main beam and dipped headlight with side light and direction indicator
05005	Left main beam and dipped headlight with side light and direction indicator
05008	Right headlight, main beam and dipped with side light
05009	Left headlight, main beam and dipped with side light
05013	Fuel consumption sensor
05015	Right foglight
05016	Left foglight
05410	Right front direction indicator
05411	Left front direction indicator
05412	Right front side indicator
05413	Left front side indicator
05640	Number plate light
05671	Right rear light cluster: side light, direction indicator, brake light, reversing light
05684	Left rear light cluster: side light, direction indicator, brake light, rear foglight
05690	Right rear light cluster, sidelight, direction indicator, brake light, rear foglight
05691	Left rear light cluster, sidelight, direction indicator, brake light, rear foglight
06000	Light on rear view mirror with switch
06005	Courtesy light on rear view mirror with switch
06026	Map reading light
06070	Ideogram light bulb
06076	Ideogram fibre optic light
06080	Heater controls light bulb
06084	Instrument panel light bulb
06088	Cigar lighter light bulb
06104	Left side direction indicator
06105	Right side direction indicator
06108	Left no. plate light bulb
06109	Right no. plate light bulb
06300	Side lights warning light
06305	Main beam headlights warning light
06310	Rear foglights warning light
06311	Foglights warning light
06315	Hazard warning lights warning light

06320	Direction indicators warning light
06335	Brake fluid level warning light
06336	Handbrake 'on' warning light
06337	Brake and handbrake warning light
06343	Insufficient engine oil pressure warning light
06344	Brake fluid level warning light
06345	Fuel reserve warning light
06350	Coolant overheating warning light
06355	Battery recharging warning light
06365	Choke warning light
06366	Rear drive engaged warning light
06368	Antiskid system failure light
06385	Heated rear windscreen warning light
06634	Timed buzzer signalling Park not engaged
06800	Horn
06801	Right horn
06802	Left horn
06887	Brake fluid and handbrake warning light
07000	Coolant level sensor
07001	Engine oil level sensor
07003	Brake fluid level sensor
07012	Electronic clutch
07015	Right front brake pad wear sensor
07016	Left front brake pad wear sensor
07020	Engine speed sensor
07021	TDC sensor
07022	Anti-knock sensor
07023	Diagnostic socket
07037	Butterfly valve (cut-off) switch
07050	Fuel gauge
07051	Fuel consumption gauge (econometer)
07052	Airflow meter
07060	Idle cut out device
07107	Roadwheel speed sensors
07109	Vacuum switch
07191	Absolute pressure sensor
07192	Vacuum switch
07400	Fuel level gauge
07410	Engine oil temperature gauge
07415	Coolant temperature gauge
07420	Engine oil pressure gauge
07430	Tachometer
07460	Clock
07461	Digital clock
08051	Ignition coil condenser
08406	Relay and fuse box
08410	7.5 A fuse box
09000	Dim-dip transformer
09008	Radiator cooling fan 1st speed resistor
09100	Heated rear windscreen
09010	Radio (wiring)
10022	Cut-off device electronic control unit
10500	Control (fuse) box
10515	Electronic injection control unit
10561	Automatic transmission electronic control unit
10571	Central locking control unit
10584	Antiskid system ECU
10586	Pressure modulators
11062	Diagnostic socket
11065	Bridge as per legislation
40086	Join between dashboard cables and rear cables
40089	Join between dashboard cables and ceiling cables
59000	Cigar lighter
59010	Radio power lead (if fitted)
60000	Instrument panel
60120	Gear selector and engagement panel
60204	Four place fusebox
60220	Fusebox
70090	General earth
70091	General earth
70092	Earth plate
70117	Right front earth
90003	Junction
A } B }	Connector block
M	Electronic control unit

PART A: UNOs PRE - 1990

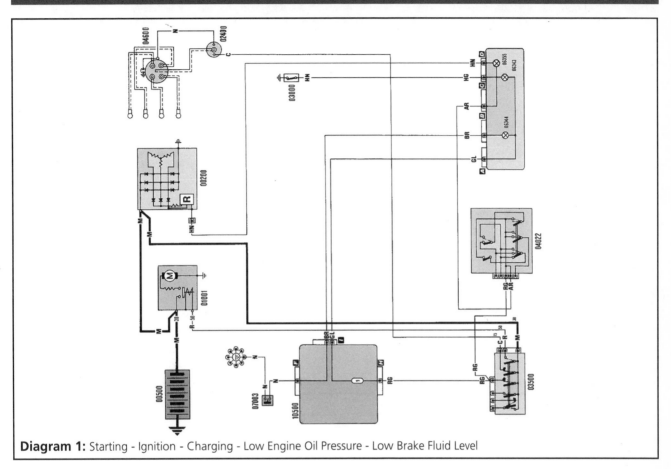

Diagram 1: Starting - Ignition - Charging - Low Engine Oil Pressure - Low Brake Fluid Level

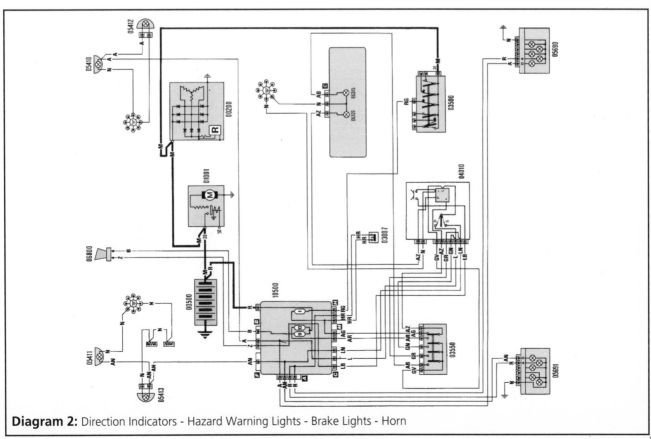

Diagram 2: Direction Indicators - Hazard Warning Lights - Brake Lights - Horn

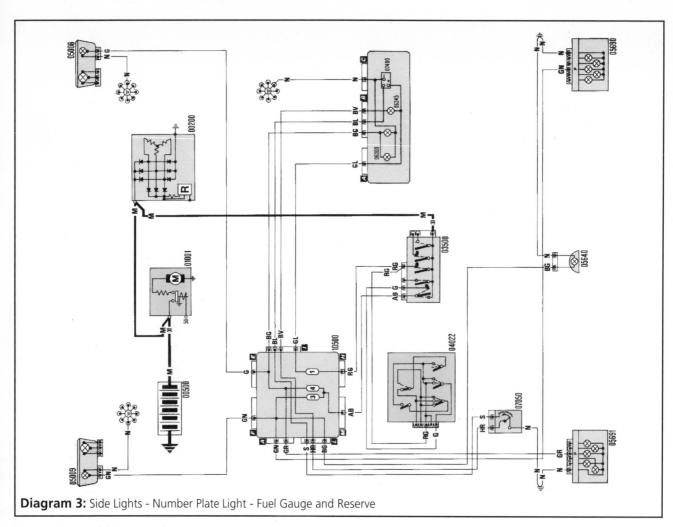

Diagram 3: Side Lights - Number Plate Light - Fuel Gauge and Reserve

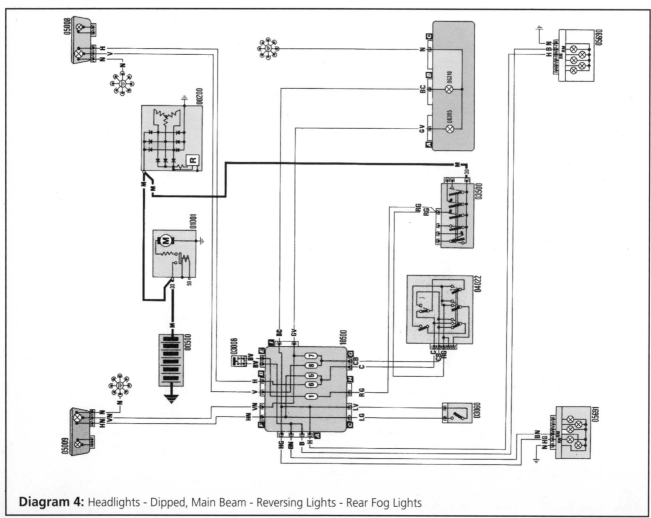

Diagram 4: Headlights - Dipped, Main Beam - Reversing Lights - Rear Fog Lights

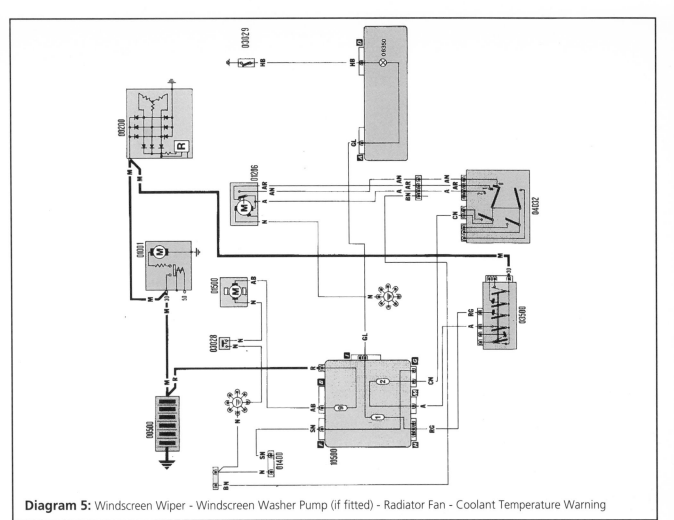

Diagram 5: Windscreen Wiper - Windscreen Washer Pump (if fitted) - Radiator Fan - Coolant Temperature Warning

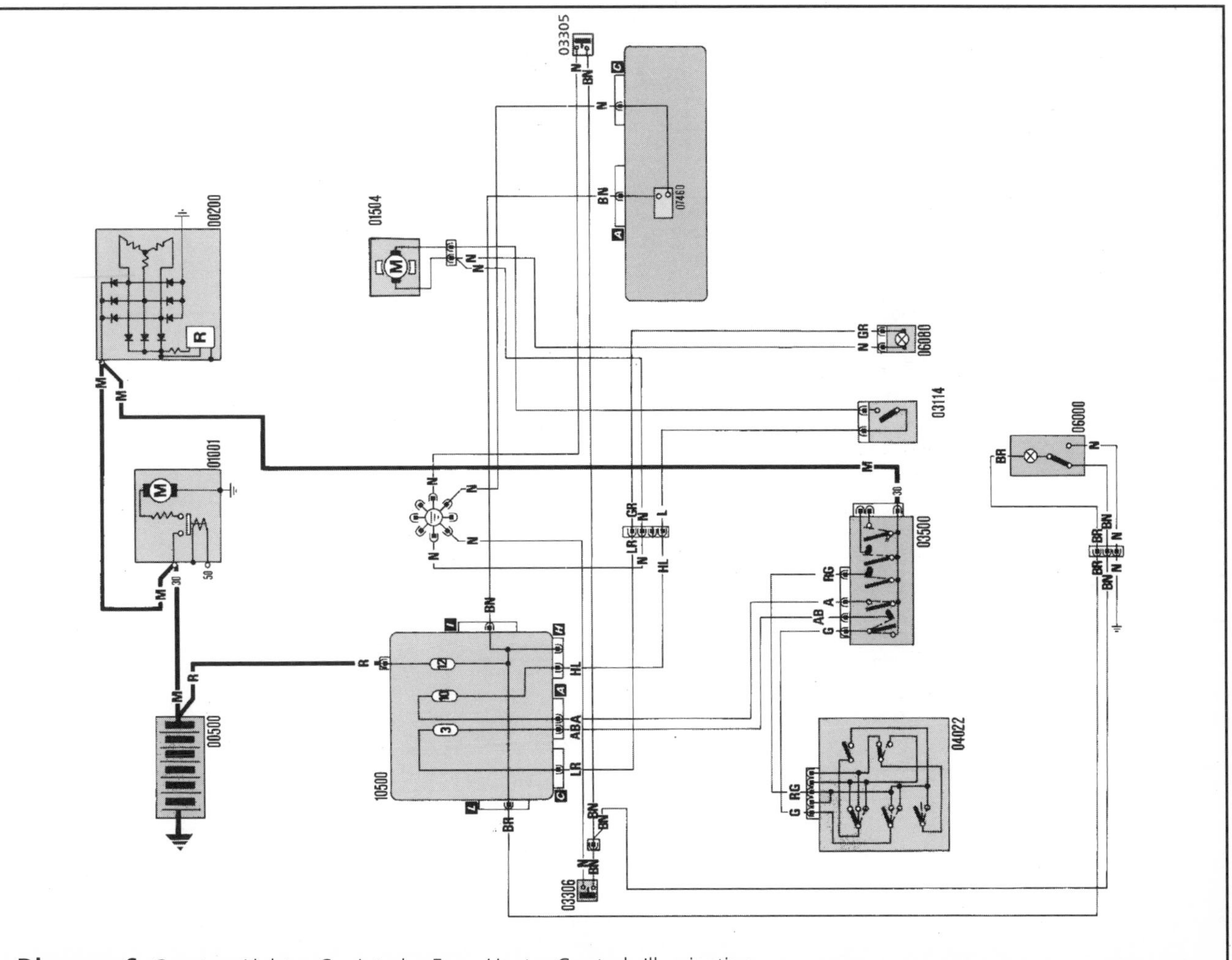

Diagram 6: Courtesy Lights - Car Interior Fan - Heater Controls Illumination

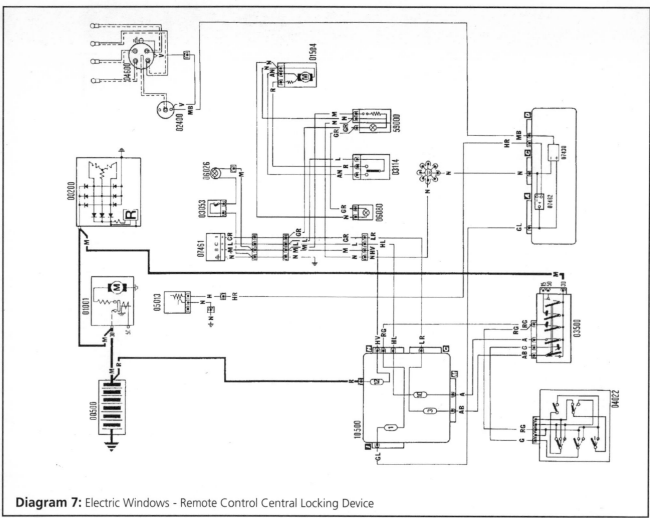

Diagram 7: Electric Windows - Remote Control Central Locking Device

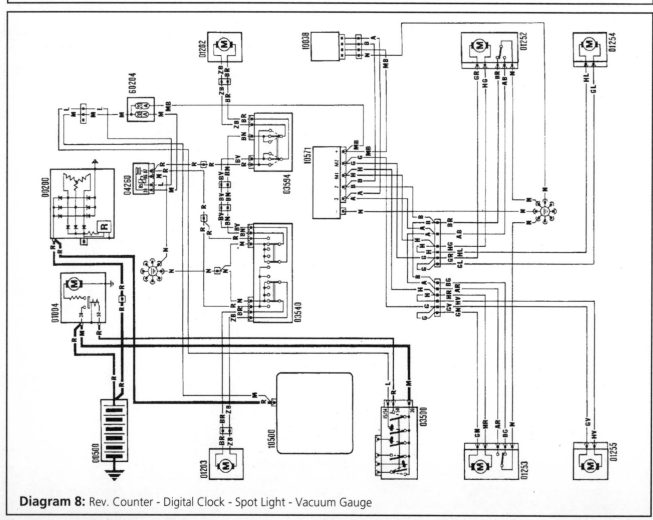

Diagram 8: Rev. Counter - Digital Clock - Spot Light - Vacuum Gauge

PART B: 1301cc TURBO i.e.

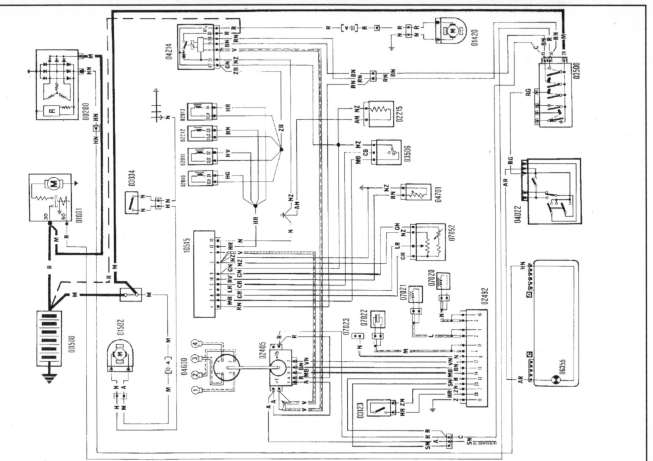

Diagram 9: Starting - Microplex Electronic Ignition - Charging - LE2-Jetronic Electronic Ignition - Electric Fuel Pump - Injector Cooling Fan

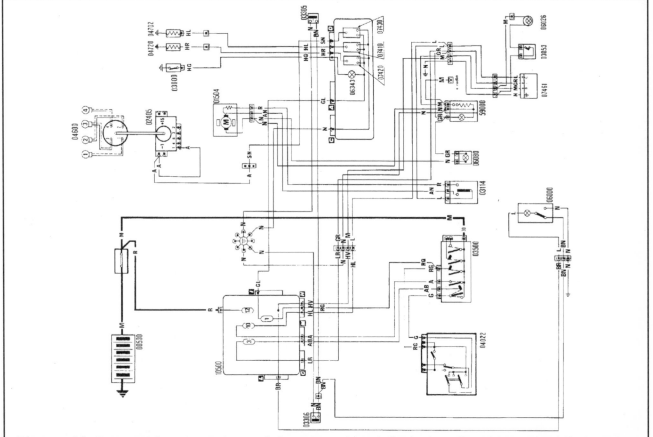

Diagram 10: Courtesy Lights - Car Interior Ventilation - Heater Controls Illumination - Cigar Lighter - Digital Clock - Radio Wiring - Low Engine Oil Pressure - Engine Oil Pressure - Oil Temperature Gauge - Rev. Counter

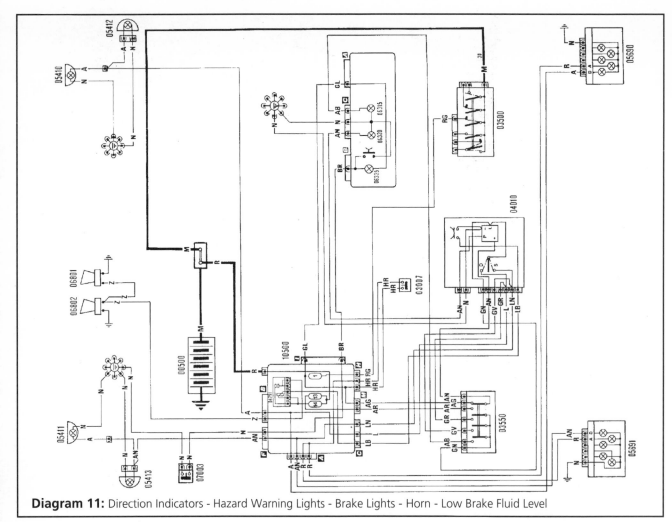

Diagram 11: Direction Indicators - Hazard Warning Lights - Brake Lights - Horn - Low Brake Fluid Level

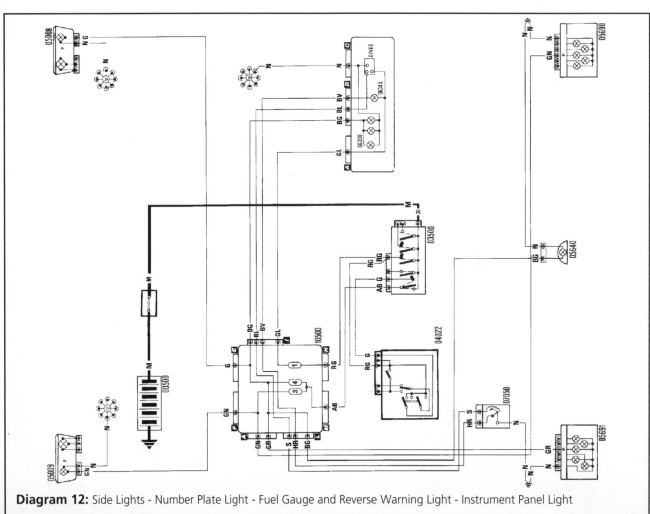

Diagram 12: Side Lights - Number Plate Light - Fuel Gauge and Reverse Warning Light - Instrument Panel Light

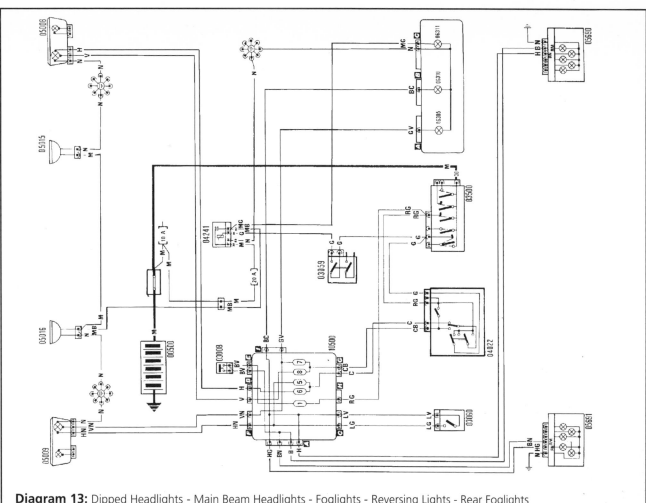

Diagram 13: Dipped Headlights - Main Beam Headlights - Foglights - Reversing Lights - Rear Foglights

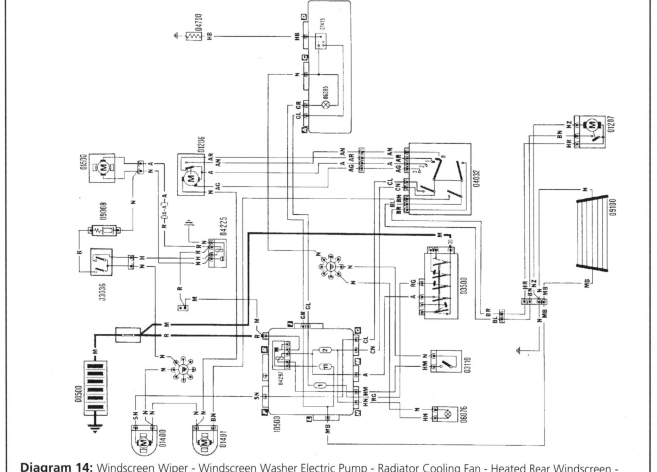

Diagram 14: Windscreen Wiper - Windscreen Washer Electric Pump - Radiator Cooling Fan - Heated Rear Windscreen - Ideogram Fibre Optic Light - Coolant Temperature Gauge - Rearscreen Washer Electric Pump

KEY: COMPONENT NUMBERS MKII UNOs 1990-0N Note: Not all the items listed will be fitted to all models

No.	Description
1	Injector cooling fan
2	Left front light cluster
3	Left foglight
4	Left front engine compartment earth
5	Radiator cooling fan
6	Double contact thermostatic switch on engine radiator
6A	Thermostatic switch on engine radiator
7	Left horn
8	Right horn
9	Resistor for engaging radiator fan 1st speed
10	Right front light cluster
11	Right foglight
12	Right front engine compartment earth
13	Battery
14	Ignition coil
15	Ignition distributor with magnetic impulse generator
16	Left front side direction indicator
17	Ignition power module
18	MPi electronic injection control unit
19	Join between injection/ignition cables in engine compartment
20	Battery cables join in engine compartment
21	Antiskid braking system wiring join
22	Starting go-ahead relay
23	Earth for battery
24	Radiator coolant temperature sender unit for electronic injection
25	Anti-knock sensor
26	Injection system diagnostic socket
27	Switch signalling insufficient engine oil pressure
28	Radiator coolant temperature sender unit
29	Engine oil temperature sender unit
30	Engine oil pressure sender unit
31	Right front side direction indicator
32	Engine oil temperature sender unit cable join
33	Battery recharging signal cable join
34	Windscreen washer pump
35	Rear screen washer pump
36	Reversing switch
37	Fuel injectors relay feed
38	Insufficient brake fluid level sensor
39	Left brake pad wear sensor
40	Microplex electronic ignition control unit
41	Injection cables join in engine compartment
42	Ignition cables join in engine compartment
43	Join between battery cable and injection cables
44	Join between engine cable and battery cables
45	Left front brake pad cables join
46	Starter motor
47	Windscreen wiper motor
48	Headlight washer pump
49	Fuel injector
50	Fuel injector
51	Fuel injector
52	Fuel injector
53	Supplementary air valve
54	Spark plug
55	Spark plug
56	Spark plug
57	Spark plug
58	Excess supercharging pressure switch
59	Throttle position switch
60	Engine speed sensor
61	Ignition diagnostic socket
62	Connector block
63	Connector block
64	Alternator
65	Thermostatic switch for injector cooling fan
66	Right brake pad wear sensor
67	TDC sensor
68	Connector block
69	Connector block
70	Connector block
71	Connector block
72	Join with right brake pad cables
73	Electronic earth
74	Power earth
75	Brake stop-light switch
76	20 A fuse for central locking
77	10 A fuse for electric fuel pump
78	30 A fuse for radiator cooling fan
79	30 A fuse for electric windows
80	10 A fuse for injector cooling fan
81	20 A fuse for headlight wash/wipe
82	20 A fuse for foglights
83	Junction box with fuses and relays:
E1	Horn relay (for single tone horns bridge between 86 and 87)
E2	Heated rear screen relay

No.	Description
E3	Heater (bridge between 85 and 30)
84	Join between front cable and rear cables
85	Join between front cable and door open sensor cables
86	Earth on dashboard, left hand side
87	Earth on dashboard, right hand side
88	Choke warning light switch
89	Ignition switch
90	Hazard warning lights switch
91	Steering column switch unit
A	Rear screen wash/wipe switch
B	Horn button
C	Direction indicators switch
D	Windscreen wiper intermittent speed selector switch
E	Windscreen/headlight washer control switch
F	Rear foglights/headlight washer intermittent device switch
G	Headlight dip switch
H	External lights switch
I	Flasher switch
92	Foglight relay
93	Electric fuel pump relay
94	Electric windows relay feed
95	Headlight wash/wipe intermittent device
96	Direction indicators/hazard warning lights flasher unit
97	Central locking receiver
98	Central locking control unit
99	Join with brake pad cables
100	Join between engine cable and dashboard cables
101	Automatic heater cable join
102	Instrument panel
A	Foglights warning light
B	Main beam headlights warning light
C	Side lights warning light
D	Rear foglights warning light
E	Heated rear screen warning light
F	Hazard warning lights warning light
G	Direction indicators warning light
H	Handbrake applied and insufficient brake fluid level warning light
I	Choke warning light
K	Instrument panel light bulbs
L	Battery recharging warning light
M	Insufficient engine oil pressure warning light
O	Antiskid braking system failure warning light
P	Maximum turbocharging pressure warning light
Q	Brake pad wear warning light
R	Door open warning light
U	Fuel level gauge
V	Engine oil pressure gauge
W	Engine oil temperature gauge
Y	Tachometer
Z	Coolant temperature gauge
103	Join with remote control central locking cables
104	Cigar lighter
105	Radio receiver
106	Heater unit
107	Switch unit
A	Heated rear screen switch
B	Rear foglights switch
C	Switch unit light bulb
D	Rear screen wiper switch
E	Foglights switch
F	Clock
108	Left front electric window motor
109	Left front central locking geared motor
110	Switch signalling left front door open
111	Push button on left front pillar for centre courtesy light
112	Front electric windows switch panel, driver's side
113	Join between dashboard cable and adjustable map reading light cable
114	Join with left front electric window cables
115	Join between dashboard cable and rear cables
116	Join between rear cable and courtesy light cables
117	Left front speaker
118	Handbrake 'on' switch
119	Centre courtesy light bulb
119A	Adjustable map reading light on rear view mirror
120	Right front electric window motor
121	Right front central locking geared motor
122	Switch signalling right front door open
123	Push button on right front pillar for centre courtesy light
124	Electric windows control panel, passenger side
125	Fuel level gauge
126	Join with right front electric window cables
127	Join between engine cable and dashboard cables

No.	Description
128	Right front speaker
129	Left rear light cluster
130	Join between rear cable and luggage compartment courtesy light
131	Windscreen washer pump wiring join
132	Rear screen washer pump wiring join
133	Left rear earth
134	Rear screen wiper motor
135	Electric fuel pump
136	Rear number plate light
137	Heated rear screen
138	Right rear light cluster
139	Rear foglight go-ahead switch
140	Join between front cable and antiskid brakes cables
141	Join between front cable and antiskid brakes cables
142	25 A fuse for antiskid brakes
143	Antiskid braking system control unit
144	Left modulator for antiskid brakes
145	Right modulator for antiskid brakes
146	Sensor on left front wheel
147	Sensor on right front wheel
148	10 A fuse for antiskid braking system
149	Vacuum switch for antiskid braking system
150	Antiskid braking system engagement relay
151	Antiskid braking system failure signalling switch
152	Digiplex electronic ignition control unit
153	Bosch SPI Mono-Jetronic injection system control unit
155	Join between engine cable and injection cables
156	Join between engine cable and rear cables for SPI system
157	Idle adjustment actuator
158	Throttle position switch
159	Injector current restriction resistor (SPI)
162	Engine cut-out solenoid
163	Idle cut-out solenoid valve
168	Tachometer electro-magnetic sensor
169	Automatic heater control unit
170	Heater fan
171	Outside temperature sensor
172	Mixed air temperature sensor
173	Air mixture flap electrical control motor
174	Diagnostic socket for automatic heater
175	Connector block
176	Connector block
177	Join with cables for automatic heater
178	Radiator coolant circulation solenoid valve
179	Automatic heater unit:
A	Temperature control potentiometer
B	Fan speed control potentiometer
C	Heater controls light bulbs
D	Ideogram signalling automatic function engaged
E	Automatic function engaged switch
180	Horn
181	Check Panel:
A	Insufficient engine oil level warning light
B	Insufficient coolant level warning light
C	Failure with side lights/rear foglight/rear number plate light/braking lights warning light
D	Insufficient brake fluid level warning light
E	Door open warning light
F	Brake pad wear warning light
182	Earth on dashboard
183	Join with cables for central locking
184	Join with cables for central locking
185	Left rear central locking geared motor
186	Right rear central locking geared motor
187	Contact on choke lever
188	Resistor for inlet manifold heating
189	Pre-heating thermal switch
191	Heated Lambda sensor
192	Lambda sensor protective fuse
193	Silicon diode
194	Join between front cable and injection cable
197	Connector block
198	Rear cable join
199	Insufficient engine oil level sensor
200	Insufficient coolant level sensor
201	Switch signalling left rear door open
202	Switch signalling right rear door open
203	Switch on gear selector
204	Light for gear selector panel signalling gear engaged
205	Parking signal not on
206	Connector block
207	Join in engine compartment with injection cables
208	Petrol vapour cut out-solenoid valve

KEY: COMPONENT NUMBERS MKII UNOs 1990-0N   Continued

No.	Description	No.	Description	No.	Description
209	Petrol vapour cut out-solenoid valve	217	Join between front cable and emission control cable	229	Dim-dip circuit 7.5 A protective fuse
210	Airflow meter			230	Driver's side seat heated pad
211	Speedometer relay	218	Join between front cable and battery cable	231	Driver's seat backrest heated pad
212	LE2 Jetronic electronic injection control unit	219	Injection system air temperature sensor	232	10 A protective fuse for driver's seat heated pads
213	Connector block	220	Ignition control unit relay feed	233	Foglights go-ahead switch
214	Connector block	225	Front cable join	234	Driving lights cut out switch
215	Connector block	226	Front cable join	235	Dipped headlights relay
216	Ignition cable join	227	Dim-dip circuit cut out switch	236	Main beam headlights relay
		228	Dim-dip circuit resistance	237	Join between engine cable and dashboard cables

PART C: 'MKII' UNOs 1990-On

* To the rev counter (Only for the 999 SX - 1108 SX)   ** Non existent for the 903

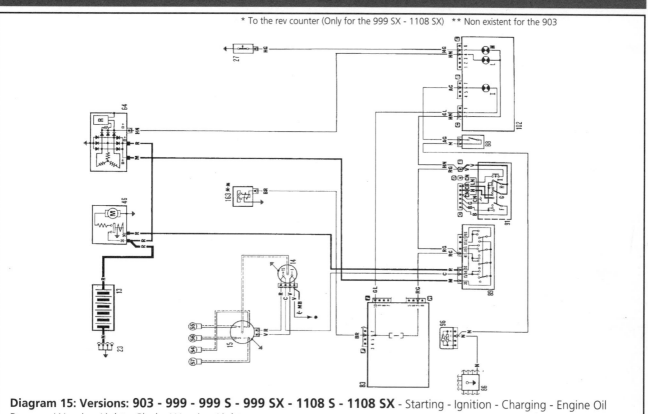

Diagram 15: Versions: 903 - 999 - 999 S - 999 SX - 1108 S - 1108 SX - Starting - Ignition - Charging - Engine Oil Pressure Warning Light - Choke Warning Light

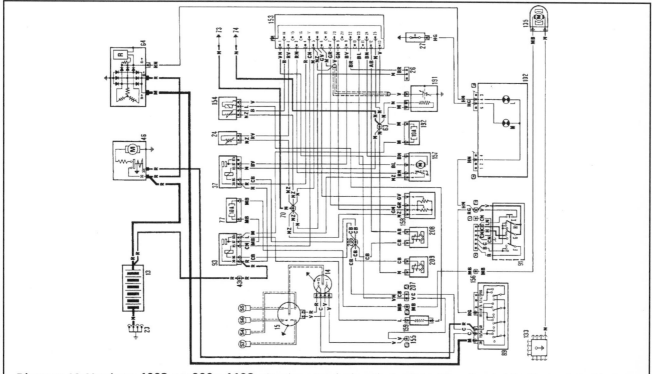

Diagram 16: Versions: 1993-on 999 - 1108 - Starting - Breakerless Electronic Ignition - Bosch S.P.I. Electronic Ignition - Charging - Electric Fuel Pump - Low Engine Oil Pressure Warning Light

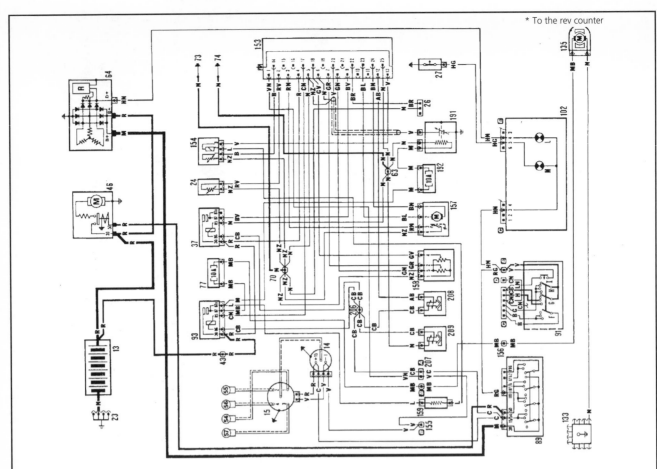

Diagram 17: Versions: 1993-on 1372 - 1498 - Starting - Digiplex 2 Electronic Ignition - Bosch S.P.I. Electronic Ignition - Charging - Electric Fuel Pump - Low Engine Oil Pressure Warning Light

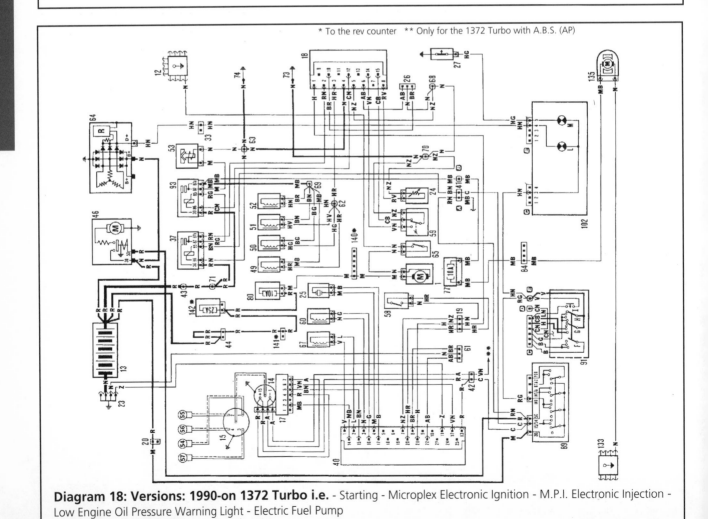

Diagram 18: Versions: 1990-on 1372 Turbo i.e. - Starting - Microplex Electronic Ignition - M.P.I. Electronic Injection - Low Engine Oil Pressure Warning Light - Electric Fuel Pump

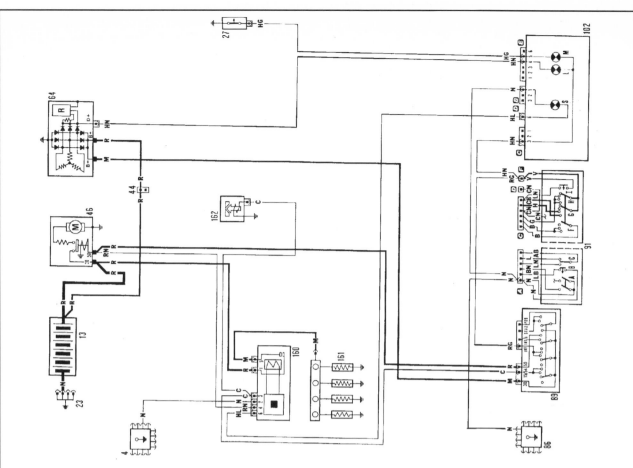

Diagram 19: Versions: 1697 D - Starting - Pre-heating System and Heater Plugs Warning Light - Charging - Low Engine Oil Pressure Warning Light

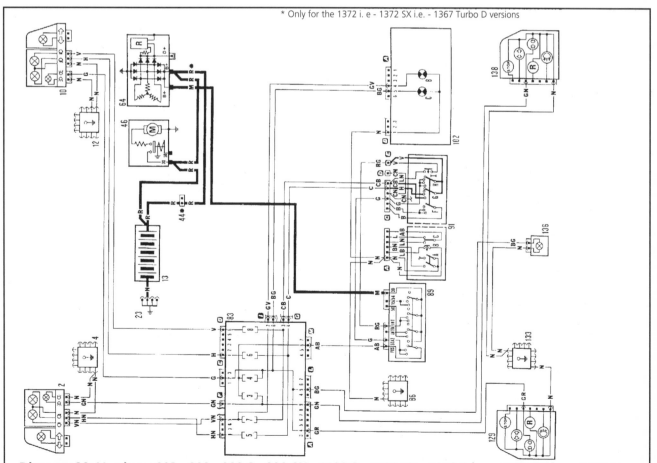

* Only for the 1372 i. e - 1372 SX i.e. - 1367 Turbo D versions

Diagram 20: Versions: 903 - 999 - 999 S - 999 SX - 1108 S - 1108 SX - 1372 S i.e. - 1372 SX i.e. - 1301 D - 1697 D - 1367 Turbo D - Parking Lights and Warning Lights - Dipped Beam Headlights - Main Beam Headlights and Warning Light - Headlight Flasher - Number Plate Light

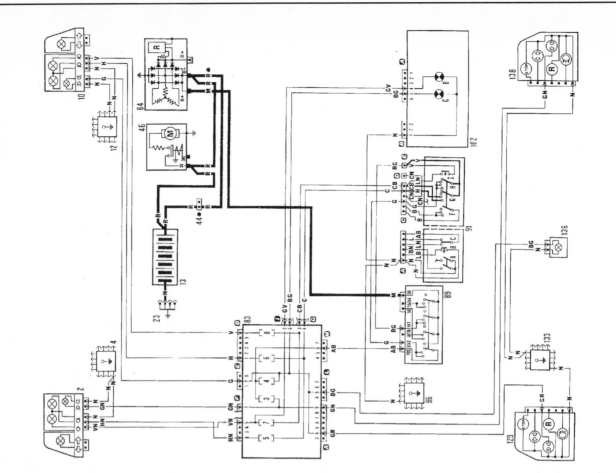

Diagram 21: Versions: 1372 Turbo - Parking Lights and Warning Light - Dipped Beam Headlights - Main Beam Headlights and Warning Light - Headlight Flasher - Number Plate Light

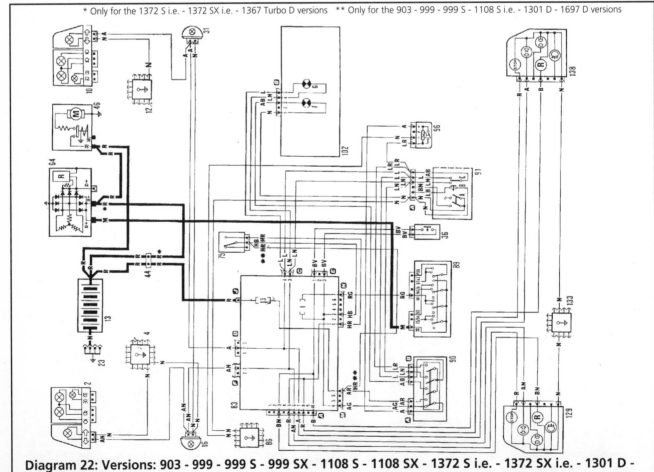

* Only for the 1372 S i.e. - 1372 SX i.e. - 1367 Turbo D versions   ** Only for the 903 - 999 - 999 S - 1108 S i.e. - 1301 D - 1697 D versions

Diagram 22: Versions: 903 - 999 - 999 S - 999 SX - 1108 S - 1108 SX - 1372 S i.e. - 1372 SX i.e. - 1301 D - 1697 D - 1367 Turbo D - Direction Indicators and Warning Light - Hazard Warning Lights and Warning Light - Reversing Lights - Brake Lights

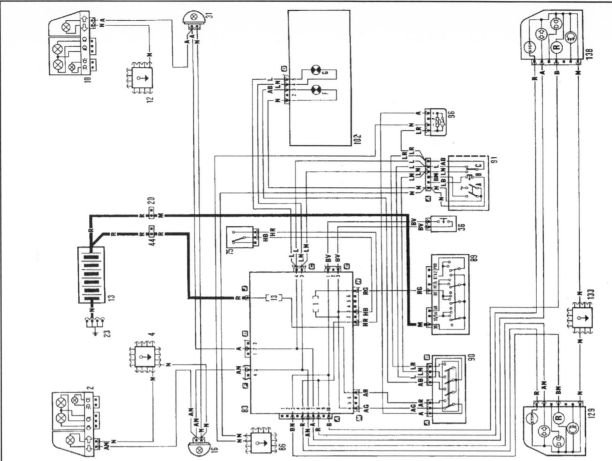

Diagram 23: Version 1372 Turbo - Direction Indicators and Warning Light - Hazard Warning Lights and Warning Light - Reversing Lights - Braking Lights

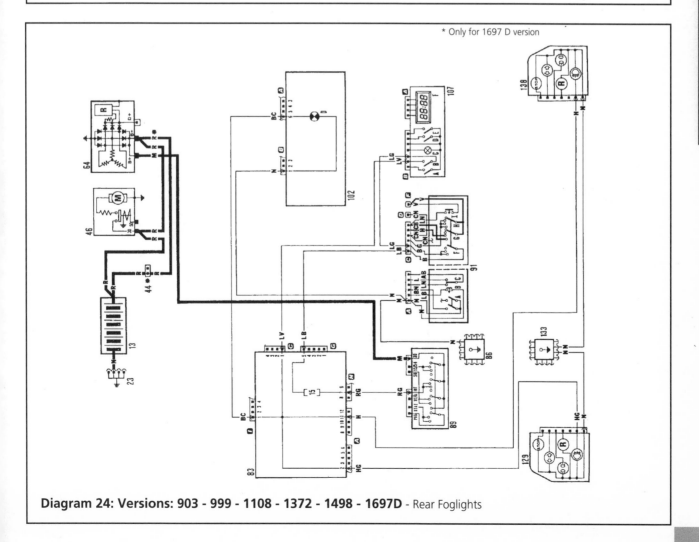

* Only for 1697 D version

Diagram 24: Versions: 903 - 999 - 1108 - 1372 - 1498 - 1697D - Rear Foglights

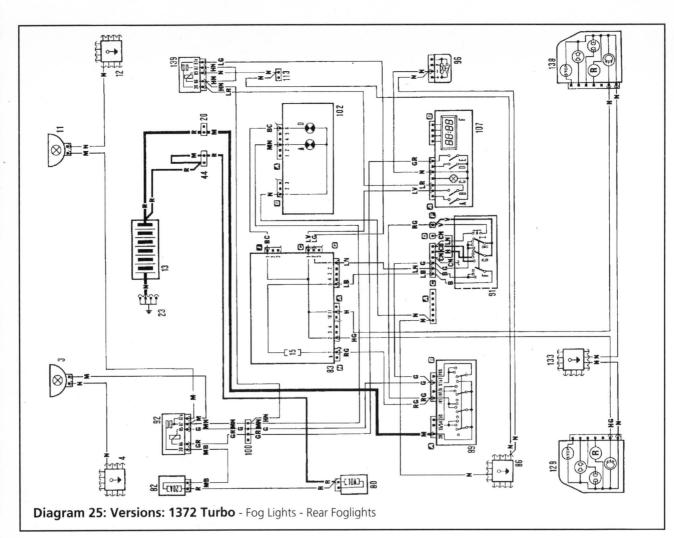

Diagram 25: Versions: 1372 Turbo - Fog Lights - Rear Foglights

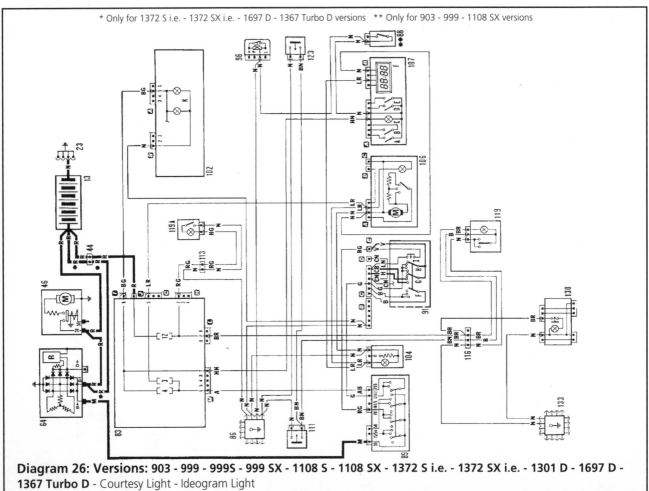

* Only for 1372 S i.e. - 1372 SX i.e. - 1697 D - 1367 Turbo D versions   ** Only for 903 - 999 - 1108 SX versions

Diagram 26: Versions: 903 - 999 - 999S - 999 SX - 1108 S - 1108 SX - 1372 S i.e. - 1372 SX i.e. - 1301 D - 1697 D - 1367 Turbo D - Courtesy Light - Ideogram Light

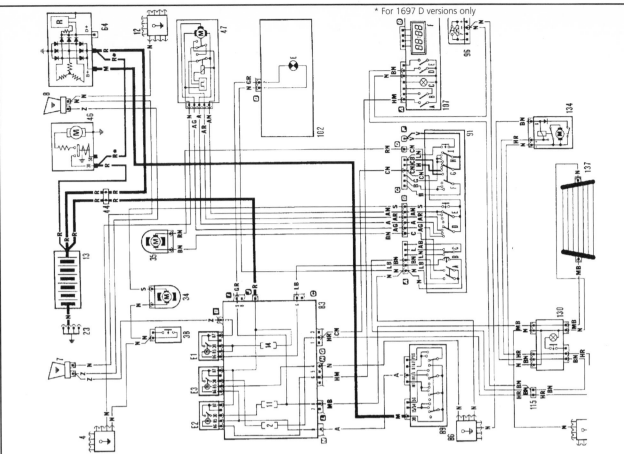

* For 1697 D versions only

Diagram 27: Versions: 903 - 999 - 1108 - 1372 - 1498 - 1697 D - Electric Horns - Heated Rear Windscreen and Warning Light - Windscreen Wiper - Rearscreen Wash/Wipe - Electric Windscreen Washer Pump - Electric Pump for Rearscreen Washer

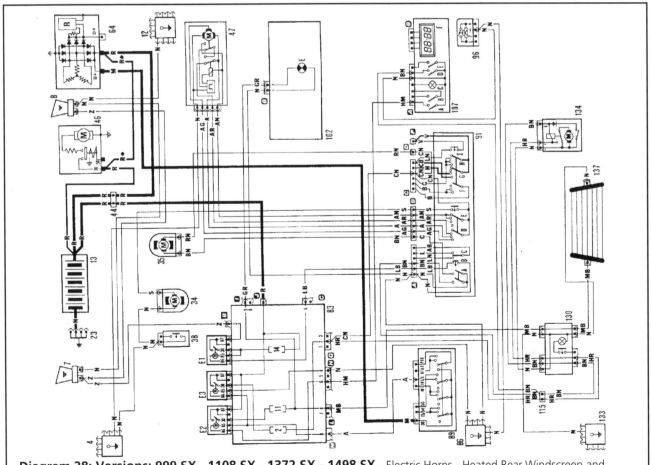

Diagram 28: Versions: 999 SX - 1108 SX - 1372 SX - 1498 SX - Electric Horns - Heated Rear Windscreen and Warning Light - Windscreen Wiper - Rearscreen Wiper - Electric Windscreen Washer Pump - Electric Pump for Rearscreen Washer

* For SX versions only   ** For 1372 - 1498 versions only   ▲ For basic versions with 999 engine warning light only

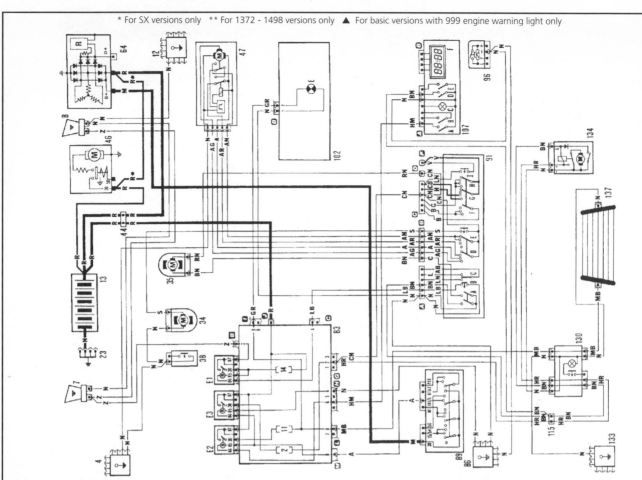

Diagram 29: Versions: 903 - 999 - 1108 - 1372 - 1498 - Engine Radiator Cooling - Car Interior Ventilation - Radio - Cigar Lighter

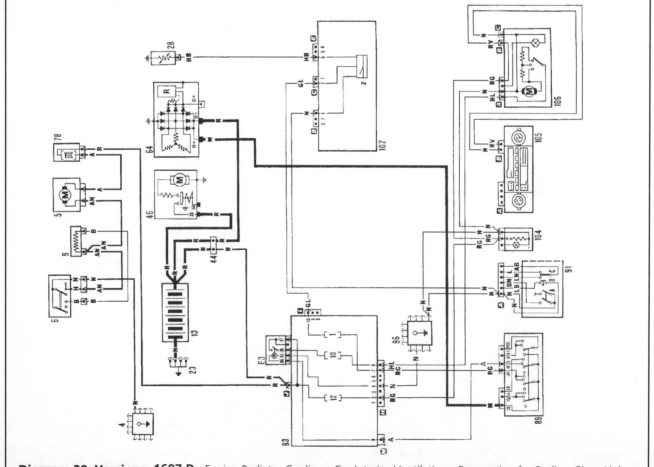

Diagram 30: Versions: 1697 D - Engine Radiator Cooling - Car Interior Ventilation - Preparation for Radio - Cigar Lighter

* Only for 1372 - 1498 - 1697 D versions ** Only for 1697 D version ▲ Only for 999 - 1108 - 1372 - 1498 versions

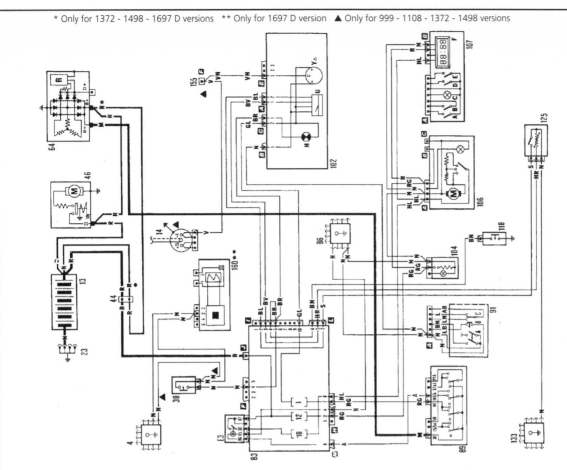

Diagram 31: Versions: 903 - 999 - 1108 - 1372 - 1498 - 1697 D - Fuel Level Gauge - Low Brake Fluid Level and Handbrake Warning Light - Rev. Counter - Digital Clock

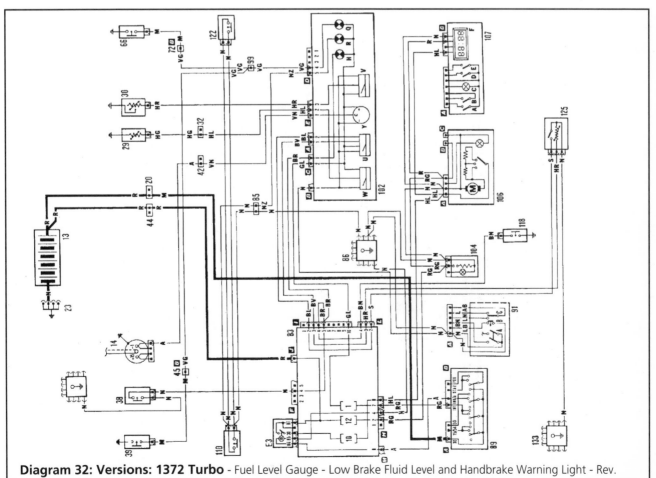

Diagram 32: Versions: 1372 Turbo - Fuel Level Gauge - Low Brake Fluid Level and Handbrake Warning Light - Rev. Counter - Digital Clock - Brake Pad Wear Warning Light - Door Open Warning Light - Engine Oil Pressure Gauge - Engine Oil Temperature Gauge

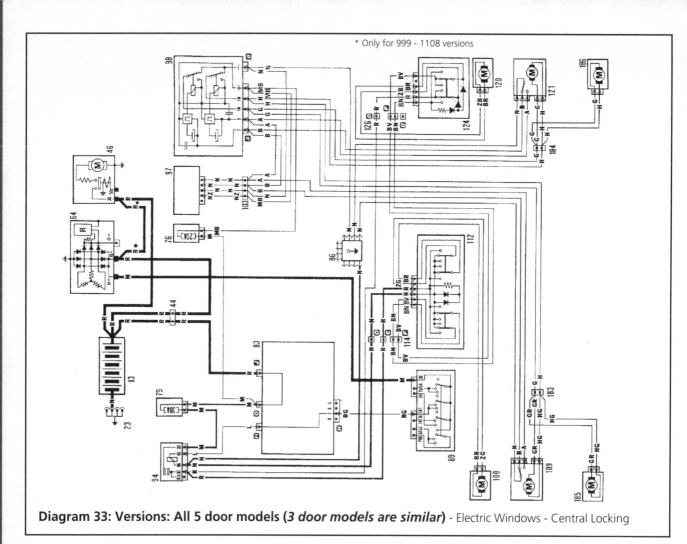

Diagram 33: Versions: All 5 door models (*3 door models are similar*) - Electric Windows - Central Locking

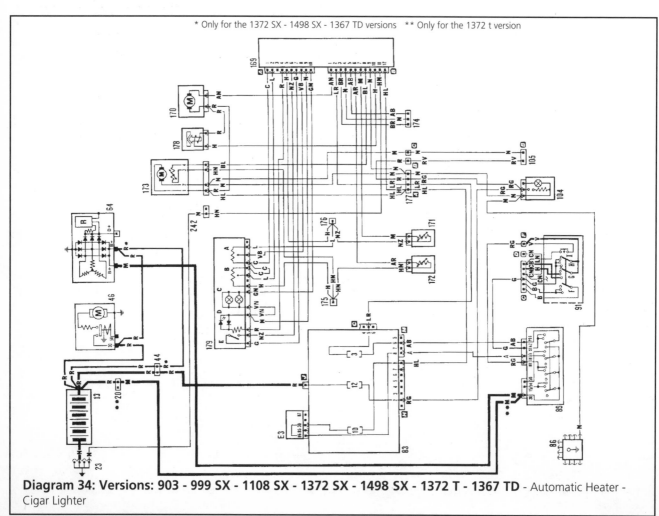

Diagram 34: Versions: 903 - 999 SX - 1108 SX - 1372 SX - 1498 SX - 1372 T - 1367 TD - Automatic Heater - Cigar Lighter

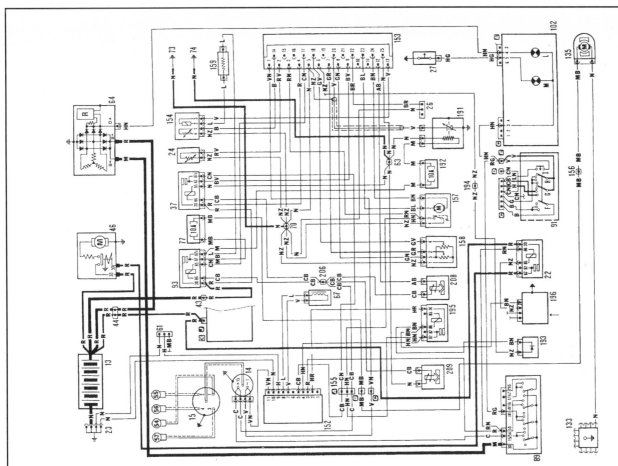

Diagram 35: Versions: 1498 Selecta - Starting - Digiplex 2 Electronic Ignition - Bosch S.P.I. Electronic Injection - Charging - Electric Fuel Pump - Low Engine Oil Pressure Warning Light

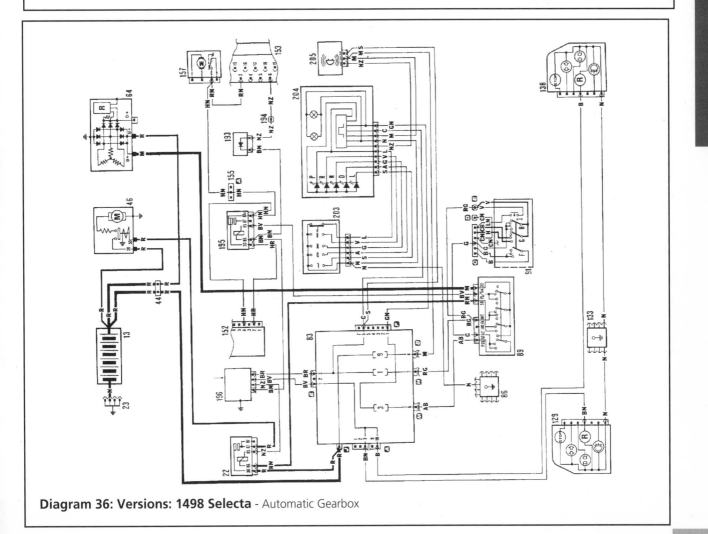

Diagram 36: Versions: 1498 Selecta - Automatic Gearbox

* Only for the 1372 - 1498 versions

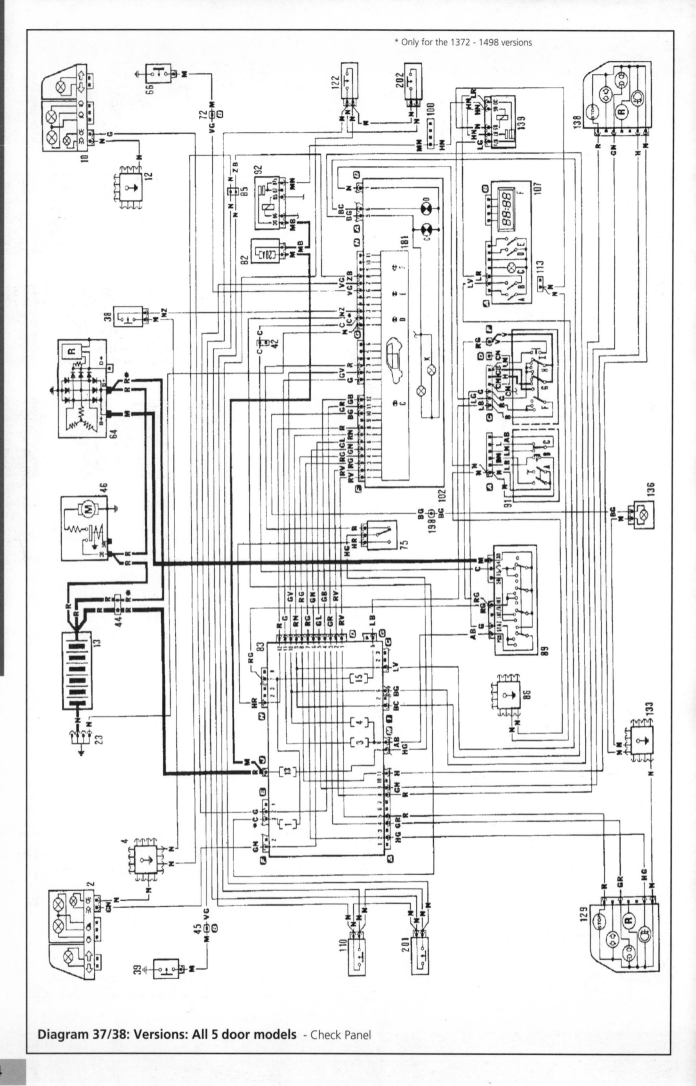

Diagram 37/38: Versions: All 5 door models - Check Panel